What
We Know
About
Grading

What
We Know
About
Grading

What Works,
What Doesn't,
and What's Next

Edited by

THOMAS R. GUSKEY
SUSAN M. BROOKHART

Alexandria, Virginia USA

1703 N. Beauregard St. • Alexandria, VA 22311-1714 USA
Phone: 800-933-2723 or 703-578-9600 • Fax: 703-575-5400
Website: www.ascd.org • E-mail: member@ascd.org
Author guidelines: www.ascd.org/write

Ronn Nozoe, *Interim CEO and Executive Director;* Stefani Roth, *Publisher;* Genny Ostertag, *Director, Content Acquisitions;* Julie Houtz, *Director, Book Editing & Production;* Miriam Calderone, *Editor;* Judi Connelly, *Associate Art Director;* Masie Chong, *Graphic Designer;* Valerie Younkin, *Senior Production Designer;* Mike Kalyan, *Director, Production Services;* Trinay Blake, *E-Publishing Specialist;* Audra Jefferson, *Production Specialist*

All web links in this book are correct as of the publication date below but may have become inactive or otherwise modified since that time. If you notice a deactivated or changed link, please e-mail books@ascd.org with the words "Link Update" in the subject line. In your message, please specify the web link, the book title, and the page number on which the link appears.

PAPERBACK ISBN: 978-1-4166-2723-4   ASCD product #118062   n2/19
PDF E-BOOK ISBN: 978-1-4166-2724-1; see Books in Print for other formats.
Quantity discounts are available: e-mail programteam@ascd.org or call 800-933-2723, ext. 5773, or 703-575-5773. For desk copies, go to www.ascd.org/deskcopy.

Library of Congress Cataloging-in-Publication Data
Names: Guskey, Thomas R., editor. | Brookhart, Susan M., editor.
Title: What we know about grading : what works, what doesn't, and what's next / [edited by] Thomas R. Guskey and Susan M. Brookhart.
Description: Alexandria, VA : ASCD, [2019] | Includes bibliographical references and index.
Identifiers: LCCN 2018048688 (print) | LCCN 2018059495 (ebook) | ISBN 9781416627241 (PDF) | ISBN 9781416627234 (pbk.)
Subjects: LCSH: Grading and marking (Students)
Classification: LCC LB3063 (ebook) | LCC LB3063 .W55 2019 (print) | DDC 371.27/2—dc23
LC record available at https://lccn.loc.gov/2018048688

27 26 25 24 23 22 21 20 19   1 2 3 4 5 6 7 8 9 10 11 12

We dedicate this book to the school leaders, teachers, and researchers around the world who are working to understand and improve grading and reporting, especially those with whom we've had the privilege to work. Their dedication and commitment to doing what is right and better for students are a constant inspiration to us.

What We Know About Grading

Introduction

Thomas R. Guskey and Susan M. Brookhart

Grading is one of the most hotly debated topics in education today. If you want to start an argument about some aspect of education, you need only bring up the way teachers grade. Everyone who has gone to school has experienced some form of grading, usually beginning in early elementary school, and most of us have negative associations with it. We remember a disappointment, a frustration, a wrongdoing, or an injustice. Common refrains include "The grade didn't reflect what I learned," "The teacher didn't like me and gave me a bad grade," and "It just wasn't fair!" (Guskey, 2006).

Grades are the symbols assigned to individual pieces of student work or to composite measures of student performance created for report cards and other summative documents. Grades can be letters, numbers, figures, or any set of descriptors that designate different levels of performance. They are used in preschool and kindergarten through graduate and professional schools throughout the world.

Grading is typically the last element addressed in education reform efforts. Most reform initiatives begin with the articulation of curriculum goals or standards—that is, what we want students to learn and be able to do as a result of their experiences in school. Next, we consider what evidence best reflects that learning and examine issues associated with student assessments. After that, we focus on the quality of instruction and how best to help students achieve the established goals or standards. Finally, we turn to grading—the matter of effectively communicating assessment results and other measures of learning to students, parents, and families. We take grading on last and always with some reluctance, because changing grading policies and practices means challenging some of education's longest-held traditions.

Most of us have strong opinions about grading based on our personal experiences in school. And because those experiences vary widely, so do our opinions. In light of this reality, it is extremely important that grading policies and practices be based on trustworthy research evidence rather than personal experience.

Educators involved in grading reform today often take guidance from education books and blogs. In the past 15 years, dozens of books have been published on the topic, all offering guidance to educators in their reform efforts. A quick Google search identifies a multitude of blogs on grading issues. There are even Facebook pages and regular Twitter chats devoted to the topic of grading.

Busy, overworked educators often assume that these book authors and bloggers have studied the research on grading in detail and thoroughly understand the knowledge base derived from the body of evidence on grading amassed over the past century. But that is seldom the case. Some grading book authors fail to cite *any* significant research on grading, and most grading bloggers do the same. Others cite research they clearly have not read, drawing inferences from summaries that may or may not be accurate. This problem is exacerbated when well intentioned but only partially informed consultants offer passionate and inspiring presentations on grading issues filled with "I believe," "I think," or "In my opinion" statements based on their personal philosophies about grading.

Although we admire the passion and commitment of authors, bloggers, and consultants who devote their time to grading issues, arguments based solely on personal philosophies or opinions are rarely convincing to teachers, students, or their families. They also do not win the support of skeptical policymakers or school board members, who fittingly ask, "Where's the evidence?" Advice with no firm grounding in reliable research will simply not advance reform efforts.

Unfortunately, grading practices today are largely based on tradition rather than on a thorough understanding of the research literature. We do what we do simply because "we've always done it that way." In fact, some of the longest-held traditions in education involve the way we grade students and the consequences we attach to grades. Successfully challenging those long-held traditions requires strong, defensible evidence showing that recommended reforms are actually better and provide specific benefits for students, parents, and families.

Despite efforts to convince them otherwise, most students and their families do not share educators' interest in the philosophy behind grading. Unless they are personally affected, they generally don't care too much about any inequity built into policies and practices. Further, they do not consider grading reform a "moral imperative," as some writers and consultants suggest. What students and their parents want to know from educators, especially at the middle and high school levels, is straightforward: how to get the highest grade possible or, more specifically, how to get an *A* (Guskey, 2016). This is understandable, as final grades follow students to different schools, go to college admissions departments, and may even be viewed by potential employers.

When considering change in well-established grading policies and practice, all stakeholders want to know "Why?" They want to know what evidence supports the change and how trustworthy that evidence is. They want to know whether the evidence comes from contexts similar to theirs. Most important, they want to know the probable outcomes of the change and whether the reforms will truly benefit students or potentially harm them. In other words, they want to know what research supports the change and how that evidence informs the change process.

About the Research

Although grading has been a part of education since antiquity, only in recent years has it become a major focus of education practitioners, policymakers, and researchers. This new attention has revealed that the grading policies and practices used in most schools today have remained relatively unchanged for decades (Brookhart, 2009; Guskey, 2000, 2001; Haladyna, 1999). And this is not because they are especially effective, but because they are steeped in traditions that many stakeholders believe have served us well (Guskey, 2013). As a result, changing the way we grade and report on student learning progress in school often becomes the most challenging aspect of any educational reform effort.

Some reformers believe the solution to most grading issues lies in technology. Educators today have their choice from a slew of online grading programs that use mathematical algorithms to calculate grades, thus limiting teacher decision making and offering the pretense of objectivity (Guskey, 2002a, 2002b). Other reformers believe breaking grades down into specific components related to different learning standards will solve the problem—an approach known as "standards-based grading" (Guskey, 2009). Still others want to abandon grading completely, believing the process debases learning, causing students to focus more on earning high grades than on improving their skills and understanding (Kohn, 1999). Regardless of their stances, few educators today know about the long history of grading research and its implications for more effective practice, having lacked a truly comprehensive guide to the most up-to-date literature on the subject. This book is designed to be just that.

Understanding the extensive knowledge base on grading is essential to making informed decisions about any policy changes. Students today generally perceive grades to be something they "earn" for their achievement in school (Brookhart, 1993). As such, grades have a pervasive influence on how students regard school and how they see themselves as learners (Pattison, Grodsky, & Muller, 2013). Grades also predict important future educational consequences, such as dropping out of school (Bowers, 2010; Bowers & Sprott, 2012; Bowers, Sprott, & Taff, 2013) and applying to, attending, and succeeding in college (Atkinson & Geiser, 2009; Bowers, 2010; Thorsen & Cliffordson, 2012). Grades are especially predictive of academic success in higher education institutions with more open admission policies (Sawyer, 2013).

These are but a small sample of the results of hundreds of research studies on grading and reporting conducted over the past century. Today we know more than ever before about what grades mean to teachers, students, and parents. We know what purposes different types of grades serve well and what purposes they impede. We know a great deal about the effect of grades on student cognition, behavior, and emotional health. This knowledge provides an evidence-based foundation for making better and more informed decisions about effective grading policies and practices.

The Birth of Our Project

The American Educational Research Association (AERA), one of the premier educational research organizations in the world, celebrated its 100th anniversary in 2016. As part of that celebration, AERA invited members to prepare syntheses of research from the past 100 years on topics holding special significance to educators at all levels. These syntheses would be reviewed by scholars in the field, and a select few would be chosen for publication in *Review of Educational Research* (*RER*), AERA's most prestigious journal. Upon learning of this endeavor, Susan M. Brookhart of Duquesne University and Thomas R. Guskey of the University of Kentucky assembled a distinguished team of scholars to prepare a synthesis of the research on grading. The completed synthesis was reviewed and selected as a major entry in the special anniversary edition of *RER* (see Brookhart et al., 2016).

Immediately following publication, we were contacted by educators around the world asking if we could prepare an expanded version of our review for school leaders and teachers involved in grading reform initiatives, and we set out to do just that. We expanded our team to include scholars in important areas of grading that were not addressed in our original review due to space limitations, and asked them to prepare succinct but thorough summaries highlighting practical implications for practice.

The Scope of Our Work

In developing this book, we did our best to describe research findings in ways that are meaningful to a broad range of stakeholders. We first identified eight major areas of grading research. For each area, we then selected exceptionally talented researchers to summarize the results from relevant studies. These outstanding scholars are not only intimately familiar with the research in these areas, but also major contributors to that research. We have long admired their excellent work in these areas and frequently cite their publications. We asked them to describe why their area of focus is important, what the major research findings are, and how those findings might be leveraged to improve grading policy and practices.

Following are brief summaries of the eight chapters in this book, each of which concentrates on a different major area of grading research.

Chapter 1: Reliability in Grading and Grading Scales

In this chapter, Susan M. Brookhart and Thomas R. Guskey review early studies on the reliability of grades and various perspectives on what grades represent. They find that teachers have historically varied greatly in terms of the criteria they consider and the procedures they use to assign grades. Many early studies that reach this conclusion have a "what's wrong with teachers" undertone that today would likely be seen as researcher bias. Nonetheless, this collection of studies offers an important basis for discussing the sources of variation among teachers, even those who teach at the same grade level or subject area in the same school.

Chapter 2: Report Card Grades and Educational Outcomes

Alex J. Bowers of Teachers College, Columbia University, turns attention to quantitative studies of K–12 report card grades. He shows that whereas early studies of the relationship between grades and assessment results typically examined the correlation between grades and intelligence test scores, more recent investigations compare grades to standardized achievement assessment results. These studies show that teachers include factors beyond the achievement represented by standardized assessments in determining students' grades. Bowers also examines how grades relate to other indices such as high school graduation, college admission, and college grade point average (GPA).

Chapter 3: The Composition of Grades: Cognitive and Noncognitive Factors

Sarah M. Bonner and Peggy P. Chen of Hunter College, City University of New York (CUNY), examine studies of the cognitive and noncognitive factors teachers consider when assigning grades. This research shows that teachers typically give weight to "enabling behaviors" such as completing homework assignments and participating in class discussions as well as to "compliance behaviors" such as turning in assignments on time and following established class-room procedures. The authors discuss how this mixture of factors can muddle the interpretation of grades at all instructional levels.

Chapter 4: Surveys of Teachers' Grading Practices and Perceptions

Many studies have surveyed teachers to determine their perceptions of grading and the specific grading practices they employ. In this chapter, James H. McMillan of Virginia Commonwealth University describes the results of these many surveys and offers further insight into the multifaceted nature of grades. He also explains the important differences among teachers who teach at different levels of education and what the implications are for grading reform efforts.

Chapter 5: Standards-Based Grading

As the name implies, standards-based grading emphasizes communicating student progress on grade-level or subject-area learning standards. Megan E. Welsh of the University of California–Davis examines research on the advantages and challenges of this approach to grading as well as the conditions necessary for reporting achievement separate from work habits and behavior.

Chapter 6: Grading Students with Learning Differences

For families of students with learning differences, accurate accounts of their children's progress in school are essential to providing effective interventions and making wise placement decisions. Lee Ann Jung, the founder of Lead Inclusion, reviews research on determining fair and accurate grades for students with learning differences and offers a five-step process for linking IEP (individualized education plan) goals to general curriculum standards and reporting student learning clearly and meaningfully.

Chapter 7: Leadership for Grading Reform

Laura J. Link of Purdue University–Fort Wayne describes research on the implementation of grading reforms and the special leadership challenges involved. She addresses the difficulties of making changes to long-standing policies and practices, relevant legal issues, and factors identified in the research as essential to successful reform.

Chapter 8: Grading in Higher Education

Fair and accurate grading at the college and university level poses unique challenges because relatively few faculty members are trained in pedagogy, assessment, or grading. Jeffrey K. Smith and Lisa F. Smith of the University of Otago in Dunedin, New Zealand, examine research on grading in higher education, paying special attention to differences across countries, the relation between grades and course evaluations, expectations for grade distributions, and evidence on grade inflation.

Our Goal

Our goal for this book is to present the broadest and most comprehensive summary of research on grading and reporting practices available to date. We did our best to organize, interpret, and synthesize the entire corpus of research on grading and reporting student learning. In plain and direct language, the authors of each chapter describe the research in each area; distinguish critical issues from those that are less consequential or downright trivial; outline the history of the research, contrasting various points of view and interpretations; and discuss the implications for better practice.

We hope that this book prompts a critical review of current grading practices and adoption of policies and practices the research shows to be better for students. We hope it helps consultants to advocate for evidence-based reforms—and to be more honest about reforms for which the evidence is slim or nonexistent. We hope it steers researchers to expand our body of knowledge and provide a foundation for improved grading policy and practice at all levels.

If sharing the work of the dedicated researchers in this book means more students will have positive rather than negative memories of their grading experiences, we will consider it a success.

References

Atkinson, R. C., & Geiser, S. (2009). Reflections on a century of college admissions tests. *Educational Researcher, 38,* 665–676.

Bowers, A. J. (2010). Analyzing the longitudinal K–12 grading histories of entire cohorts of students: Grades, data-driven decision making, dropping out, and hierarchical cluster analysis. *Practical Assessment Research and Evaluation, 15*(7), 1–18.

Bowers, A. J., & Sprott, R. (2012). Examining the multiple trajectories associated with dropping out of high school: A growth mixture model analysis. *The Journal of Educational Research, 105,* 176–195.

Bowers, A. J., Sprott, R., & Taff, S. (2013). Do we know who will drop out? A review of the predictors of dropping out of high school: Precision, sensitivity and specificity. *The High School Journal, 96,* 77–100.

Brookhart, S. M. (1993). Teachers' grading practices: Meaning and values. *Journal of Educational Measurement, 30,* 123–142.

Brookhart, S. M. (2009). *Grading* (2nd ed.). New York: Merrill Pearson Education.

Brookhart, S. M., Guskey, T. R., Bowers, A. J., McMillan, J. H., Smith, J. K., Smith, L. F., et al. (2016). A century of grading research: Meaning and value in the most common educational measure. *Review of Educational Research, 86*(4), 803–848.

Guskey, T. R. (2000). Grading policies that work against standards... and how to fix them. *NASSP Bulletin, 84*(620), 20–29.

Guskey, T. R. (2001). Helping standards make the grade. *Educational Leadership, 59*(1), 20–27.

Guskey, T. R. (2002a). Computerized gradebooks and the myth of objectivity. *Phi Delta Kappan, 83*(10), 775–780.

Guskey, T. R. (2002b). *How's my kid doing? A parent's guide to grades, marks, and report cards.* San Francisco: Jossey-Bass.

Guskey, T. R. (2006). "It wasn't fair!" Educators' recollections of their experiences as students with grading. *Journal of Educational Research and Policy Studies, 6*(2), 111–124.

Guskey, T. R. (Ed.). (2009). *Practical solutions for serious problems in standards-based grading.* Thousand Oaks, CA: Corwin.

Guskey, T. R. (2013). Beyond tradition: Teachers' views of crucial grading and reporting issues. *Journal of Educational Research and Policy Studies, 13*(1), 32–49.

Guskey, T. R. (2016, August 18). Rubrics are fine, but how do I get an *A*? *Education Week Blog.* Retrieved from http://blogs.edweek.org/edweek/finding_common_ground/2016/08/rubrics_are_fine_but_how_do_i_get_an_a.html

Haladyna, T. M. (1999). *A complete guide to student grading.* Boston: Allyn & Bacon.

Kohn, A. (1999). *Punished by rewards: The trouble with gold stars, incentive plans, As, and other bribes.* Boston: Houghton Mifflin.

Pattison, E., Grodsky, E., & Muller, C. (2013). Is the sky falling? Grade inflation and the signaling power of grades. *Educational Researcher, 42,* 259–265.

Sawyer, R. (2013). Beyond correlations: Usefulness of high school GPA and test scores in making college admissions decisions. *Applied Measurement in Education, 26,* 89–112.

Thorsen, C., & Cliffordson, C. (2012). Teachers' grade assignment and the predictive validity of criterion-referenced grades. *Educational Research and Evaluation, 18,* 153–172.

1

Reliability in Grading and Grading Scales

Susan M. Brookhart and Thomas R. Guskey

Few people today would question the premise that students' grades should reflect the quality of their work and not depend on whether their teachers are "hard" or "easy" graders. But how much subjectivity on the part of teachers is involved in the grading process, and what do we know about its influence? The earliest research on grading dates to the 1800s and was concerned with this very issue. These early studies questioned the reliability of teachers' grading.

Why Is This Area of Research Important?

Reading the research on grading gives present-day educators cause for consternation. On the one hand, early studies of grading reliability clearly were motivated by dissatisfaction, and sometimes disdain, by researchers for teachers' unreliable practices. Our reaction to this, of course, is indignation: That's not right! On the other hand, the extent of the unreliability in grading identified in these early studies was huge. Grades for the same work varied dramatically from teacher to teacher, resulting in highly divergent conclusions about students, their learning, and their future studies. That's not right, either.

In this chapter, we describe these early studies of grade reliability as well as one contemporary study that replicated an early study. We gently critique some of the underlying bias in these studies, and then offer some practical suggestions for applying the studies' results to grading practices today. Despite their biases and flaws, these early studies do offer several clear implications for practice.

What Significant Studies Have Been Conducted in This Area?

In our review of the research, we found 16 individual studies of grading reliability from the early 20th century, plus two early reviews of grading studies by Kelly (1914) and Rugg (1918). These are described in Figure 1.1 (pp. 16–17). We reference these early reviews because they include dozens of early studies in addition to the published studies we were able to locate. Some of the studies Kelly and Rugg reviewed were unpublished reports from school districts or universities that are unavailable to us a century later. In addition, we found an early statistical treatise on the subject by Edgeworth (1888) that we describe first because it set the stage for the research that followed.

The earliest investigation we could find is a statistical study published by the *Journal of the Royal Statistical Society* in the United Kingdom and rarely cited in the U.S. grading literature. And it's a doozy—the study begins with a table of contents outlining 26 separate points the author wants to make! Professor F. Y. Edgeworth (1888), author of the study, made an important contribution to both statistics and grading research by applying normal curve theory— he called it the "Theory of Errors" (p. 600)—to the case of grading examinations. Normal curve theory was fairly new at the time.

Mathematician Carl Friedrich Gauss introduced the theory in the early 1800s and pointed out its usefulness for estimating the size of error in any measure. Edgeworth deserves a lot of credit for realizing this advance in statistics could help us with practical problems in education.

Unlike some of the researchers who followed him, Edgeworth's motivation was not to criticize teachers and professors, but rather to make things fairer for students. He explained that when students' performance is poorly measured, bad decisions result, including mistakes in identifying students for "honours" upon graduation (by which Edgeworth meant "'successful candidates' in an open competition for the Army or the India or Home Civil Service" [p. 603]). Thus, unreliable grades had real consequences for students.

Edgeworth described the plight of those whose achievement was good enough for these important future opportunities but whose grades did not confirm it: "There are some of the pass men as good as some of the honour men; but, like the unsung brave 'who lived before Agamemnon,' they are huddled unknown amongst the ignominious throng, for want, not of talent, or learning, or industry, or judgment, but luck" (p. 616). Edgeworth considered this part of an argument for improving grading reliability. We love Edgeworth's poetic and righteous indignation.

Normal curve theory allowed Edgeworth to measure the amount of error in grades due to chance, which in itself was a contribution to research. But Edgeworth went beyond that to tease out different sources of grading error: (1) chance, (2) personal differences among graders regarding the whole exam and individual items on the exam, and (3) "taking [the examinee's] answers as representative of his proficiency" (p. 614). He did this by using both hypothetical and real data to calculate the probable amount of error in examination grades, under different conditions and for different exams.

The idea that multiple factors led to unreliable grades was a huge step forward. It gave educators a window into things they could

FIGURE 1.1 | **Early Studies of the Reliability of Grades**

Studies	Participants	Main Findings
Ashbaugh (1924)	University education students	• Grading the same 7th grade arithmetic paper on three occasions, the mean remained constant, but the scores got closer together. • Inconsistencies among graders increased over time. • After discussion, graders devised a point scheme for each problem and grading variability decreased.
Bolton (1927)	6th grade arithmetic teachers	• Average deviation was 5 points out of 100 on 24 papers. • Lowest-quality work presented the greatest level of variation.
Brimi (2011)	English teachers	• Range of scores was 46 points out of 100 and covered all five letter-grade levels.
Eells (1930)	Teachers in a college measurement course	• Elementary teachers displayed grading inconsistency over time grading three geography and two history questions. • Estimated reliability was low. • Most agreement was found on one very poor paper.
Healy (1935)	6th grade written compositions from 50 different teachers	• Format and usage errors were weighed more heavily in grades than the quality of ideas.
Hulten (1925)	English teachers	• Teacher inconsistency was revealed over time grading five compositions. • 20 percent changed from pass to fail or vice versa on the second marking.
Jacoby (1910)	College astronomy professors	• There was little disagreement on grades for five high-quality exams.
Lauterbach (1928)	Teachers grading handwritten and typed papers	• Student work quality was a source of grade variability. • In absolute terms, there was much variation by teacher for each paper. • In relative terms, teachers' marks reliably ranked students.
Shriner (1930)	High school English and algebra teachers	• Teachers' grading was reliable. • There was greater teacher disagreement in grades for the poorer papers.
Silberstein (1922)	Teachers grading one English paper that originally passed in high school but was failed by the New York Regents	• When teachers regraded the same paper, they changed their grade. • Scores on individual questions on the exam varied greatly, explaining the overall grading disagreement (except on one question about syntax, where grades were more uniform).

Sims (1933)	Reanalysis of four studies of grading arithmetic, algebra, high school English, and psychology exams	• There were two kinds of variability in teachers' grades: (1) differences in students' work quality, and (2) "differences in the standards of grading found among school systems and among teachers within a system" (p. 637). • Teachers disagreed significantly on grades. • Changing from a 100-point scale to grades reduced disagreements.
Starch (1913)	College freshman English instructors	• Teacher disagreement was significant, especially for the two poorest papers. • Four sources of variation were found and probable error reported for each: (1) differences among the standards of different schools (no influence), (2) differences among the standards of different teachers (some influence), (3) differences in the relative values placed by different teachers upon various elements in a paper, including content and form (larger influence), and (4) differences due to the pure inability to distinguish between closely allied degrees of merit (larger influence).
Starch (1915)	6th and 7th grade teachers	• Average teacher variability of 4.2 (out of 100) was reduced to 2.8 by forcing a normal distribution using a five-category scale (*poor, inferior, medium, superior,* and *excellent*).
Starch & Elliott (1912)	High school English teachers	• Teacher disagreement in assigning grades was large (a range of 30–40 out of 100 points). • Teachers disagreed on rank order of papers.
Starch & Elliott (1913a)	High school mathematics teachers	• Teacher disagreement on a mathematics exam was larger than it was on the English papers in Starch and Elliott (1912). • Teachers disagreed on the grade for one item's answer about as much as they did on the composite grade for the whole exam.
Starch & Elliott (1913b)	High school history teachers	• Teacher disagreement on one history exam was larger than for the English or math exams in prior Starch and Elliott studies (1912, 1913a). • Study concluded that variability isn't due to subject, but "the examiner and method of examination" (p. 680).

Source: From "A Century of Grading Research: Meaning and Value in the Most Common Educational Measure," by S. M. Brookhart, T. R. Guskey, A. J. Bowers, J. H. McMillan, J. K. Smith, L. F. Smith, et al., 2016, *Review of Educational Research, 86*(4), pp. 803–848. Copyright 2016 by American Educational Research Association. Adapted with permission.

do about the problem. We can't really do much about the fact that measures tend to vary by chance. We can, however, take steps to help graders develop a shared view of what knowledge and skills the items and tasks on an exam are supposed to measure. We also can take steps to make sure the items and tasks on an exam really are representative of what we would now call desired learning outcomes.

What Questions Have Been Addressed in This Research? What Have the Results of Those Studies Revealed?

As we have noted, the most valuable early studies of grading reliability investigated sources of variation in grading. The least valuable of these studies simply investigated whether variability in grading existed at all, found that it did (of course it did), and simply proclaimed it a bad thing. More valuable studies investigated whether grading variability was affected by the quality of the student work or its format (e.g., by asking whether teachers find it easier to agree on grades for good papers or poor ones). Other studies investigated whether changing the grading scale would make grading more reliable. In the early 20th century, the most prevalent grading scale was the 0 to 100 percentage scale, which proved to be exceedingly unreliable. Teachers were much more consistent when using grading scales with fewer categories, especially those with five categories or fewer.

The main finding from these early studies was that great variation existed in the grades teachers assign to students' work (Ashbaugh, 1924; Brimi, 2011; Eells, 1930; Healy, 1935; Hulten, 1925; Lauterbach, 1928; Silberstein, 1922; Sims, 1933; Starch, 1913, 1915; Starch & Elliott, 1912, 1913a, 1913b). This finding agrees with the two early reviews of grading studies by Kelly (1914) and Rugg (1918). Not every early study, however, was quite so pessimistic. Studies by Jacoby (1910), Bolton (1927), and Shriner (1930) argued that grading was not as unreliable as commonly believed at the time.

Early researchers attributed the inconsistency in teachers' grades to one or more of the following sources:

- The criteria for evaluating the work (Ashbaugh, 1924; Brimi, 2011; Healy, 1935; Silberstein, 1922; Sims, 1933; Starch, 1915; Starch & Elliott, 1913a, 1913b)

- The quality of students' work (Bolton, 1927; Healy, 1935; Jacoby, 1910; Lauterbach, 1928; Shriner, 1930; Sims, 1933)

- Teacher severity or leniency (Shriner, 1930; Silberstein, 1922; Sims, 1933; Starch, 1915; Starch & Elliott, 1913b)

- Differences in tasks (Silberstein, 1922; Starch & Elliott, 1913a)

- The grading scale (Ashbaugh, 1924; Sims, 1933; Starch, 1913, 1915)

- Teacher error (Brimi, 2011; Eells, 1930; Hulten, 1925; Lauterbach, 1928; Silberstein, 1922; Starch & Elliott, 1912, 1913a, 1913b)

Starch (1913; Starch & Elliott, 1913b) found that teacher error and the use of different criteria were the two largest sources of variation.

For our purposes here, we grouped the studies into three sections based on these factors. Some overlap exists because some studies investigated several of these factors.

Criteria and Scales for Evaluation

Most of the studies investigating teachers' grading reliability sent examination papers to teachers and asked them to assign grades without any specific grading criteria. Today, this lack of clear criteria would be seen as a shortcoming in the assessment design. In the early 1900s, however, researchers assumed that asking teachers to "grade" or "mark" an examination, which usually consisted of a set of constructed-response or essay questions, meant assigning a score on a scale of 0 to 100. Sometimes this was done for the entire exam, and at other times it was done by marking each question separately and then adding up the points.

Two aspects of the criteria for grading are worth considering here: (1) lack of clarity about what those criteria should be, and (2) differences among teachers regarding which criteria are emphasized. In his review of 17 monographs (including one summarizing 39 additional articles), Rugg (1918) concluded, "Teachers' marks are variable and inconsistent primarily because *teachers* in marking pupils *do not measure the same trait*, secondarily because teachers *do not have a common scale* for the evaluation of definite amounts of the traits measured" (p. 705, italics in original).

The most prolific authors of studies documenting teacher variability in grading, and the ones most remembered today, are Daniel Starch and Edward Elliott (1912, 1913a, 1913b; Starch, 1913, 1915). They conducted a series of studies that involved grading papers in English, mathematics, and history. In each study, they sent completed examinations composed of sets of questions to high school teachers. The same two freshman English papers were graded independently by 152 English teachers (Starch & Elliott, 1912); the same geometry exam by 138 math teachers (Starch & Elliott, 1913a); and the same history exam by 114 history teachers (Starch & Elliott, 1913b). The teachers were from different high schools in the Midwestern United States.

In each study, Starch and Elliot showed the distribution of marks and calculated probable error as the typical deviation from average marks, as Edgeworth (1888) had. The results were shocking. The grades assigned by history teachers on the same exam, for example, ranged from 43 to 92 (Starch & Elliott, 1913b). The authors turned to considering (1) what factors contributed to such great discrepancies, and (2) what could be done about it (p. 681).

To answer the first question, Starch (1913) conducted a small study involving 10 university freshman English final examination papers, each graded by 10 freshman English instructors. He also analyzed smaller data sets of psychology, mathematics, English, and German exams. He hypothesized that four major factors produce the variability in grades:

1. Differences among the standards of different schools,
2. Differences among the standards of different teachers,
3. Differences in the relative values placed by different teachers upon various elements in a paper, including content and form, and
4. Differences due to the pure inability to distinguish between closely allied degrees of merit. (p. 630)

He then analyzed his data sets to isolate these factors.

Starch (1913) found the average probable error of a grade was 5.4 on a 100-point scale across instructors and schools. Of these 5.4 points, he estimated that "the fourth factor contributes 2.2 points, the third 2.1 points, the second 1.0 point, and the first practically nothing toward the total" (p. 632). In other words, teacher error and differences in criteria were the main sources of variation in teachers' grades. Given a probable error of around 5 in a 100-point scale, he suggested the use of a 9-point scale (*A+, A−, B+, B−, C+, C−, D+, D−,* and *F*) to improve grading reliability.

Two years later, Starch (1915) proposed three additional strategies to help teachers address the problem of unreliability in grades: (1) teachers could study how they mark and discuss their findings in a faculty meeting, (2) departments could agree on common plans for marking certain types of work and common student errors, and (3) marks could be distributed according to either the normal curve or another distribution. He presented a small study (24 compositions by 6th and 7th graders marked by 12 teachers) to show that forcing grades into five categories based on the normal distribution reduced the variability of grades from 4.2 to 2.8.

Ashbaugh (1924) set out to find other ways to reduce the variability in teachers' grades besides altering the scale from 100 points to just five categories, the most common solution suggested at that time. He had 55 of his preservice teachers and graduate students grade a 7th grade math test three times at four-week intervals. The test consisted of 10 10-point problems. Ashbaugh found that the median grade remained about the same over the four times, but the variability among graders decreased over the occasions.

What followed next makes Ashbaugh's study unique among these early grading studies. Being a teacher education professor, he presented the data to his class to consider. The class discussed the type of errors made and then proposed what today would be called a point scheme for grading. Specifically, students assigned "4 [points] for correct computation, 5 for correct principle, 1 for no variation from correct mathematical statement" (p. 196). Rescoring the papers with this new scheme greatly reduced the variability in assigned grades. Today, standard recommendations for grading student work include being clear about criteria. Apparently this was a new insight in 1924—and we love that it was teacher education students who came up with this answer!

For her study, Healy (1935) collected five compositions from 50 6th grade teachers. The papers had been graded using a five-category scale (*excellent, superior, average, poor,* and *failure*), but included no comments. Three trained judges regraded the compositions. Healy (1935) applied a rubric-like "analysis chart" to discover which criteria (ideas, organization, self-expression, sentence sense, and vocabulary) contributed to the grades. She found that teachers weighted format and usage errors (language, format, spelling, punctuation, and capitalization, which were not on the chart) more heavily in their grades than the quality of ideas. This suggests that the relative emphasis among criteria is a factor in grading variability.

Brimi (2011) is the only contemporary study in this group of investigations of the reliability of grades. It belongs with this group because Brimi replicated Starch and Elliott's 1912 study. Seventy-three high school teachers who had just completed a workshop on the 6 + 1 Trait Writing Rubric were asked to grade a student writing sample on a 100-point scale. Despite their training, the teachers focused on elements of student work they could mark wrong rather than using criteria for good writing, resulting in grades that ranged from 50 to 96 for the same paper. While demonstrating the importance of clear criteria in ensuring reliability in grades, the procedure used in this study also may have been confusing for teachers who had just studied characteristics of good writing in the context of using a descriptive rubric and were, for this experiment, asked to grade on the conventional 100-point scale.

The Quality of Students' Work

Results were mixed regarding whether good-quality work or poor-quality work led to more variability in teachers' grades. Studies by Jacoby (1910), Bolton (1927), and Shriner (1930) suggest that good work was easier for teachers to grade reliably. However, another study by Eells (1930) suggests poor work was easier to grade reliably.

Jacoby (1910) selected 11 midterm exams to be graded independently by six professors of astronomy. All of the papers received high grades, and there was good agreement among the professors. Jacoby (1910) interpreted this result as evidence of grader agreement, but it also may illustrate the influence of students' work quality.

Bolton (1927) found that variability in grades was greater for poor papers than for good papers, suggesting student work quality was a factor. In Bolton's study, 6th grade teachers prepared an arithmetic test for their own pupils, administered it, and then agreed to grade a set of 20 additional papers of the same test. Bolton's research was designed to give teachers some personal investment in the grading, which he perceived as a flaw in previous studies. Grading variability was low, which means that reliability was generally good.

Lauterbach's (1928) study was designed to see if the appearance of students' papers (typed versus handwritten) affected teachers' grading. He selected and typed 60 8th grade students' compositions, creating four sets of 30 papers each. Each set included 15 typed and 15 handwritten papers, with no composition duplicated in a set. Sixteen teachers then graded each set. The typewritten papers had more variability in grades, receiving both more high grades and more low grades. In addition, there was great teacher variability. Teachers were more consistent in making comparative judgments (i.e., this paper is better than that one) than absolute judgments (i.e., this is a good paper and that is a bad paper). In this experiment, then, both characteristics of students' work (typed versus handwritten) and differences among teachers were significant sources of variation.

Sims (1933) discussed two issues related to variability in teachers' grades: (1) "the subjective nature of the pupil response," which he interpreted as differences in students' work quality, and (2) "differences in the standards of grading found among school systems and among teachers within a system" (p. 637). The second issue cited by Sims here seems to conflate teacher severity/leniency with differences in the criteria teachers used to evaluate student work.

Teacher Severity or Leniency, Other Teacher Error, and Random Error

Most of these early studies of grading conflate random error and teacher inability to judge student work appropriately, considering both to fall under the category of "teacher error."

Silberstein's (1922) study had a practical motivation. In 1920, Stuyvesant High School in New York City experienced a high failure rate on the Regents Exam among fourth-year English students. Silberstein selected one paper for study. This paper had received a 73 from the English department, although it failed the Regents. The paper was typewritten and distributed back to English department members for regrading. Overall and question-by-question analyses showed great variability in grading. Silberstein interpreted the variability as due to differences in criteria, the task (e.g., the grammar task exhibited less variability than essays), teachers' personality and "natural prejudices" (which today might be called teacher error), and teachers' severity or leniency as markers.

Teacher severity/leniency also played a role in studies by Shriner (1930) and Sims (1933). Shriner (1930) sampled 25 sophomore algebra exams and 25 freshman English exams from the same high school. He then had 25 English and 25 algebra teachers, respectively, grade the exams. Relative agreement among teachers for both the algebra and English exams was high; that is, teachers agreed overall on which papers were better and which were poorer. However, there was large variation in the percentage of pupils the teachers would fail (algebra: 8 to 56 percent; English: 4 to 56 percent). In other words, despite agreeing on which papers were better and poorer, teachers disagreed on which were good enough to pass. Shriner (1930) concluded grading was not the source of unreliability, but rather some graders were more severe than others. He also found that greater ranges of grades occurred for the poorer papers, suggesting another source of variation is student work quality.

Eells (1930) investigated the stability of teachers' grading over time. Sixty-one teachers, graduate students of the author, graded answers to three grammar school geography and two history questions that had been used in previous research. They graded these papers at the start of a summer quarter course in measurement and again at the end of the quarter, 11 weeks later. Answers to the second geography question were particularly poor, and 55 (90 percent) of the teachers gave it a score of 0 (on a scale of 0 to 10) both times. Excluding that question, no teachers gave the same grade twice on the four other questions. Only two teachers gave the same grade twice on three questions. Statistical measures of reliability were also low. This suggests teacher inconsistency over time is a source of variation in grading. Greater consistency on the poor paper also shows there is variation by level of student work.

Finally, in his investigation of variability in teachers' grades, Hulten (1925) sent five compositions representing standard work for students in 6th through 10th grade to 30 English teachers. The teachers were told the papers were written by 8th graders and were asked to grade them using a 100-point scale on which 75 was considered passing. Two months later, the same compositions in different order were sent to the same teachers. The grades on each occasion varied widely for the compositions. Twenty percent of grades changed from pass to fail or vice versa on the second marking. Hulten (1925) interpreted his findings to show that variation was due to teacher inconsistency or teacher error.

What Are the Implications of These Research Findings for Improvement in Grading Policy and Practice?

The overall finding of these many studies that "grades are unreliable" has given grades a bad reputation that continues to this day. It's also one of the reasons the general public prefers standardized test scores to grades as measures of student achievement (Brookhart, 2013). Educators have struggled for over a century to reform grading (Crooks, 1933; Kelly, 1914; Kirschenbaum, Napier, & Simon, 1971; Rugg, 1918; Smith & Dobbin, 1960) with modest success. Ironically, the current standards-based reform movement may have given educators a renewed opportunity. Teaching toward achievement of specific standards implies that educators should be able to measure and report that achievement accurately. Thus, clarity and press for transparency are the basis of the standards-based reform movement (Guskey, 2015).

Addressing the reliability of grades is a foundational issue. No amount of reform in grading policies or report card formats will improve grading if the grades reported are not reliable. Despite their age, the early research findings about the reliability of grading give us several practical suggestions for today. The three most important relate to criteria, consistency, and categories in grading.

Be Clear About Criteria

Our biggest takeaway from the early studies of reliability was the expectation that somehow English teachers, mathematics teachers, history teachers—any teachers—would just "know" how to grade a piece of student work. In Starch's (1913) analysis, one of the most important factors contributing to unreliability in grading was the difference in emphases teachers placed on different criteria while grading. There are three steps to solving this problem: (1) clearly define the criteria, (2) clearly specify the weight or relative emphasis each criterion should contribute to the grade for the piece of student work, and (3) apply the criteria and weights consistently.

Assessment theory has made great strides in the last century, and clarity of criteria is now an important, known foundation for good assessment. More current research has shown that individuals can be trained to judge examinee work accurately and reliably, according to established criteria (Myford, 2012). This same research offers insights into the factors associated with reliable and fair grading.

Our practical work with teachers suggests, however, that identifying and describing clear criteria is one of the most difficult things teachers strive to do (Brookhart, 2016). Teachers also must make sure these criteria describe students' learning and not simply how well they followed directions. In other words, the criteria should describe the quality of students' performance rather than students' compliance with directions and classroom procedures. Many teachers struggle to make criteria specific and clear enough to guarantee students' understanding and at the same time support grader agreement.

Be Consistent

Another takeaway from the early research on grading reliability is that teachers must be deliberately consistent across all possible factors that could influence grading. In the years between the earliest studies of grading and today, many recommendations for improving grading consistency have been made, including these by Brookhart and Nitko (2008):

- Use a scoring guide (a rubric, checklist, or point scheme) to focus decisions on criteria and performance-level requirements.
- Use a model answer as a reference for your expectations of students.
- For constructed-response assessments, grade all students' responses to one question before moving on to the next question.
- Bracket and evaluate separately (whether with a score or feedback) qualities of the work other than those in the criteria (e.g., neatness, format, grammar, and mechanics).
- Grade work anonymously. For example, cover students' names when grading papers.
- Every so often, ask a knowledgeable colleague to regrade some of the work you have graded.

The challenge before us is to find ways to help teachers at all levels to learn about these practices and then incorporate them on a regular basis in their classrooms.

Use Simple Scales with a Few Distinct Categories

Several studies found that the probable error on the 0 to 100 scale is plus or minus five to six points or even greater. This occurs largely because the 0 to 100 scale looks more precise than it really is. Another way of expressing this range of probable error is to say that teachers can't make reliable distinctions within about 10 to 12 points on a scale that includes 101 distinct levels of performance. There are two takeaways from this finding. One, don't overinterpret percentage grades because they look more precise than they in fact are. Two, it's better to use simpler scales with fewer categories (like *A, B, C, D,* and *F* or proficiency categories like *advanced, proficient,* and *basic*) that don't require such fine distinctions that are likely to be inaccurate.

Historically, this suggestion was taken. In the early 20th century, schools began to shift from reporting percentages to the familiar letter-grade scale (Guskey, 2015). The proficiency scales commonly used with contemporary standards-based grading reforms are similarly scales that include fewer categories, usually three or four. These changes may cause educators to have to contend with more borderline grades, but in fact, as the number of categories decreases, so do the number of potential borderline cases that must be considered (see discussion in Guskey & Bailey, 2001, pp. 72–74). The generally accepted recommendation for dealing with borderline cases is to look at additional evidence of student learning for the standard or learning goal (Brookhart & Nitko, 2008). The current resurgence of the 100-point percentage grade scale has been attributed to the use of computerized grading programs that typically are developed by software engineers who have scant knowledge of this history of their unreliability (Guskey, 2013).

Conclusion

The early research on grading is fascinating. In some ways it's like a slow-motion car wreck in a movie: you know what's going to happen, and there's nothing you can do about it except watch the impending disaster. In other ways it's like watching students learn: the studies detail the thinking and development that eventually brought grading to where it is today.

We favor the second perspective. While early studies of grading reliability did indeed draw some conclusions quite critical of grading practices at the time, they also succeeded in identifying several factors in the grading process that we can do something about. This is productive information for educators at every level. The most important of these factors are (1) use clear criteria, (2) take steps to ensure consistency, and (3) use scales that don't require finer distinctions than you can reliably make. Taking these steps will help educators make grades more reliable, more accurate, more meaningful, and far more defensible.

References

Ashbaugh, E. J. (1924). Reducing the variability of teachers' marks. *The Journal of Educational Research, 9,* 185–198.

Bolton, F. E. (1927). Do teachers' marks vary as much as supposed? *Education, 48,* 28–39.

Brimi, H. M. (2011). Reliability of grading high school work in English. *Practical Assessment, Research & Evaluation, 16*(17).

Brookhart, S. M. (2013). The use of teacher judgment for summative assessment in the USA. *Assessment in Education, 20,* 69–90.

Brookhart, S. M. (2016). In assessment, you see what you are looking for. *New Hampshire Journal of Education.* Retrieved: http://nhje.plymouth.edu/?article=in-assessment-you-see-what-you-are-looking-for

Brookhart, S. M., & Nitko, A. J. (2008). *Assessment and grading in classrooms.* Upper Saddle River, NJ: Pearson Education.

Crooks, A. D. (1933). Marks and marking systems: A digest. *The Journal of Educational Research, 27,* 259–272.

Edgeworth, F. Y. (1888). The statistics of examinations. *Journal of the Royal Statistical Society, 51,* 599–635.

Eells, W. C. (1930). Reliability of repeated grading of essay type examinations. *Journal of Educational Psychology, 21,* 48–52.

Guskey, T. R. (2013). The case against percentage grades. *Educational Leadership, 7*(1), 68–72.

Guskey, T. R. (2015). *On your mark: Challenging the conventions of grading and reporting.* Bloomington, IN: Solution Tree.

Guskey, T. R., & Bailey, J. M. (2001). *Developing grading and reporting systems for student learning.* Thousand Oaks, CA: Corwin.

Healy, K. L. (1935). A study of the factors involved in the rating of pupils' compositions. *Journal of Experimental Education, 4,* 50–53.

Hulten, C. E. (1925). The personal element in teachers' marks. *The Journal of Educational Research, 12,* 49–55.

Jacoby, H. (1910). Note on the marking system in the astronomical course at Columbia College, 1909–1910. *Science, 31,* 819–820.

Kelly, F. J. (1914). *Teachers' marks: Their variability and standardization.* Contributions to Education No. 66. New York: Teachers College, Columbia University.

Kirschenbaum, H., Napier, R., & Simon, S. B. (1971). *Wad-ja-get? The grading game in American education.* New York: Hart.

Lauterbach, C. E. (1928). Some factors affecting teachers' marks. *Journal of Educational Psychology, 19,* 266–271.

Myford, C. (2012). Rater cognition research: Some possible directions for the future. *Educational Measurement: Issues and Practice, 31*(3), 48–49.

Rugg, H. O. (1918). Teachers' marks and the reconstruction of the marking system. *The Elementary School Journal, 18,* 701–719.

Shriner, W. O. (1930). The comparison factor in the evaluation of examination papers. *Teachers College Journal, 1,* 65–74.

Silberstein, N. (1922). The variability of teachers' marks. *English Journal, 11,* 414–424.

Sims, V. M. (1933). Reducing the variability of essay examination marks through eliminating variations in standards of grading. *The Journal of Educational Research, 26,* 637–647.

Smith, A. Z., & Dobbin, J. E. (1960). Marks and marking systems. In C. W. Harris (Ed.), *Encyclopedia of educational research* (3rd ed.) (pp. 783–791). New York: Macmillan.

Starch, D. (1913). Reliability and distribution of grades. *Science, 38*(983), 630–636. doi:10.1126/science.38.983.630

Starch, D. (1915). Can the variability of marks be reduced? *School and Society, 2,* 242–243.

Starch, D., & Elliott, E. C. (1912). Reliability of the grading of high-school work in English. *School Review, 20,* 442–457.

Starch, D., & Elliott, E. C. (1913a). Reliability of grading work in mathematics. *School Review, 21,* 254–259.

Starch, D., & Elliott, E. C. (1913b). Reliability of grading work in history. *School Review, 21,* 676–681.

2

Report Card Grades and Educational Outcomes

Alex J. Bowers

Over the last 100 years, researchers have criticized teacher-assigned grades as subjective and unreliable measures of student academic achievement (Allen, 2005; Banker, 1927; Carter, 1952; Evans, 1976; Hargis, 1990; Kirschenbaum, Napier, & Simon, 1971; Quann, 1983; Simon & Bellanca, 1976), referring to them as "hodge-podge" (Brookhart, 1991) or "kitchen sink" practices (Cizek, 2000; Cizek, Fitzgerald, & Rachor, 1996). When teachers are asked what they are assessing with their grades, they consistently say not only student academic knowledge and achievement but also student persistence, behavior, participation, and effort (Henke, Chen, Goldman, Rollefson, & Gruber, 1999; Randall & Engelhard, 2009, 2010).

Why Is This Area of Research Important?

Mixing academic and nonacademic information in one grade results in a measure that is hard to interpret. However, as Cross and Frary (1999) note,

We must ask, if hodgepodge grading is so deplorable, why haven't students, parents and administrators or the general public called for reform? It may well be that they share a common understanding that grades often do, in fact, represent a hodgepodge of attitude, effort, conduct, growth, and achievement and that is what they expect and endorse. (p. 70)

Despite 100 years of research on the subjective nature of grades, mixed grading practices continue unabated alongside the rise of standardized testing responsibilities (Busick, 2000; Farr, 2000; Trumbull, 2000). The research shows that grades can be useful indicators of a host of factors besides academic progress (Bisesi, Farr, Greene, & Haydel, 2000; Folzer-Napier, 1976; Linn, 1982); as Swineford (1947) noted in a study on middle and high school grading practices, "the data clearly show that marks assigned by teachers in this school are reliable measures of *something* but there is apparently a lack of agreement on just what that something should be" (p. 47). Indeed, over the past 100 years, a strong line of research has attempted to understand the different components represented by grades as a means to inform decision making in schools and classrooms (Bowers, 2009; Parsons, 1959). Additionally, a persistent finding across this literature is that while standardized test scores have low criterion validity for overall schooling outcomes, such as graduation from high school and admission to postsecondary institutions, grades have consistently been the strongest predictors of K–12 educational persistence, completion, and transition from high school to college (Atkinson & Geiser, 2009; Bowers, Sprott, & Taff, 2013).

In this chapter, I will review the quantitative research over the past 100 years regarding what this "something" is that teacher-assigned grades represent, beyond the fundamental academic skills assessed by standardized test scores. I will also examine recent research in this area over the last few decades showing that teacher-assigned grades and marks assess not just student achievement but also persistence, behavior, and substantive engagement in the schooling process. Finally, I will review the research on how grades align to educational outcomes.

What Significant Studies Have Been Conducted in This Area?

To investigate these issues, I have reviewed studies of the research on K–12 grades as predictors of educational outcomes. My goal was to include studies from the past 100 years that (1) examined the relationship of K–12 grades to other schooling outcomes (e.g., test scores, dropout rates), (2) were quantitative, and (3) analyzed data from actual student assessments rather than focusing on teacher perspectives. For a detailed description of the literature I reviewed, please see Brookhart and colleagues (2016). I reviewed the article titles from the searches and then read the articles that matched the aim of this chapter.

What Have the Results of Those Studies Revealed?

The studies offer insight into both the relationship between grades and test scores and the use of grades as multidimensional assessments.

The Relationship Between Grades and Test Scores

Scholars researching the relationship between grades and test scores have tended to focus on the relationship of average grades (usually GPA) to standardized test scores. In the early 20th century, scholars began correlating standardized test scores to grades, first using small intact samples of students and the intelligence tests available at the time (Ross & Hooks, 1930; Unzicker, 1925) and then progressing to larger or more nationally generalizable samples and multiple standardized tests across subjects (Pattison, Grodsky, & Muller, 2013).

Although the perception remains that grades and test scores should logically approach a correlation of 1.0 (Allen, 2005; Duckworth, Quinn, & Tsukayama, 2012; Stanley & Baines, 2004), the research tells us that the correlation is in fact more moderate (closer to 0.5). As noted by Willingham, Pollack, and Lewis (2002):

> Understanding these characteristics of grades is important for the valid use of test scores as well as grade averages because, in practice, the two measures are often intimately connected.... [There is a] tendency to assume that a grade average and a test score are, in some sense, mutual surrogates; that is, measuring much the same thing, even in the face of obvious differences. (p. 2)

The research can be divided into two distinct eras: (1) studies from the early 20th century, and (2) studies from the late 20th century and early 21st century, when there was a resurgent interest in the topic. As an example of work in the first era, Unzicker (1925) examined the relationship between the grades of 425 7th, 8th, and 9th graders in the same school and their scores on the Otis intelligence test. He found that average grades across English, mathematics, and history had a 0.47 correlation with the tests.

Ross and Hooks (1930) provided the most comprehensive review of the research available in 1930, analyzing 20 studies from 1920 through 1929 on the degree of correlation between the intelligence tests and report card grades students received and their marks across a variety of subjects in 7th, 8th, and 9th grades. Samples across the studies included mostly single-school intact samples of 49 to 157 students and a range of popular intelligence assessments including the Illinois, Otis, and National tests (Brooks, 1929). Ross and Hooks (1930) found the correlation for the relationships of intelligence tests and grades given in the same 7th grade year ranged from 0.38 to 0.44, and drew the following conclusion:

> Data from this and other studies indicate that... the grade school record affords a more reliable or consistent basis of prediction [of

high school achievement] than any other available, the correlations in three widely-scattered school systems showing remarkable stability; and that without question the grade school record of the pupil is the most usable or practical of all bases for prediction, being available wherever cumulative records are kept, without cost and with a minimum expenditure of time and effort. (p. 195)

Subsequent studies compared grades to standardized achievement tests rather than intelligence tests. For example, Moore (1939) directly compared an analysis of about 200 5th and 6th graders in Wyoming and Colorado with similar studies from the time (Dickinson, 1925; Heilman, 1928; Kertes, 1932), identifying the correlation between the students' average grades to their average scores on the new Stanford Achievement Test as 0.61. Similarly, Carter (1952) examined the relationship between 235 student grades from a high school in Pennsylvania and standardized algebra achievement scores, finding a 0.52 correlation. A study by McCandless, Roberts, and Starnes from 1972, between the two dominant eras of research, examined the correlations between the average grades of 433 Atlanta 7th graders and their scores on the Metropolitan Achievement Test, tabulating differences by student socioeconomic status (SES), ethnicity, and gender. The researchers found that the overall correlation between grades and the standardized test was 0.31. Clearly, the first 50 or so years of research were marked by a focus on intelligence testing versus achievement testing, reflecting a desire to figure out the "something" that teacher-assigned grades represent (Ross & Hooks, 1930).

Research from the late 20th and early 21st centuries has replicated and extended the early findings using much larger and more representative samples and more modern standardized tests and methods (Brennan, Kim, Wenz-Gross, & Siperstein, 2001; Woodruff & Ziomek, 2004). Using data from 736 8th graders from across six Boston schools, Brennan and colleagues (2001) compared students' scores on the Massachusetts Comprehensive Assessment System reading test to their grades in mathematics, English, and science classes, reporting correlations of 0.54, 0.59, and 0.54 respectively.

In a study using a small intact sample of 140 8th graders, Duckworth and Seligman (2006) compared students' GPAs to their scores on the TerraNova Second Edition California Achievement Test, finding a correlation of 0.66. Subsequently, Duckworth and colleagues (2012) examined the data from 1,364 9th grade students and 510 8th grade students, comparing reading and math scores on standardized tests to GPAs, finding correlations between 0.62 and 0.66. Woodruff and Ziomek (2004) compared the data from all high school students who took the ACT college entrance exam between 1991 and 2003—about 700,000 students per year—and found consistently strong correlations of average GPAs and overall composite ACT scores ranging from 0.56 to 0.58, and specific correlations of math grades to ACT scores between 0.54 and 0.57, and of English scores to ACT scores between 0.45 and 0.50. One critique of this study is that the students self-reported their GPAs (Woodruff & Ziomek, 2004). Pattison and colleagues (2013) examined data from students who completed high school taken from nationally generalizable longitudinal studies from the National Center for Education Statistics (NCES), including the National Longitudinal Study of the High School Class of 1972 (NLS72), the High School and Beyond sophomore cohort (HS&B), the National Educational Longitudinal Study of 1988 (NELS), and the Educational Longitudinal Study of 2002 (ELS), comparing high school GPA from reading, mathematics, science, and social studies to the NCES standardized tests in 10th grade reading and mathematics. These data consist of tens of thousands of student achievement patterns across four decades (Pattison et al., 2013). The authors found GPA correlations consistent with the past research, including 0.52 to 0.64 for mathematics and 0.46 to 0.54 for reading comprehension.

More than 100 years of research strongly suggest that teacher-assigned grades correlate at about 0.5 to standardized measures of achievement. While there is some variance from year to year and across core subjects, when considering large nationally representative data sets, the correlation is neither very weak (indicating that teacher grades aren't completely subjective) nor very strong (indicating that teacher grades aren't perfect measures of fundamental academic knowledge). Rather, the correlation between grades and tests appears to be consistently moderate. This consistent moderate relationship persists across a significant amount of time and studies and despite large shifts across the educational system, especially in relation to accountability and standardized testing (Linn, 1982). When this moderate correlation is squared, about 25 percent of a teacher-assigned grade appears to address the fundamental academic knowledge measured by standardized tests (Bowers, 2011), with the remaining 75 percent at least partly attributable to separate factors.

Grades as Multidimensional Assessments

The research shows that grades appear to assess not just academic knowledge but substantive engagement and persistence as well (see Figure 2.1, pp. 40–41). In one early study, Sobel (1936) calculated the difference between students' standardized test scores and classroom grades, categorizing the students as "mark-superior" (high grades and low test scores), "test-superior" (low grades and high test scores), or "middle group" (average grades and test scores). Sobel noted that "mark-superior" students "are apparently outstanding in penmanship, attendance, punctuality, and effort marks. They also rank high in teachers' ratings on certain personality traits—industry, perseverance, dependability, cooperation, and ambition" (p. 239).

Miner (1967) examined 671 students' achievement variables from three high schools in a Midwestern city, including academic grades in 1st, 3rd, 6th, 9th, and 12th grades; achievement tests in 5th, 6th, and 9th grades; and classroom citizenship grades in 1st, 3rd, and 6th grades. She found that the variables separated into three factors:

(1) objective achievement as measured through standardized assessments, (2) early classroom citizenship (measuring a behavior factor), and (3) high school achievement as measured through grades. In this study, Miner demonstrated that grades could be identified as a factor separate from other achievement and behavior measures.

In attempting to understand the components of teacher-assigned grades, Farkas, Grobe, Sheehan, and Shuan (1990) examined the grades of 486 8th grade students. They also included a teacher survey of measures of each student's basic skills, absenteeism, work habits, disruptiveness, appearance and dress, and coursework mastery as measured by a district curriculum-referenced test on subject-specific skills. The authors show that student work habits and basic skills were the strongest noncognitive social and emotional predictors of grades:

> Most striking is the powerful effect of student work habits upon course grades. This confirms the notion that . . . teacher judgments of student noncognitive characteristics are powerful determinants of course grades, even when student cognitive performance is controlled. (p. 140)

Willingham and colleagues (2002) analyzed the second follow-up to the National Center for Educational Statistics' NELS:88 data set, examining the data from the full high school transcripts of 8,454 students across 581 schools. The authors examined the relationship between grades and a host of variables, including standardized tests, school skills, initiative, activities such as television watching and socializing, family background, and student attitudes toward school. Beyond the moderate correlation between grades and tests, the authors found strong positive relationships between grades and student motivation, engagement, completion of work assigned, and persistence. The authors found that grades provide a useful assessment of both conative factors (e.g., interest, volition, and self-regulation; see Snow, 1989) and cognitive student factors.

FIGURE 2.1 | **Studies of K–12 Report Card Grades as Multidimensional Measures of Academic Knowledge, Engagement, and Persistence**

Studies	Participants	Main Findings
Bowers (2009)	High school students	• Grades were multidimensional, separating core and noncore grades from state standardized assessments in science, mathematics, and reading.
Bowers (2011)	High school students	• Three main grading factors were identified: (1) a cognitive factor that describes the relationship between tests and core subject grades, (2) an engagement factor between core subject grades and noncore subject grades, and (3) a factor that described the difference between grades in art and physical education.
Casillas et al. (2012)	7th and 8th graders	• 25 percent of the explained variance in GPA was attributable to standardized assessments. • Academic discipline and commitment to school were strongly related to GPA.
Farkas, Grobe, Sheehan, & Shuan (1990)	8th graders and their teachers	• Student work habits were the strongest noncognitive predictors of grades.
Kelly (2008)	6th, 7th, and 8th grade students	• Positive and significant effects of students' substantive engagement were found on subsequent grades, but no relationship with procedural engagement.
Klapp Lekholm & Cliffordson (2008)	Swedish students	• Grades consisted of two major factors: (1) a cognitive achievement factor and (2) a noncognitive "common grade dimension."
Klapp Lekholm (2011) Klapp Lekholm & Cliffordson (2009)	Swedish students	• The cognitive achievement factor of grades consists of student self-perception of competence, self-efficacy, coping strategies, and subject-specific interest. The noncognitive factor consists of motivation and a general interest in school.
Miner (1967)	High school students	• The study examined academic grades in 1st, 3rd, 6th, 9th, and 12th grade; achievement tests in 5th, 6th, and 9th grades; and citizenship grades in 1st, 3rd, and 6th grades. Three factors were found: (1) objective achievement, (2) behavior factor, and (3) high school achievement as measured through grades.

Sobel (1936)	Not reported	• Students were categorized into three groups based on comparing grades and achievement test levels: (1) grade-superior, (2) middle-group, and (3) mark-superior.
Thorsen (2014)	Students in Sweden	• The study generally replicated Klapp Lekholm and Cliffordson (2009) in examining norm-referenced grades.
Thorsen & Cliffordson (2012)	9th grade students in Sweden	• The study generally replicated Klapp Lekholm and Cliffordson (2009).
Willingham, Pollack, & Lewis (2002)	High school students	• A moderate relationship between grades and tests was identified, as were strong positive relationships between grades and student motivation, engagement, completion of work assigned, and persistence.

Source: From "A Century of Grading Research: Meaning and Value in the Most Common Educational Measure," by S. M. Brookhart, T. R. Guskey, A. J. Bowers, J. H. McMillan, J. K. Smith, L. F. Smith, et al., 2016, *Review of Educational Research, 86*(4), pp. 803–848. Copyright 2016 by American Educational Research Association. Adapted with permission.

One critique of using grades to assess conative factors is that teachers may award grades based on students *appearing* engaged but just going through the motions (procedural engagement) rather than on legitimate effort and participation that leads to increased learning (substantive engagement). To address this issue, Kelly (2008) examined the data of 1,653 6th, 7th, and 8th graders related to grades, achievement, family background, and student effort. Student engagement was assessed through observation and coding of an extensive set of video-recorded classroom observations. Kelly found a significant correlation between substantive engagement and higher classroom grades but a statistically nonsignificant relationship between procedural engagement and grades, concluding that "most teachers successfully use grades to reward achievement-oriented behavior and promote a widespread growth in achievement" (p. 45). Kelly continued:

> The misperception that teachers base grades on the appearance of cooperation, rather than on legitimate effort, lends support to the use of high-stakes tests as the sole criterion for promotion

decision by advancing the myth that standardized tests are inherently objective, while teachers' assessments are inherently subjective and likely to be biased. (p. 46)

As a researcher myself, I used multidimensional scaling to examine the relationship between grades and standardized tests, first with a small intact sample of 195 students from two small school districts (Bowers, 2009) and again with a sample from the NCES ELS:2002 data set of 4,520 students (Bowers, 2011). These studies examined the difference not just between grades and standardized test scores in each semester in high school, but also between grades in core subjects (mathematics, English, science, and social studies) and noncore subjects (foreign/non-English languages, art, and physical education). In my analysis, I found strong evidence of three factors at play: (1) the cognitive factor for the relationship between tests and core subject grades, (2) the conative factor for the relationship between core subject grades and noncore subject grades (termed a "Success at School Factor, SSF"), and (3) a factor related specifically to the difference between grades in art and physical education. I was able to show that much of the variance in grades was not attributable to the moderate correlation between tests and grades, but rather to teachers assessing students' ability to navigate the social processes of schooling using substantive engagement and persistence. Subsequently, Duckworth and colleagues (2012) used structural equation modeling of data for 510 New York City 5th–8th graders to show that the engagement and persistence factor is mediated through teacher evaluations of student conduct and homework completion.

Analyzing a sample of 4,660 7th and 8th graders across 24 middle schools from the Midwest and South, Casillas and colleagues (2012) examined the relationship between students' classroom grades and scores on ACT's middle-grades English, mathematics, science, and reading assessments and a range of psychosocial characteristics (student motivation through academic discipline and commitment to school, social control such as positive family and personal relationships, self-regulation and orderly conduct, and behaviors such as absenteeism and amount of time spent on homework). The authors found that 25 percent of students' GPA was attributable to standardized assessments, with 30 percent attributable to prior grades, 23 percent to psychosocial factors, 10 percent to behavioral indicators, 9 percent to demographics, and 3 percent to school factors. Of the psychosocial factors, academic discipline and commitment to school had the strongest relationship to GPA.

A strong set of recent studies hails from Sweden (see, for example, Cliffordson, 2008; Klapp Lekholm, 2011; Klapp Lekholm & Cliffordson, 2008, 2009; Thorsen, 2014; Thorsen & Cliffordson, 2012) and analyzes data sets of about 100,000 Swedish students. Klapp Lekholm and Cliffordson (2008) examined data for the entire population of 99,070 Swedish students who left compulsory school in 2003 across 1,246 schools and showed that grades in mathematics, English, and Swedish consisted of two major factors: (1) a cognitive achievement factor and (2) a noncognitive "common grade dimension." In a follow-up study (Klapp Lekholm & Cliffordson, 2009), the authors reanalyzed the same with a focus on multiple student and school characteristics that influenced both factors. For the cognitive achievement factor of grades, the following characteristics were most important: student self-perception of competence, self-efficacy, coping strategies, and subject-specific interest. By contrast, for the noncognitive "common grade dimension" related to higher grades across all three subjects, the most important student variables were motivation and a general interest in school. These results were then replicated across three full population-level cohorts in Sweden representing all 9th grade students in the years 2003 (99,085), 2004 (105,697), and 2005 (108,753) (Thorsen & Cliffordson, 2012), as well as in comparison to both norm-referenced and criterion-referenced grading systems using a data set of 3,855 students (Thorsen, 2014). Klapp Lekholm and Cliffordson (2009) noted:

> The relation between general interest or motivation and the common grade dimension seems to recognize that students who are motivated often possess both specific and general goals and approach new phenomena with the goal of understanding them, which is a student characteristic awarded in grades. (p. 19)

These findings provide strong evidence in replication of Kelly's (2008), Bowers's (2009, 2011), and Casillas and colleagues' (2012) findings that substantive engagement in the process of schooling is an important component of grades unrelated to the component of grades that is measured well by standardized tests.

Thus, grades are not and have never been a valid measure of academic achievement. Rather, they are a multidimensional assessment of *both* academic achievement (cognitive factors) *and* substantive engagement in the schooling process (noncognitive/conative factors). This makes grading a very useful assessment, particularly when augmented by standardized test score data. As the goals of education are far broader than acquiring the fundamental academic knowledge and skills represented by scores on standardized achievement tests (Cusick, 1983; Labaree, 1997, 2012; Nichols & Berliner, 2007), it is a strength and a benefit of the system that schools already possess both tests and grades for assessing multiple and sometimes conflicting goals of schooling. Grades appear to be very useful as assessments of noncognitive social and emotional behavior factors that are well-known to predict educational outcomes (Heckman & Rubinstein, 2001; Levin, 2013). This is important, as contemporary researchers have postulated that while noncognitive skills help to build cognitive skills, the reverse may not be the case (Cunha & Heckman, 2008).

Grades as Predictors of Educational Outcomes

Teacher-assigned grades are known predictors of high school graduation (Bowers, 2014) and college attendance (Atkinson & Geiser, 2009; Cliffordson, 2008). This is not surprising, as satisfactory grades historically have been one of the main criteria for a high school diploma (Rumberger, 2011). Many studies have used grades in early elementary school to identify students categorized as "at-risk" (Gleason & Dynarski, 2002; Pallas, 1989). Early studies in this domain (Fitzsimmons, Cheever, Leonard, & Macunovich, 1969; Lloyd, 1974, 1978; Voss, Wendling, & Elliott, 1966) identified teacher-assigned grades as among the strongest predictors of whether or not a student would reach graduation. Subsequent studies combined these findings with multiple other variables, such as absences and misbehavior; however, grades remained a strong predictor (Barrington & Hendricks, 1989; Cairns, Cairns, & Neckerman, 1989; Ekstrom, Goertz, Pollack, & Rock, 1986; Ensminger & Slusarcick, 1992; Finn, 1989; Hargis, 1990; Morris, Ehren, & Lenz, 1991; Rumberger, 1987; Troob, 1985). More recent research regards low or failing grades as having a cumulative effect over years on students deciding to drop out of school (Alexander, Entwisle, & Kabbani, 2001; Jimerson, Egeland, Sroufe, & Carlson, 2000; Pallas, 2003; Roderick & Camburn, 1999). Figure 2.2 presents a summary of this research.

The more recent research focuses on the influence of low grades and of a continuous scale of grades (such as GPA) on students deciding to drop out. For example, studies of students in Chicago have shown that failing a core subject course in 9th grade is highly correlated with dropping out of school (Allensworth, 2013; Allensworth & Easton, 2005, 2007), and at the middle school level, there is a correlation between grades and transitioning from middle school to high school (Allensworth, Gwynne, Moore, & de la Torre, 2014). Using data from Philadelphia, Balfanz, Herzog, and MacIver (2007) showed a strong relationship between failing core courses in 6th grade and dropping out. In my own work, I have found the strongest predictor of dropping out, after grade retention, to be receipt of *D*s and *F*s (Bowers, 2010b).

Many studies also consider the full GPA scale in predicting school completion (Rumberger & Palardy, 2005). However, few

FIGURE 2.2 | **Studies of Grades as Predictors of Educational Outcomes**

Studies	Participants	Main Findings
Alexander, Entwisle, & Kabbani (2001)	9th grade students	• Student background, grade retention, academic performance, and behavior are strongly related to dropping out of school.
Allensworth & Easton (2007)	9th grade students in Chicago	• GPA and failing a course in early high school strongly predicted dropping out of school.
Allensworth, Gwynne, Moore, & de la Torre (2014)	8th grade Chicago students	• Middle school grades and attendance are stronger predictors of high school performance in comparison to test scores, and middle school grades are a strong predictor of students on or off track for high school success.
Balfanz, Herzog, & MacIver (2007)	6th grade students from Philadelphia	• Predictors of dropping out of high school included failing mathematics or English, low attendance, and poor behavior.
Barrington & Hendricks (1989)	High school students	• GPA, number of low grades, intelligence test scores, and student mobility significantly predicted dropout.
Bowers (2010a)	Students tracked from 1st grade through high school	• Having low grades over time across all types of course subjects correlated with dropping out and not taking the ACT.
Bowers (2010b)	Students tracked from 1st grade through high school	• Receiving low grades (*D* or *F*) and being held back in a grade strongly related to dropping out.
Bowers & Sprott (2012)	10th grade students	• Noncumulative GPA trajectories in early high school were strongly predictive of dropping out.
Bowers, Sprott, & Taff (2013)	Review of 36 previous studies	• Dropout flags focusing on GPA were some of the most accurate dropout flags across the literature.
Cairns, Cairns, & Neckerman (1989)	7th grade students	• Beyond student demographics, student aggressiveness and low levels of academic performance were associated with dropping out.

Studies	Participants	Main Findings
Cliffordson (2008)	Swedish students	• Grades predicted achievement in higher education more strongly than the Swedish Scholastic Aptitude Test, and criterion-referenced grades were slightly better predictors than norm-referenced grades.
Ekstrom, Goertz, Pollack, & Rock (1986)	10th grade students	• Grades and problem behavior were identified as the most important variables for identifying dropping out, even higher than test scores.
Ensminger & Slusarcick (1992)	1st grade students from historically disadvantaged communities	• Low grades and aggressive behavior were related to eventually dropping out, with low SES skewing relationships negatively.
Fitzsimmons, Cheever, Leonard, & Macunovich (1969)	High school students	• Students receiving low grades (D or F) in elementary or middle school were at much higher risk of dropping out.
Jimerson, Egeland, Sroufe, & Carlson (2000)	Children tracked from birth through age 19	• Home environment, quality of parent caregiving, academic achievement, student problem behaviors, peer competence, and intelligence test scores were significantly related with dropping out.
Lloyd (1978)	3rd grade students	• Grades and marks significantly correlated with dropping out.
Morris, Ehren, & Lenz (1991)	Students in 7th through 12th grade	• Dropping out was predicted by absences, low grades (D or F), and mobility.
Roderick & Camburn (1999)	Chicago 9th grade students	• Significant predictors of course failure included low attendance and found failure rates varied significantly at the school level.
Troob (1985)	New York City high school students	• Low grades and high absences corresponded to higher levels of dropping out.

Source: From "A Century of Grading Research: Meaning and Value in the Most Common Educational Measure," by S. M. Brookhart, T. R. Guskey, A. J. Bowers, J. H. McMillan, J. K. Smith, L. F. Smith, et al., 2016, *Review of Educational Research, 86*(4), pp. 803–848. Copyright 2016 by American Educational Research Association. Adapted with permission.

studies have focused on grades alone as the only predictor of graduation or dropping out, rather examining patterns in grades (Bowers, 2010a; Bowers & Sprott, 2012). A recent review of the research on the accuracy of dropout flags and predictors showed that longitudinal GPA trajectories were among the most accurate predictors in the literature to date (Bowers et al., 2013).

What Are the Implications of These Research Findings for Improvement in Grading Policy and Practice?

A century of quantitative studies on K–12 classroom grades shows that teacher-assigned grades are a multidimensional assessment of student cognitive and noncognitive/conative factors. Grades represent the academic knowledge represented in standardized test scores as well as substantive engagement, persistence, and positive school behaviors. Grades and standardized tests are moderately correlated, and the assumption that grades and tests should have a strong relationship is misplaced, as these two assessments have never been shown to have a strong relationship. Rather, grades are a useful assessment of multiple factors that teachers value in student work, and thus useful in identifying students who may face either academic or socio-behavioral challenges in the future. The research, especially over the last two decades, suggests that when combined with standardized tests, teacher-assigned grades provide a rich multidimensional assessment of student performance. From a policy perspective, then, both grades and standardized test scores should be considered when making major decisions about students.

Unfortunately, policy and practice discussions often confuse standardized tests and grades. Do they measure the same thing? Are grades more or less subjective than tests? I started this chapter by relating early research that maligns teacher-assigned grades as subjective and unreliable, while accepting standardized test scores as objective measures of fundamental academic knowledge. This perspective, promulgated by the testing industry, can lead teachers, principals, and districts to think there is something wrong with grades and focus on standardized assessments. However, just from a logic and efficiency standpoint, if a school already has tests to assess fundamental academic knowledge, why would it need to create another one by aligning grades and tests? As I have described throughout this chapter, grades are not subjective and unreliable; the research is very clear that teachers are quite good at assessing student engagement and persistence through grades. Rather, grades are multidimensional, with about 25 percent of any grade assessing fundamental knowledge and the balance assessing engagement. It is this remaining 75 percent that correlates to overall life outcomes such as graduating from high school and college.

Of course, grades are not perfect, and there is room for improvement in the system. However, as we attempt to clarify the signal and meaning of grades to students and parents, let us remember that a century of research shows assessing engagement to be an important component of grading that is valued by students, parents, schools, employers, and communities.

References

Alexander, K. L., Entwisle, D. R., & Kabbani, N. S. (2001). The dropout process in life course perspective: Early risk factors at home and school. *The Teachers College Record, 103*(5), 760–822.

Allen, J. D. (2005). Grades as valid measures of academic achievement of classroom learning. *The Clearing House, 78*(5), 218–223.

Allensworth, E. M. (2013). The use of ninth-grade early warning indicators to improve Chicago schools. *Journal of Education for Students Placed at Risk (JESPAR), 18*(1), 68–83. doi:10.1080/10824669.2013.745181

Allensworth, E. M., & Easton, J. Q. (2005). *The on-track indicator as a predictor of high school graduation* (Vol. 2006). Chicago: University of Chicago, Consortium on Chicago School Research.

Allensworth, E. M., & Easton, J. Q. (2007). *What matters for staying on-track and graduating in Chicago public high schools: A close look at course grades, failures, and attendance in the freshman year.* Chicago: University of Chicago, Consortium on Chicago School Research.

Allensworth, E. M., Gwynne, J. A., Moore, P., & de la Torre, M. (2014). *Looking forward to high school and college: Middle grade indicators of readiness in Chicago Public Schools.* Chicago: University of Chicago, Consortium on Chicago School Research.

Atkinson, R. C., & Geiser, S. (2009). Reflections on a century of college admissions tests. *Educational Researcher, 38*(9), 665–676. doi:10.3102/0013189x09351981

Balfanz, R., Herzog, L., & MacIver, D. J. (2007). Preventing student disengagement and keeping students on the graduation path in urban middle-grades schools: Early identification and effective interventions. *Educational Psychologist, 42*(4), 223–235. doi:10.1080/00461520701621079

Banker, H. J. (1927). The significance of teachers' marks. *The Journal of Educational Research, 16*(3), 159–171. doi:10.1080/00220671.1927.10879778

Barrington, B. L., & Hendricks, B. (1989). Differentiating characteristics of high school graduates, dropouts, and nongraduates. *The Journal of Educational Research, 82*(6), 309–319.

Bisesi, T., Farr, R., Greene, B., & Haydel, E. (2000). Reporting to parents and the community. In E. Trumbull & B. Farr (Eds.), *Grading and reporting student progress in an age of standards* (pp. 157–183). Norwood, MA: Christopher-Gordon Publishers.

Bowers, A. J. (2009). Reconsidering grades as data for decision making: More than just academic knowledge. *Journal of Educational Administration, 47*(5), 609–629. doi:10.1108/09578230910981080

Bowers, A. J. (2010a). Analyzing the longitudinal K–12 grading histories of entire cohorts of students: Grades, data driven decision making, dropping out and hierarchical cluster analysis. *Practical Assessment Research and Evaluation, 15*(7), 1–18.

Bowers, A. J. (2010b). Grades and graduation: A longitudinal risk perspective to identify student dropouts. *The Journal of Educational Research, 103*(3), 191–207. doi:10.1080/00220670903382970

Bowers, A. J. (2011). What's in a grade? The multidimensional nature of what teacher-assigned grades assess in high school. *Educational Research and Evaluation, 17*(3), 141–159. doi:10.1080/13803611.2011.597112

Bowers, A. J. (2014). Student risk factors. In D. J. Brewer & L. O. Picus (Eds.), *Encyclopedia of education economics and finance.* Thousand Oaks, CA: Sage.

Bowers, A. J., & Sprott, R. (2012). Examining the multiple trajectories associated with dropping out of high school: A growth mixture model analysis. *The Journal of Educational Research, 105*(3), 176–195. doi: 10.1080/00220671.2011.552075

Bowers, A. J., Sprott, R., & Taff, S. (2013). Do we know who will drop out? A review of the predictors of dropping out of high school: Precision, sensitivity and specificity. *The High School Journal, 96*(2), 77–100.

Brennan, R. T., Kim, J., Wenz-Gross, M., & Siperstein, G. N. (2001). The relative equitability of high-stakes testing versus teacher-assigned grades: An analysis of the Massachusetts Comprehensive Assessment System (MCAS). *Harvard Educational Review, 71*(2), 173–215.

Brookhart, S. M. (1991). Letter: Grading practices and validity. *Educational Measurement: Issues and Practice, 10*(1), 35–36.

Brookhart, S. M., Guskey, T. R., Bowers, A. J., McMillan, J. H., Smith, J. K., Smith, L. F., et al. (2016). A century of grading research: Meaning and value in the most common educational measure. *Review of Educational Research, 86*(4), 803–848.

Brooks, F. D. (1929). *The psychology of adolescence.* Oxford, England: Houghton Mifflin.

Busick, K. (2000). Grading and standards-based assessment. In E. Trumbull & B. Farr (Eds.), *Grading and reporting student progress in an age of standards* (pp. 71–86). Norwood, MA: Christopher-Gordon Publishers.

Cairns, R. B., Cairns, B. D., & Neckerman, H. J. (1989). Early school dropout: Configurations and determinants. *Child Development, 60,* 1437–1452.

Carter, R. S. (1952). How invalid are marks assigned by teachers? *Journal of Educational Psychology, 43*(4), 218–228. doi:10.1037/h0061688

Casillas, A., Robbins, S., Allen, J., Kuo, Y.-L., Hanson, M. A., & Schmeiser, C. (2012). Predicting early academic failure in high school from prior academic achievement, psychosocial characteristics, and behavior. *Journal of Educational Psychology, 104*(2), 407–420. doi:10.1037/a0027180

Cizek, G. J. (2000). Pockets of resistance in the assessment revolution. *Educational Measurement: Issues and Practice, 19*(2), 16–23.

Cizek, G. J., Fitzgerald, S. M., & Rachor, R. E. (1995). Teachers' assessment practices: Preparation, isolation, and the kitchen sink. *Educational Assessment, 3*(2), 159–179.

Cliffordson, C. (2008). Differential prediction of study success across academic programs in the Swedish context: The validity of grades and tests as selection instruments for higher education. *Educational Assessment, 13*(1), 56–75. doi:10.1080/10627190801968240

Cross, L. H., & Frary, R. B. (1999). Hodgepodge grading: Endorsed by students and teachers alike. *Applied Measurement in Education, 12*(1), 53–72.

Cunha, F., & Heckman, J. J. (2008). Formulating, identifying, and estimating the technology of cognitive and noncognitive skill formation. *Journal of Human Resources, 43*(4), 738–782. doi:10.3368/jhr.43.4.738

Cusick, P. A. (1983). *The egalitarian ideal and the American high school: Studies of three schools.* New York: Longman.

Dickinson, C. E. (1925). A study of the relation of reading ability to scholastic achievement. *The School Review, 33*(8), 616–626. doi:10.1086/438215

Duckworth, A. L., Quinn, P. D., & Tsukayama, E. (2012). What No Child Left Behind leaves behind: The roles of IQ and self-control in predicting standardized achievement test scores and report card grades. *Journal of Educational Psychology, 104*(2), 439–451. doi:10.1037/a0026280

Duckworth, A. L., & Seligman, M. E. P. (2006). Self-discipline gives girls the edge: Gender in self-discipline, grades, and achievement test scores. *Journal of Educational Psychology, 98*(1), 198–208. doi: 10.1037/0022-0663.98.1.198

Ekstrom, R. B., Goertz, M. E., Pollack, J. M., & Rock, D. A. (1986). Who drops out of high school and why? Findings from a national study. *Teachers College Record, 87*(3), 356–373.

Ensminger, M. E., & Slusarcick, A. L. (1992). Paths to high school graduation or dropout: A longitudinal study of a first-grade cohort. *Sociology of Education, 65*(2), 91–113.

Evans, F. B. (1976). What research says about grading. In S. B. Simon & J. A. Bellanca (Eds.), *Degrading the grading myths: A primer of alternatives to grades and marks* (pp. 30–50). Washington, DC: Association for Supervision and Curriculum Development.

Farkas, G., Grobe, R. P., Sheehan, D., & Shuan, Y. (1990). Cultural resources and school success: Gender, ethnicity, and poverty groups within an urban school district. *American Sociological Review, 55*(1), 127–142. doi: 10.2307/2095708

Farr, B. P. (2000). Grading practices: An overview of the issues. In E. Trumbull & B. Farr (Eds.), *Grading and reporting student progress in an age of standards* (pp. 1–22). Norwood, MA: Christopher-Gordon Publishers.

Finn, J. D. (1989). Withdrawing from school. *Review of Educational Research, 59*(2), 117–142.

Fitzsimmons, S. J., Cheever, J., Leonard, E., & Macunovich, D. (1969). School failures: Now and tomorrow. *Developmental Psychology, 1*(2), 134–146.

Folzer-Napier, S. (1976). Grading and young children. In S. B. Simon & J. A. Bellanca (Eds.), *Degrading the grading myths: A primer of alternatives to grades and marks* (pp. 23–27). Washington, DC: Association for Supervision and Curriculum Development.

Gleason, P., & Dynarski, M. (2002). Do we know whom to serve? Issues in using risk factors to identify dropouts. *Journal of Education for Students Placed at Risk, 7*(1), 25–41. doi:10.1207/S15327671ESPR0701_3

Hargis, C. H. (1990). *Grades and grading practices: Obstacles to improving education and helping at-risk students.* Springfield, IL: Charles C. Thomas.

Heckman, J. J., & Rubinstein, Y. (2001). The importance of noncognitive skills: Lessons from the GED testing program. *The American Economic Review, 91*(2), 145–149. doi:10.1257/aer.91.2.145

Heilman, J. D. (1928). The relative influence upon educational achievement of some hereditary and environmental factors. In *The twenty-seventh yearbook of the National Society for the Study of Education: Nature and nurture, part II—Their influence upon achievement* (pp. 35–65). Bloomington, IL: Public School Publishing Co.

Henke, R. R., Chen, X., Goldman, G., Rollefson, M., & Gruber, K. (1999). *What happens in classrooms? Instructional practices in elementary and secondary schools, 1994–1995.* Washington, DC: U.S. Department of Education, National Center for Education Statistics.

Jimerson, S. R., Egeland, B., Sroufe, L. A., & Carlson, B. (2000). A prospective longitudinal study of high school dropouts examining multiple predictors across development. *Journal of School Psychology, 38*(6), 525–549.

Kelly, S. (2008). What types of students' effort are rewarded with high marks? *Sociology of Education, 81*(1), 32–52. doi:10.1177/003804070808100102

Kertes, F. (1932). Ability grouping in the high school. *The Mathematics Teacher, 25*(1), 5–16.

Kirschenbaum, H., Napier, R., & Simon, S. B. (1971). *Wad-ja-get? The grading game in American education.* New York: Hart Publishing.

Klapp Lekholm, A. (2011). Effects of school characteristics on grades in compulsory school. *Scandinavian Journal of Educational Research, 55*(6), 587–608. doi:10.1080/00313831.2011.555923

Klapp Lekholm, A., & Cliffordson, C. (2008). Discrepancies between school grades and test scores at individual and school level: Effects of gender and family background. *Educational Research and Evaluation, 14*(2), 181–199.

Klapp Lekholm, A., & Cliffordson, C. (2009). Effects of student characteristics on grades in compulsory school. *Educational Research and Evaluation, 15*(1), 1–23. doi:10.1080/13803610802470425

Labaree, D. F. (1997). Public goods, private goods: The American struggle over educational goals. *American Educational Research Journal, 34*(1), 39–81. doi:10.3102/00028312034001039

Labaree, D. F. (2012). *Someone has to fail: The zero-sum game of public schooling.* Cambridge, MA: Harvard University Press.

Levin, H. M. (2013). The utility and need for incorporating noncognitive skills into large-scale educational assessments. In M. von Davier, E. Gonzalez, I. Kirsch, & K. Yamamoto (Eds.), *The role of international large-scale assessments: Perspectives from technology, economy, and educational research* (pp. 67–86). Dordrecht, the Netherlands: Springer.

Linn, R. L. (1982). Ability testing: Individual differences, prediction, and differential prediction. In A. K. Wigdor & W. R. Garner (Eds.), *Ability testing: Uses, consequences, and controversies* (pp. 335–388). Washington, DC: National Academy Press.

Lloyd, D. N. (1974). Analysis of sixth grade characteristics predicting high school dropout or graduation. *JSAS Catalog of Selected Documents in Psychology, 4,* 90.

Lloyd, D. N. (1978). Prediction of school failure from third-grade data. *Educational and Psychological Measurement, 38*(4), 1193–1200.

McCandless, B. R., Roberts, A., & Starnes, T. (1972). Teachers' marks, achievement test scores, and aptitude relations with respect to social class, race, and sex. *Journal of Educational Psychology, 63*(2), 153–159. doi:10.1037/h0032646

Miner, B. C. (1967). Three factors of school achievement. *The Journal of Educational Research, 60*(8), 370–376. doi:10.1080/00220671.1967.10883518

Moore, C. C. (1939). The elementary school mark. *The Pedagogical Seminary and Journal of Genetic Psychology, 54*(2), 285–294. doi:10.1080/08856559.1939.10534336

Morris, J. D., Ehren, B. J., & Lenz, B. K. (1991). Building a model to predict which fourth through eighth graders will drop out in high school. *Journal of Experimental Education, 59*(3), 286–293.

Nichols, S. L., & Berliner, D. C. (2007). *Collateral damage: How high stakes testing corrupts America's schools.* Cambridge, MA: Harvard Education Press.

Pallas, A. M. (1989). Conceptual and measurement issues in the study of school dropouts. In K. Namboodiri & R. G. Corwin (Eds.), *Research in the sociology of education and socialization* (Vol. 8, pp. 87–116). Greenwich, CT: JAI Press.

Pallas, A. M. (2003). Educational transitions, trajectories, and pathways. In J. T. Mortimer & M. J. Shanahan (Eds.), *Handbook of the life course.* New York: Kluwer Academic/Plenum Publishers.

Parsons, T. (1959). The school class as a social system: Some of its functions in American society. *Harvard Educational Review, 29*(4), 297–318.

Pattison, E., Grodsky, E., & Muller, C. (2013). Is the sky falling? Grade inflation and the signaling power of grades. *Educational Researcher, 42*(5), 259–265. doi:10.3102/0013189x13481382

Quann, C. J. (1983). *Grades and grading: Historical perspectives and the 1982 AACRAO study* (p. 75). Washington, DC: American Association of Collegiate Registrars and Admissions Officers.

Randall, J., & Engelhard, G. (2009). Examining teacher grades using Rasch Measurement Theory. *Journal of Educational Measurement, 46*(1), 1–18. doi:10.1111/j.1745-3984.2009.01066.x

Randall, J., & Engelhard, G. (2010). Examining the grading practices of teachers. *Teaching and Teacher Education, 26*(7), 1372–1380. doi:10.1016/j.tate.2010.03.008

Roderick, M., & Camburn, E. (1999). Risk and recovery from course failure in the early years of high school. *American Educational Research Journal, 36*(2), 303–343. doi:10.3102/00028312036002303

Ross, C. C., & Hooks, N. T. (1930). How shall we predict high-school achievement? *The Journal of Educational Research, 22*(3), 184–196. doi:10.1080/00220671.1930.10880085

Rumberger, R. W. (1987). High school dropouts: A review of issues and evidence. *Review of Educational Research, 57*(2), 101–121.

Rumberger, R. W. (2011). *Dropping out: Why students drop out of high school and what can be done about it.* Cambridge, MA: Harvard University Press.

Rumberger, R. W., & Palardy, G. J. (2005). Test scores, dropout rates, and transfer rates as alternative indicators of high school performance. *American Educational Research Journal, 42*(1), 3–42. doi:10.3102/00028312042001003

Simon, S. B., & Bellanca, J. A. (1976). *Degrading the grading myths: A primer of alternatives to grades and marks.* Washington, DC: Association for Supervision and Curriculum Development.

Snow, R. E. (1989). Toward assessment of cognitive and conative structures in learning. *Educational Researcher, 18*(9), 8–14. doi:10.3102/0013189x018009008

Sobel, F. S. (1936). Teachers' marks and objective tests as indices of adjustment. *Teachers College Record, 38*(3), 239–240.

Stanley, G., & Baines, L. (2004). No more shopping for grades at B-Mart: Re-establishing grades as indicators of academic performance. *The Clearing House: A Journal of Educational Strategies, Issues and Ideas, 77*(3), 101–104. doi:10.1080/00098650409601237

Swineford, F. (1947). Examination of the purported unreliability of teachers' marks. *The Elementary School Journal, 47*(9), 516–521. doi:10.1086/462367

Thorsen, C. (2014). Dimensions of norm-referenced compulsory school grades and their relative importance for the prediction of upper secondary school grades. *Scandinavian Journal of Educational Research, 58*(2), 127–146. doi:10.1080/00313831.2012.705322

Thorsen, C., & Cliffordson, C. (2012). Teachers' grade assignment and the predictive validity of criterion-referenced grades. *Educational Research and Evaluation, 18*(2), 153–172. doi:10.1080/13803611.2012.659929

Troob, C. (1985). *Longitudinal study of students entering high school in 1979: The relationship between first term performance and school completion.* New York: New York City Board of Education.

Trumbull, E. (2000). Why do we grade—and should we? In E. Trumbull & B. Farr (Eds.), *Grading and reporting student progress in an age of standards* (pp. 23–44). Norwood, MA: Christopher-Gordon Publishers.

Unzicker, S. P. (1925). Teachers' marks and intelligence. *The Journal of Educational Research, 11*(2), 123–131. doi:10.1080/00220671.1925.10879537

Voss, H. L., Wendling, A., & Elliott, D. S. (1966). Some types of high school dropouts. *The Journal of Educational Research, 59*(8), 363–368.

Willingham, W. W., Pollack, J. M., & Lewis, C. (2002). Grades and test scores: Accounting for observed differences. *Journal of Educational Measurement, 39*(1), 1–37.

Woodruff, D. J., & Ziomek, R. L. (2004). *High school grade inflation from 1991 to 2003.* (Research report series 2004–05.) Iowa City, IA: ACT.

3

The Composition of Grades: Cognitive and Noncognitive Factors

Sarah M. Bonner and Peggy P. Chen

In grading student work and reporting grades, teachers employ a deliberate system to rate and classify the quality of students' classroom performance into ordered categories. These categories may be labeled from *A* to *F,* from *highly proficient* to *below proficiency,* or in other ways.

Broadly defined, measurements quantify theoretical attributes or constructs, the meanings of which are socially or culturally negotiated. Thus, educational outcomes are defined through social negotiation. As Haertel (1985) argued 30 years ago about all educational outcomes, "They are artificial, designed deliberately to equip students with a repertoire of appropriate responses to the complex settings and symbols of our culture" (p. 28). Because of the cultural nature of constructs, the way we define achievement and educational outcomes varies across different settings or cultures as well as over time due to societal change.

This process of contextual negotiation over construct definition is particularly evident in grades. Within the United States, grading practices vary considerably. Teacher effectiveness varies by region, as do the levels of achievement represented by high marks. Grades awarded in different locales may not be calibrated against a common criterion but awarded to students based on their performance in comparison with that of other students in the same locale (Farkas, Grobe, Sheehan, & Shuan, 1990). Definitions of achievement may also differ by content area (Bowers, 2011), student developmental level (Bonner & Chen, 2009), school or district grading policies (Carey & Carifio, 2012), and teachers' beliefs about learning (Chen & Bonner, 2017). Finally, all grades contain a measure of unpredictability due to the specific idiosyncrasies of the teachers who award them.

Given the largely subjective nature of grades, stakeholders sometimes disagree about how to interpret them. This may seem strange given the ubiquity of grades in U.S. schools; most people *think* they know what grades mean. Most parents probably would not claim to be able to interpret a scale score of 420 on the 8th grade State of New York exam in English/language arts, but they know (or *think* they know) the difference between an *A* and a *C*. However, parents and others may be misled in their interpretations when teachers grade according to different standards, principles, or beliefs. One teacher's *A* can mean something quite different from another teacher's. Without a shared understanding of what grades actually measure, how can they be accurately interpreted?

Why Is This Area of Research Important?

Poor interpretability is problematic for any kind of educational measurement, but particularly so for grades, which are the most common means of communicating student academic performance in the United States and Canada. They communicate information about performance status to students (Pattison, Grodsky, & Muller,

2013) and carry emotional valence that can affect student self-image (Thomas & Oldfather, 1997). Course grades have immediate and long-term academic consequences for students. They influence students' placement in classes (e.g., advanced placement, remediation) and grade promotion. They affect selection for awards and honors, which in turn affect postsecondary opportunities (Tyson & Roksa, 2017). According to the National Association for College Admission Counseling (2016), grades are the most important factor that colleges and universities use in admitting students. Grades are also significant at the administrative and school leadership levels; because they influence school and course promotion, they affect graduation rates and school performance indices. For instance, in New York State, metrics of school accountability include the four-year graduation rate, which is determined by the rate at which students pass courses to achieve the required credits (New York State Education Department, 2017). Finally, parents and families make decisions based on school grades. After seeing poor grades, parents may chide their children to perform better, hire a tutor to assist in making improvements, or contest a grade if they believe it is inaccurate or unfair.

Despite the important role of academic grades in decision making at many levels, their overall validity is questionable. In educational measurements, validity is largely established by employing large data sets, objective scoring, and standardization to control for contextual influences. But grades are not assigned on a large scale, involve teacher subjectivity in their composition, and are not determined under standardized settings. Thus, it is difficult to evaluate their validity.

When validity cannot be adequately established, school leaders and other stakeholders may doubt whether grade-based decisions are fair and appropriate (Tierney, 2013). They need more information about what grades mean before they know how to use them. They must then turn to the source—teachers—for information about how to interpret grades. Teachers are the people most directly responsible for how the educational outcomes measured by grades are defined and related to behaviors (American Educational Research Association [AERA], American Psychological Association [APA], & National Council on Measurement in Education [NCME], 2014). The question then is, what do teachers mean to measure when they assign grades?

The purpose of this chapter is to explore how and why teachers, in their capacity as grade developers, draw on achievement as well as factors unrelated to achievement in grading. We look for possible relationships among these factors and teachers' beliefs about the nature of learning. Our aim is to identify systems of teacher reasoning that relate to grading beliefs and practices. We believe that if school leaders and teachers view grades as the products of professional judgment, based on legitimate systems of values and beliefs, they will be able to engage in fruitful discussions about improving the interpretability of grades.

Using Learning Theory to Find Order in a Hodgepodge

Academic achievement has repeatedly been identified as the dominant type of performance that correlates with teachers' grades (Brookhart, 2015). But quantitative analyses also demonstrate that assigned grades significantly relate to factors other than achievement, including work habits (Farkas et al., 1990); completion of work, academic self-control, or "getting it done" (Duckworth, Quinn, & Tsukayama, 2012; McMillan, Myran, & Workman, 2002); attitude, engagement, and interest (Russell & Austin, 2010; Willingham, Pollack, & Lewis, 2002); and effort and behavior (Cross & Frary, 1996; Randall & Engelhard, 2010). Grading practices have been shown to vary among teachers and even within a single teacher's practice (Cizek, Fitzgerald, & Rachor, 1996).

For at least the last two decades, research has overwhelmingly concluded that teachers assign grades in an unpredictable manner, considering both cognitive and noncognitive factors. The construct that grades represent, therefore, is considered multidimensional (Brookhart et al., 2016). It has also been referred to as a "hodge-podge" (Brookhart, 1991).

Relatively little research has shed light on *why* teachers include factors other than achievement in grading. McMillan (2003) discussed educational philosophy as one of five themes that appeared to influence grading, noting that educational philosophies may be formed out of teachers' "foundational beliefs and values about education in general" (p. 37). In this chapter, we seek to identify systems underneath the apparent "hodgepodge" of teachers' grading practices by examining grading from the perspective of implicit or explicit learning theories.

What Significant Studies Have Been Conducted in This Area?

Theories of learning have evolved considerably over the decades. In the sections below, we frame the evidence about how teachers interpret and evaluate students when they assign grades in terms of three general theories of learning: knowledge acquisition, constructivism, and behaviorism. These are well-known theoretical frameworks of learning to which teachers are likely exposed in their certification programs.

First, we relate the learning theory of knowledge acquisition to teacher grading practice. This perspective was dominant in the 1970s, when research shifted focus from animal learning to human learning in laboratory environments. Under this approach, learning is seen to occur when individuals absorb information and store it in their memory systems. Teachers can organize and represent information using structures like graphic organizers that facilitate learning. They can evaluate students' acquisition of knowledge by testing them on the information they have stored about content. Student acquisition of knowledge is the central goal of education.

Constructivism is another view of learning. Constructivists view students as active agents in the learning process who are strategic, select relevant information, make interpretations, and construct their own understanding or knowledge. Over time, with advances in understanding the complex nature of learning, the constructivist view has taken natural settings (i.e., classrooms) into consideration. Contemporary constructivists' view of learning considers the interactions of learners' own cultural and social backgrounds, instructional factors and the meaningfulness of materials, the context of the classroom, and the dynamics of the larger system of education (Schunk, 2012).

Finally, behaviorism is an enduring theory of learning with applications that are continually observed in classrooms. In the behaviorist view, learning is seen as a direct connection between what is manipulated and the response to it. Behaviorists often see learners as passive recipients of knowledge imparted in the classroom. Learned responses are distinct from and can occur without cognition. Positive and negative reinforcement (including reward and punishment) are strong determinants of school-related behaviors and habits, as are behaviors outside the classroom (Schunk, 2012).

Although there is undoubtedly a unique, unpredictable, and idiosyncratic element to teacher grading, we suggest that teachers' views on the subject may vary along the same lines as learning theories. We do not claim that variations in grading practices are actually *caused* by different theories of learning. The theories serve to organize our review of research on factors teachers consider in grading. A summary of empirical studies we have reviewed is presented in Figure 3.1 (pp. 64–67).

What Questions Have Been Addressed in This Research?

In this section we examine how grades relate to knowledge acquisition, constructivist theory, and behaviorist theory.

How Do Grades Relate to Knowledge Acquisition?

Experts and well-known classroom assessment textbooks generally suggest that grades should represent and communicate students' academic achievement. This perspective appears to relate best to the theory of learning as knowledge acquisition. It defines the construct that grades measure as academic achievement. Other variables such as motivation may inform us about how to support learning, but the purpose of grades is to tell us whether and to what extent students have learned. Under this paradigm, grades should be readily interpretable indicators of knowledge and skills in a content area (e.g., math, English language, sciences, social studies). They should be awarded according to reasonably uniform criteria, so that student learning can be quantified, compared, and evaluated (Brookhart, 2004). Content achievement should be the sole component in assigning student grades.

Abundant studies demonstrate that teachers, by and large, assign grades according to an implicit theory of learning as knowledge acquisition. Students' academic outcomes are the main source of evidence that teachers use in grading. This is evidenced by teacher self-report in surveys (see Brookhart et al., 2016, for a recent review). Correlational studies have also shown a robust relationship between grades and other measures of achievement, usually standardized achievement test scores. Recent research reports a median correlation of 0.57 between high school grade point average (HSGPA) and standardized tests of achievement, with a range from 0.50 to 0.68 (Casillas et al., 2012; Duckworth et al., 2012; Duckworth & Seligman, 2006; Pattison et al., 2013; Woodruff & Ziomek, 2004). Looking at course- and content-specific grades and standardized test scores, Brennan, Kim, Wenz-Gross, and Siperstein (2001) reported correlations of 0.54 in mathematics, 0.54 in science, and 0.59 in English in a sample of 8th graders. Willingham and colleagues (2002) conducted analyses to explain variance in HSGPA based on student engagement, initiative, and completing activities as well as standardized

FIGURE 3.1 | **Reviewed Studies Related to Cognitive and Noncognitive Factors in Grading**

Studies	Participants	Main Findings
Bonner & Chen (2009)	Preservice teacher candidates	• Teacher candidates considered effort and improvement more than classroom behavior in their grades. • Consideration of effort and improvement and student choice was associated with constructivist teaching approaches. • Formal coursework in grading policies led to reduced support in noncognitive-based grading.
Bowers (2011)	High school students	• Variance in grades reflected student academic knowledge and socially relevant behaviors such as class participation. • The relationship of test-measured academic achievement with grades is stronger for core subjects than for noncore subjects like PE and art.
Brennan, Kim, Wenz-Gross, & Siperstein (2001)	8th grade students	• Academic achievement was consistently associated with teacher-assigned grades (r of 0.54 to 0.58). • Standardized testing is less equitable than teacher-assigned grading as shown by tests' consistently greater gender and ethnic/racial gaps. • Teacher-assigned grades correlated strongly regardless of content area (r of 0.58 to 0.80), suggesting the presence of underlying nonacademic factors.
Casillas, Robbins, Allen, Kuo, Hanson, & Schmeiser (2012)	Middle school students	• Early high school GPA was significantly related to middle school grades ($r = 0.64$) and to standardized tests of academic achievement ($r = 0.56$). • The amount of variance in high school GPA predicted by psychosocial and behavioral factors was comparable to the proportion predicted by prior grades (about 30 percent).
Chen & Bonner (2017)	Novice teachers K–12	• In grading decision making, teachers wanted to prepare students for real-world consequences and motivate them through their grading practice. • Teachers associated academic-enabling practices with instruction focused more on skill development than mastery.
Cizek, Fitzgerald, & Rachor (1996)	Elementary and high school teachers	• A large majority of teachers drew on achievement measures like test scores in assigning grades. • The extent of teacher use of achievement factors in grading varied based on the grade level they teach. • Teachers also considered student aptitude, ability, conduct, and goal achievement in assigning grades.

Studies	Participants	Main Findings
Cross & Frary (1996)	Middle and high school teachers, students	• Teachers commonly raised grades of lower-ability students. • Teachers raised grades for perceived effort, conduct, participation, and attitude, and many endorsed such practices. • Teachers did not always endorse sound psychometric practices. • Teachers' endorsement of a given grading practice did not always align with their actual practice.
Duckworth, Quinn, & Tsukayama (2012)	Middle school students	• Student self-control predicted changes in GPA from middle to high school. • Student IQ predicted changes in standardized test scores. • Teachers perceived the purpose of grading as providing feedback to students about mastery. • Teachers perceived the purpose of standardized testing as comparing performance among students.
Duckworth & Seligman (2006)	8th grade students	• Girls measured higher than boys in self-discipline. • This difference mediated girls' GPA but not their test performance.
Farkas, Grobe, Sheehan, & Shuan (1990)	7th and 8th grade students	• Controlling for academic achievement, poor and male students consistently received lower grades than their peers. • Black and Hispanic students also frequently received lower grades. • School context (e.g., overall test scores, overall absenteeism) affected student grades.
Kelly (2008)	Middle school students	• Students' classroom behaviors separated into "procedural" and "substantive" engagement. • Higher grades were predicted by substantive student effort and participation such as answering authentic questions. • Students in a lower-achieving class context received proportionally higher grades.
Marso & Pigge (1991)	K–12 teachers	• On teacher-constructed tests, items were most commonly multiple choice or matching questions. • Most teacher-made items (72 percent) functioned at the knowledge level.
McMillan (2001)	Middle and high school teachers	• Teachers considered effort, participation, and improvement in assigning grades ("academic enablers"). • Teacher use of academic achievement in grading differed significantly based on class ability level.
McMillan (2003)	High school teachers	• Teacher grading and assessment practices reflected tensions between their beliefs and values, the classroom context, and external factors such as testing.

FIGURE 3.1 | **Reviewed Studies Related to Cognitive and Noncognitive Factors in Grading—(*continued*)**

Studies	Participants	Main Findings
McMillan (2003)— (*continued*)	High school teachers	• Teachers used their educational philosophy to explain grading and assessment practice. • Teachers "pulled" for students by giving extra credit or changing assignment difficulty, affecting grades.
McMillan, Myran, & Workman (2002)	Elementary school teachers	• Teachers considered academic achievement and students' academic-enabling behaviors (e.g., effort, improvement) most important in assigning grades. • There was high variability in grading practices between teachers even within a given school. • Teachers reported that they used higher-order assessments over those measuring student recall.
Oescher & Kirby (1990)	High school teachers	• Teachers primarily used their own tests for summative evaluation and grade assignment. • Most teacher-made items assessed student knowledge, not higher-order thinking. • Teacher-made tests were poorly constructed in instructions, formatting, and design.
Pattison, Grodsky, & Muller (2013)	High school students	• Since 1982, GPA rose for high school but dipped at four-year colleges. • GPA and standardized tests correlated at about $r = 0.50$.
Randall & Engelhard (2010)	K–12 teachers	• A significant interaction existed among achievement, ability, behavior, and effort in teacher grading practices. • Teachers rewarded lower-ability students with higher grades when they had good behavior and work habits. • Grades improved as student behavior improved.
Russell & Austin (2010)	High school music teachers	• Music teachers gave more weight to noncognitive criteria than achievement criteria in assigning grades. • Most music teachers included attitude as a factor in grade assignment.
Sun & Cheng (2014)	High school English teachers (China)	• Teachers perceived grades as rewards for effort and improvement. • Teachers chose to lower grades for high-ability low-effort students or reward clear improvement in attitude. • Teachers may have been more concerned with the consequences of grades than the interpretation of them. • Teachers believed strictness in grading would benefit students.

Studies	Participants	Main Findings
Thomas & Oldfather (1997)	Elementary to high school students, longitudinal	• Grades and assessments affected student self-esteem, identity, and motivation. • Students believed that grades shifted their goal orientation from mastery toward performance.
Willing-ham, Pollack, & Lewis (2002)	High school students	• Student test scores were the strongest predictors of student grades, $r = 0.62$. • Grading variations and teacher ratings helped explain the discrepancy between grades and test scores. • Students' engagement (e.g., demonstrating initiative) was significantly correlated to their grades.
Woodruff & Ziomek (2004)	High school students	• From 1991 to 2003, grades inflated by around 0.23 on a scale of 0 to 4. • Grades and standardized tests were moderately correlated.

test scores, drawing from 1992 data from the National Education Longitudinal Study (1988). Achievement as measured by standardized tests was by far the strongest single predictor of student grades ($r = 0.62$), although other measured factors contributed significantly to grade variance. All these and other sources indicate that grades mostly measure acquired learning.

As for the *kinds* of acquired learning that are captured in grades, McMillan and colleagues (2002) found that teachers claimed to rely most heavily in grading on objective assessments of higher-order thinking and application of knowledge. However, studies that have analyzed the actual content of classroom tests have shown that teacher-made tests mainly measure basic knowledge. Using judges to categorize teacher-made test content by cognitive level (usually in terms of Bloom's taxonomy), researchers have found that between 72 percent (Marso & Pigge, 1991) and 91 percent (Oescher & Kirby, 1990) of items assessed student knowledge rather than higher-order thinking. These findings are also consistent with theories of simple knowledge acquisition, which stress the important role of memory and rehearsal on information retrieval.

In short, a knowledge acquisition view of learning seems to fit the way grades are generally conceived and developed. Teachers believe their grades do and should primarily reflect the information and skills that students have gained in school. Other measures of achievement correlate strongly with grades, indicating that grades represent achievement quite well. Evidence about teacher-made tests suggests that grades mostly convey information about basic kinds of learning that may be readily memorized and tested. Overall, these features suggest that the framework of knowledge acquisition is a plausible lens through which to interpret most of the variability in grades.

How Do Grades Relate to Constructivism?

Constructivist approaches to learning take into account that learners make sense of their understanding while interacting with their cultural and social environments. The primary theme of constructivists' view of learning is that knowledge is socially or culturally "constructed" and interpreted by the learner (Mayer, 2008). Teachers' beliefs about learning and teaching, especially in relation to constructivist beliefs, have been theorized to correspond to their assessment practices. In a constructivist classroom, Shepard (2001) stated, teachers implement learning activities that embed assessments, so both learning and assessments are contextual, meaningful to learners, and individualized to meet student needs.

Constructivist approaches to assessment focus on both learning process and product (Shepard, 2001; Windschitl, 2002). To align with this thinking, grades in a constructivist classroom should be individualized and incorporate rich information that includes learning-related elements beyond academic achievement (Thomas & Oldfather, 1997). From a constructivist perspective on assessment, standardizing student assessments and isolating academic achievement from other learning-related factors in grading make little sense.

Constructivist learning theory may help us understand some of the variability in grades that cannot be explained by school achievement alone. In numerous studies, teachers report they take information about student learning processes as well as outcomes into consideration when assigning grades. In studies of elementary and secondary teachers' grading practices, student effort, improvement, and participation were important to some teachers' grading decisions (McMillan, 2001; McMillan et al., 2002). The authors labeled these factors "academic enabling" and used the term to refer to behaviors that support rather than directly indicate achievement. A teacher who gives good grades to effortful and engaged students even though they have poor achievement has an academic-enabling grading approach. Academic-enabling grading rewards student behaviors that show "substantive engagement" (Kelly, 2008). (See Chapter 2 for more detailed information about the role of engagement and other factors in grading.)

In our own research, we have attempted to test the theory that academic-enabling approaches to grading may be partly explained by a constructivist orientation (Bonner & Chen, 2009). We created a survey instrument with vignettes about grading, some of which represented enabling approaches (Survey of Grading Beliefs [SGB]; Bonner & Chen, 2009; Chen & Bonner, 2017). We studied the relationship between preservice teachers' grading beliefs and their beliefs about a constructivist orientation to learning and teaching. We found that several vignettes describing grading based on effort or improvement had common variance, indicating that they could be grouped as a distinct factor in grading beliefs. We found that a majority of preservice teachers endorsed these enabling approaches to grading. Most important for our purposes here, academic enabling in grading had a significant positive correlation with favorable views of constructivism.

Continuing our work on constructivist views of teaching and grading (Chen & Bonner, 2017), we studied a group of novice teachers using an updated version of the SGB and interviews. The interview component of the study allowed us to delve into teacher decision-making processes and the beliefs underlying academic-enabling grading approaches. Teachers' responses indicated that they were readily able to infer rationales for academic-enabling grading approaches shown in the SGB vignettes, even when they did not support the practices themselves. Teachers provided two kinds of rationales for such practices, which we related to themes of real-world pragmatism and a "success orientation." Teachers' written responses indicated that effort, collaboration, and participation were behaviors very relevant to the real world. One teacher specifically pointed to collaboration as a skill emphasized in contemporary Common Core standards. Teachers' responses demonstrated a balancing act of grading: they were concerned about students' readiness to face the demands of the real world (e.g., college and workplace), as well as interested in assigning grades based on achievement-related evidence.

Some vignettes were interpreted as showing a success orientation. For instance, teachers responded to a vignette that depicted a teacher who dropped the lowest test score of each student in a class from their grade. Teachers' interpretations of this and similar vignettes indicated that they thought this type of grading practice allowed students to maximize their successes, encouraging them to persist and progress. In general, teachers tended to think that academic-enabling grading practices had social-emotional benefits including student empowerment, stress reduction, and motivation, even though they were aware that use of such practices resulted in a lack of evidence of mastery on all topics for each individual. They were often willing to trade precision for motivational benefits.

Finally, the teachers we interviewed associated academic-enabling grading with areas of instruction that focused on skill development rather than topic mastery. Other evidence has indicated that grading based on substantive engagement may be more of a factor in teachers' grades in noncore subjects like physical education (PE), music, and art (Bowers, 2011; Russell & Austin, 2010). For instance, Russell and Austin (2010) examined districtwide secondary music teachers' assessment practices and found that, on average, the teachers weighed noncognitive factors very heavily in course grades, particularly attendance, attitude, and amount of practice time. Ninety-three percent of music teachers weighed student attitude in grades, with an average weight of 27 percent. Although there is no direct evidence that PE, music, and art teachers have a special preference for a constructivist approach to teaching, teachers in these content areas appear to show through their grading practices a developmental, individualized approach that is consistent with constructivism.

To bring together our findings about constructivist views of learning and grading, we recall that under the theory of constructivism, learning is seen as an interactive process among students, teachers, and often other learners within a social and cultural context. Evidence clearly supports that grades are often assigned in ways that reflect an orientation toward constructivism. In assigning grades, many teachers consider student behaviors like effort and engagement that enable academic achievement in addition to academic achievement per se. The idea that student effort and engagement should be part of the assessment of student performance is consistent with the constructivist view that learning is a process, not an outcome. In our own research, we have detected a direct relationship between constructivist beliefs and beliefs about academic-enabling behaviors. Evidence that teachers in noncore content areas may include more academic-enabling behaviors is consistent with the constructivist view of the developmental nature of the learning process.

How Do Grades Relate to Behaviorism?

According to a behaviorist view, individuals learn to make connections between stimuli and responses through reinforcement or punishment (Schunk, 2012). Grading practices related to naïve behaviorism might involve awarding points to encourage good behavior in response to an academic task or reducing grades to discourage bad behavior. In multiple studies, teachers report using grades to reinforce compliance with classroom rules, although most research has demonstrated that such practices are not as prevalent as academic-enabling grading. Cizek and colleagues (1996), for example, found that 61 percent of surveyed teachers considered classroom conduct when assigning a final grade. McMillan and colleagues (2002) also reported that teachers sometimes use grades to reward positive student behaviors such as "paying attention" and completing ungraded homework, and to punish students for misconduct. As reported by Cross and Frary (1996), 39 percent of surveyed teachers acknowledged that they considered student conduct and attitude when awarding grades. Using experimentally manipulated scenarios in surveys, Randall and Engelhard (2010) found that teachers "boosted" grades for borderline students with good behavior (as well as effort), despite information that a student had lower achievement or ability than would merit the grade. Classroom behavior had the strongest effect on borderline grades.

It is not clear from these studies what kind of reasoning underlies the tendency to reward or punish classroom behavior through grading practices. As with the academic-enabling approaches described above, in our own research we have identified a distinctly management-oriented approach to grading, and we have tried to relate it to learning theories. We have found that management-oriented grading beliefs do not correlate with constructivist views, but they do correlate with traditional teaching perspectives and traditional management perspectives on learning and instruction (Bonner & Chen, 2009).

Examining the management approach to grading in more detail through a combination of vignettes and qualitative methods, we discovered that teachers' reasoning about the management approach had more nuance than one might expect. When asked to interpret vignettes that depicted teachers awarding or deducting grade "points" because of classroom conduct, the teachers we studied often referenced the need to establish a classroom culture of respect or establish teacher authority (Chen & Bonner, 2017). This is similar to Sun and Cheng's (2014) finding that some Chinese teachers emphasized the importance of strictness or student discipline in classrooms. Most teachers, we found, did not endorse using grades to reward or punish student behavior, and those who did often elaborated on the need to obtain additional sources of information on the child, such as grade level, subject matter, student motivation, and individual circumstances. Teachers valued taking the "whole child" into account when they assigned grades. They did not take the use of grades to reward or punish lightly. They were aware of the high consequences of grades and the meanings that grades represent to the learners, parents, teachers, schools, and society at large. Only a few teachers responded to vignettes about rewards and punishments in grading with comments like "It works." This latter kind of reasoning seems to represent naïve behaviorism, while the former views on management-oriented grading do not (Chen & Bonner, 2017). A purely behaviorist approach to grading seems to be relatively rare among teachers.

Our research suggests that school level (elementary or secondary school) may relate to whether teachers take a behaviorist view on grading. We have found statistically significant differences between childhood education and secondary education teacher candidates in management-oriented grading beliefs and traditional and behavioral-oriented beliefs about instruction, all indicating a stronger behaviorist/managerial tendency among secondary school teachers (Bonner & Chen, 2009). Cizek and colleagues (1996) also found some differences in the factors that teachers considered in grading related to school level, including student conduct. However, they did not report the direction of the differences.

What Have the Results of Those Studies Revealed?

There is general consensus that grades indicate educational achievement *and other things*. Measured classroom achievement consistently shows up as the dominant factor in teacher grading. A very high emphasis on factors other than achievement is apparent in only a few noncore content areas such as the arts and PE. However, many teachers, regardless of content area, report giving students *some* credit in grading for effort, engagement, and behavior. Correlational studies consistently reveal relationships between course grades and constructs other than achievement. This has sometimes led to perceptions of teacher grades as unreliable, unsystematic, and difficult to interpret.

In our review of the literature on teachers' ideas about grading, and especially in our own research, we have attempted to reveal systems of thinking about teaching and learning that may partially explain the variations we see in teacher grading. We framed our argument in this chapter around learning theories as a way of organizing the evidence about teacher grading that we found in the literature. We do not claim that teachers' exposure to learning theories directly causes them to grade students in certain ways. However, many teachers become acquainted with learning theories during formal teacher preparation, and such exposure influences their educational philosophy or foundational beliefs and values about teaching and learning (McMillan, 2003). Beliefs about teaching and learning, as with other beliefs, also accrue from personal experience acquired even before formal teacher preparation (Pajares, 1992). It is likely that such educational beliefs in turn influence the way teachers assign grades. Of course, school and course contexts and district policies also influence teacher grading, but our focus has been on teachers as grade developers.

In the beginning of this chapter, we asked what teachers mean to measure through grades. The evidence indicates that teachers primarily use grades to indicate students' knowledge acquisition. Secondarily, consideration of effort, improvement, and participation are important to many teachers. Such considerations are theoretically consistent with constructivist learning theory (Shepard, 2001), and we have found that constructivist views of teaching are correlated with academic-enabling grading approaches. Teachers who support academic-enabling grading practices reason that students are encouraged to succeed when they make an effort, participate, and work collaboratively. Such student behaviors support student learning and are legitimate, real-world goals of education. For a smaller number of teachers, grades also indicate whether students know how to behave in school. This behaviorist approach seems at face value to relate to more traditional approaches to teaching, but when questioned in depth, most teachers only support it within the context of "whole child" teaching. Relatively few teachers, perhaps especially at the secondary school level, hold a naïve behaviorist view on grading.

Implications of Findings for Practice

Does it *really* matter that teachers include noncognitive factors in their grades? After all, contemporary standards of school achievement and what it means to be "college-ready" more and more often include social-emotional aspects of learning: collaboration, persistence, and self-control (Conley, 2008). Also, grades as we know them—at least grade averages—work well enough for their intended purposes. They are good predictors of later success in school, and they have been demonstrated to be generally useful for decision making about student academic trajectory into higher grades, specialized programs, and beyond secondary school. Generations of students have been schooled in a system in which teachers assign grades based on all kinds of subjective factors. You, the reader, have likely thrived under this system. So is it reasonable to accept that noncognitive factors are a target of teachers' grading practice?

Should we encourage teachers to refer to their own beliefs about learning when they grade students? Here are some takeaways from our analysis of the research.

Noncognitive grading can be biased. Unfortunately, while classroom effort and behavior may be critical for 21st century success, we lack high-quality ways to measure them and theory and evidence to tell us how to weight them if we could. Without evidence-based guidelines for measurement and weighting, teachers may inappropriately identify how much effort or behavior to consider in a grade. They may, for instance, confuse boisterous behavior with lack of learning. Illustrating this kind of bias in grading, Farkas and colleagues (1990) demonstrated that being male, poor, and black or Hispanic was associated with lower course grades in many middle school content areas, controlling for achievement as measured by standardized tests. The authors attributed the grade disadvantage to "rambunctious" behavior (p. 824).

Conversely, compliant and "school-wise" behavior may be mistaken for proficiency, and socially reticent behavior for a lack thereof. For instance, Duckworth and Seligman (2006) detected a distinct advantage in grades for girls above and beyond that which could be explained by differences in achievement test scores. The authors were able to show that part of the grade advantage for girls was due to their better self-discipline. Farkas and colleagues (1990) found that grades of female and Asian students were consistently higher than predicted by test scores alone. The authors attributed this grade advantage to "teacher-pleasing" behavior.

The authors of these studies did not believe that direct bias, cultural insensitivity, or personality preferences were likely at work; instead, grading biases may be indirect effects of teachers' misconceptions and lack of access to complete information about students. However, direct or otherwise, bias in grading can result in perpetuating societal inequities and disparities in student outcomes. A system under which only certain kinds of students thrive is not a system that is fair to all.

Noncognitive grading does not improve motivation. Here, we draw attention to the fact that mixing up effort, behavior, and educational outcomes promotes neither good assessment nor student motivation. Evidence from a synthesis of studies indicates a negative effect on both intrinsic motivation and learning when teachers use grades to reward or punish (Harlen, 2004). Further, in classrooms where grades are emphasized, students tend to attribute performance to ability rather than effort (Ames, 1992). Therefore, using grades as a "carrot" to promote effort may defeat the purpose.

We know of numerous better ways to support student effort and behavior in classrooms. Classroom activities that have high utility and relevance to students' lives result in improved interest (Hulleman, Godes, Hendricks, & Harackiewicz, 2010). Allowing choice about activities or topics to study engages students and helps them become invested in their own learning (Stefanou, Perencevich, DiCintio, & Turner, 2004). Training in self-regulatory learning processes has a positive effect on intrinsic motivation, effort, attention, and other factors that support learning (Schmitz & Wiese, 2006). Indeed, there are many research- rather than grade-based strategies for motivating students to engage in learning and make an effort.

Leadership is necessary for better grading. We recognize that it is inherently difficult for teachers to translate their holistic impressions about student classroom performance into a single, uncomplicated, succinct representation (e.g., a letter grade, level, or percentage). Compartmentalizing achievement may seem antithetical to the notion of addressing the "whole child." Sometimes teachers experience internal conflict when a grade based only on achievement does not convey the nuances in their perceptions or their beliefs about learning and teaching. As teacher leaders and teacher educators, we must ask how we can help teachers grade better.

We recommend that school leaders take the initiative with grading policies. We strongly favor using grades to reflect academic achievement alone. We do not advocate using a separate grade as an indicator of noncognitive factors for several reasons. First, we are dubious that characteristics like effort, improvement, attitude, and engagement can be accurately measured. We know of no systematic way to measure these variables in classrooms with enough reliability to draw inferences about individual students. Further, separate cognitive and noncognitive grades might convey undesirable messages to students, particularly at higher levels of schooling, when students become more strategic in their thinking about grades. For example, a student with a high "Achievement" grade but a low "Effort" grade might infer he can excel effortlessly and fail to learn the importance of expending energy to meet goals. Another with the same grade profile might perceive that her effort is not recognized and appreciated. If the "Achievement" grade is low and the "Effort" grade is high, students may perceive effort as not being worth their while and be less motivated to apply themselves. Moreover, no one can predict how behavioral grades, which inevitably carry an official status and remain in a student's permanent record, might be misinterpreted and used inappropriately by other people to whom they are reported (parents, future teachers, school leaders, researchers). We recommend that instead of reporting behavioral grades, teachers have space to comment on students' report cards. This way they can communicate perceptions about engagement, effort, behavior, and so on without giving the false impression that the information is objective and reliable.

We recommend the use of standards-based grading to improve the validity of grades as measures of achievement. Standards-based grading focuses on student academic achievement in the context of common standards for instruction and student learning. It reflects the extent to which students' academic performance meets intended learning outcomes or targets at specific performance levels

(Muñoz & Guskey, 2015). Standards-based grading frameworks use performance-level descriptors (e.g., "proficient") rather than letter grades, which may reduce teachers' tendency to norm grades based on their own school context. Dimensions of learning are well defined within a domain, leading to clarity about what is and is not "counted" in the grade.

School and district leaders should do more than just mandate standards-based grading—they should actively promote the use of standards-based grading policies. School leaders should enlist the support of professional developers to help teachers implement strategies that build student motivation and promote effort and engagement. It should be made clear to teachers that disciplinary problems are not to be addressed through punitive grading and that teachers will have administrative support for enforcing classroom rules. We recommend that schools and districts provide clear guidelines about professional practices in grading that include both do's and don'ts. *Do* develop grading methods that communicate students' academic achievement in fair and valid ways. *Don't* use grades to manage student behavior, or to attempt to encourage academic-enabling processes like effort that can only be measured subjectively. We believe that a school atmosphere in which good and bad behavior, learning processes, and achievement outcomes are viewed as essential but distinct factors will lend interpretability to grades. Moreover, such an atmosphere will help all members of the learning community to find consensus on students' strengths and weaknesses and to focus on supporting student learning where they are most needed.

As we stated at the beginning of this chapter, grades carry with them a sense of finality and contribute to students' self-image (Thomas & Oldfather, 1997). For this reason, their interpretability is essential. Effort and school-appropriate behavior, while important engines for learning, are not the main outcomes of education according to learning standards such as the Common Core. Measuring noncognitive dimensions is difficult, vulnerable to hidden biases, and beyond the scope of the typical classroom teacher. Only when grades are clearly focused on a single, defined domain—namely, achievement of knowledge and skills—can they be considered fair and valid measures.

References

American Educational Research Association, American Psychological Association, & National Council on Measurement in Education. (2014). *Standards for educational and psychological testing.* Washington, DC: Authors.

Ames, C. (1992). Classrooms: Goals, structures, and student motivation. *Journal of Educational Psychology, 84*(3), 261–271.

Bonner, S. M. (2013). Validity in classroom assessment: Purposes, properties, and principles. In J. H. McMillan (Ed.), *Handbook of research on classroom assessment* (pp. 87–106). Thousand Oaks, CA: Sage.

Bonner, S. M., & Chen, P. P. (2009). Teacher candidates' perceptions about grading and constructivist teaching. *Educational Assessment, 14*(2), 57–77.

Bowers, A. J. (2011). What's in a grade? The multidimensional nature of what teacher-assigned grades assess in high school. *Educational Research and Evaluation, 17*(3), 141–159.

Brennan, R., Kim, J., Wenz-Gross, M., & Siperstein, G. (2001). The relative equitability of high-stakes testing versus teacher-assigned grades: An analysis of the Massachusetts Comprehensive Assessment System (MCAS). *Harvard Educational Review, 71*(2), 173–217.

Brookhart, S. M. (1991). Grading practices and validity. *Educational Measurement: Issues and Practice, 10*(1), 35–36. doi:10.1111/j.1745-3992.1991.tb00182.x

Brookhart, S. M. (2004). Classroom assessment: Tensions and intersections in theory and practice. *Teachers College Record, 106*(3), 429–458.

Brookhart, S. M. (2015). Graded achievement, tested achievement, and validity. *Educational Assessment, 20*(4), 268–296.

Brookhart, S. M., Guskey, T. R., Bowers, A. J., McMillan, J. H., Smith, J. K., Smith, L. F., et al. (2016). A century of grading research: Meaning and value in the most common educational measure. *Review of Educational Research, 86*(4), 803–848.

Carey, T., & Carifio, J. (2012). The minimum grading controversy: Results of a quantitative study of seven years of grading data from an urban high school. *Educational Researcher, 41*(6), 201–208.

Casillas, A., Robbins, S., Allen, J., Kuo, Y., Hanson, M. A., & Schmeiser, C. (2012). Predicting early academic failure in high school from prior academic achievement, psychosocial characteristics, and behavior. *Journal of Educational Psychology, 104*(2), 407–420.

Chen, P. P., & Bonner, S. M. (2017). Teachers' beliefs about grading practices and a constructivist approach to teaching. *Educational Assessment, 22*(1), 18–34. doi:10.1080/10627197.2016.1271703

Cizek, G. J., Fitzgerald, S. M., & Rachor, R. A. (1996). Teachers' assessment practices: Preparation, isolation, and the kitchen sink. *Educational Assessment, 3*(2), 159–179.

Conley, D. T. (2008). Rethinking college readiness. *New Directions for Higher Education, 144,* 3–13.

Cross, L. H., & Frary, R. B. (1996, April). *Hodgepodge grading: Endorsed by students and teachers alike.* Paper presented at the Annual Meeting of the National Council on Measurement in Education, New York.

Duckworth, A. L., Quinn, P. D., & Tsukayama, E. (2012). What No Child Left Behind leaves behind: The roles of IQ and self-control in predicting standardized achievement test scores and report card grades. *Journal of Educational Psychology, 104*(2), 439–451.

Duckworth, A. L., & Seligman, M. E. (2006). Self-discipline gives girls the edge: Gender in self-discipline, grades, and achievement test scores. *Journal of Educational Psychology, 98*(1), 198–208.

Farkas, G., Grobe, R. P., Sheehan, D., & Shuan, Y. (1990). Cultural resources and school success: Gender, ethnicity, and poverty groups within an urban school district. *American Sociological Review, 27*(4), 127–142.

Haertel, E. (1985). Construct validity and criterion-referenced testing. *Review of Educational Research, 55*(1), 23–46.

Harlen, W. (2004). *A systematic review of the evidence of the impact on students, teachers and the curriculum of the process of using assessment by teachers for summative purposes.* Bristol, UK: EPPI-Centre.

Hulleman, C. S., Godes, O., Hendricks, B. L., & Harackiewicz, J. M. (2010). Enhancing interest and performance with a utility value intervention. *Journal of Educational Psychology, 102*(4), 880–895.

Kelly, S. (2008). What types of students' effort are rewarded with high marks? *Sociology of Education, 81*(1), 32–52.

Marso, R. N., & Pigge, F. L. (1991). An analysis of teacher-made tests: Item types, cognitive demands, and item construction errors. *Contemporary Educational Psychology, 16*(3), 279–286.

Mayer, R. E. (2008). *Learning and instruction* (2nd ed.). Upper Saddle River, NJ: Pearson.

McMillan, J. H. (2001). Secondary teachers' classroom assessment and grading practices. *Educational Measurement: Issues and Practice, 20*(1), 20–32. doi:10.1111/j.1745-3992.2001.tb00055.x

McMillan, J. H. (2003). Understanding and improving teachers' classroom assessment decision making: Implications for theory and practice. *Educational Measurement: Issues and Practice, 22*(4), 34–43.

McMillan, J. H., Myran, S., & Workman, D. (2002). Elementary teachers' classroom assessment and grading practices. *The Journal of Educational Research, 95*(4), 203–213.

Muñoz, M. A., & Guskey, T. R. (2015). Standards-based grading and reporting will improve education. *Phi Delta Kappan, 96*(7), 64–68. doi:10.1177/0031721715579043

National Association for College Admission Counseling. (2016). *2015 state of college admissions.* Retrieved from https://indd.adobe.com/view/c555ca95-5bef-44f6-9a9b-6325942ff7cb

New York State Education Department. (2017). *ESEA accountability designation materials for 2017–18.* Retrieved from http://www.p12.nysed.gov/accountability/ESEAMaterials.html

Oescher, J., & Kirby, P. C. (1990, April). *Assessing teacher-made tests in secondary math and science classrooms.* Paper presented at the Annual Meeting of the National Council on Measurement in Education, Boston.

Pajares, M. F. (1992). Teachers' beliefs and educational research: Cleaning up a messy construct. *Review of Educational Research, 62*(3), 307–332.

Pattison, E., Grodsky, E., & Muller, C. (2013). Is the sky falling? Grade inflation and the signaling power of grades. *Educational Researcher, 42*(5), 259–265.

Randall, J., & Engelhard, G. (2010). Examining the grading practices of teachers. *Teaching and Teacher Education, 26*(7), 1372–1380.

Russell, J. A., & Austin, J. R. (2010). Assessment practices of secondary music teachers. *Journal of Research in Music Education, 58*(1), 37–54.

Schmitz, B., & Wiese, B. S. (2006). New perspectives for the evaluation of training sessions in self-regulated learning: Time-series analyses of diary data. *Contemporary Educational Psychology, 31,* 64–96.

Schunk, D. H. (2012). *Learning theories: An educational perspective* (6th ed.). Boston: Pearson.

Shepard, L. A. (2001). The role of classroom assessment in teaching and learning. In V. Richardson (Ed.), *Handbook of research on teaching* (4th ed., pp. 1066–1101). Washington, DC: American Educational Research Association.

Stefanou, C. R., Perencevich, K. C., DiCintio, M., & Turner, J. C. (2004). Supporting autonomy in the classroom: Ways teachers encourage student decision making and ownership. *Educational Psychologist, 39*(2), 97–110.

Sun, Y., & Cheng, L. (2014). Teachers' grading practices: Meaning and values assigned. *Assessment in Education: Principles, Policy & Practice, 21*(3), 326–343. doi:10.1080/0969594X.2013.768207

Thomas, S., & Oldfather, P. (1997). Intrinsic motivations, literacy, and assessment practices: "That's my grade. That's me." *Educational Psychologist, 32*(2), 107–123.

Tierney, R. D. (2013). Fairness in classroom assessment. In J. H. McMillan (Ed.), *Handbook of research on classroom assessment* (pp. 125–144). Thousand Oaks, CA: Sage.

Tyson, W., & Roksa, J. (2017). Importance of grades and placement for math attainment. *Educational Researcher, 46*(3), 140–142.

Willingham, W. W., Pollack, J. M., & Lewis, C. (2002). Grades and test scores: Accounting for observed differences. *Journal of Educational Measurement, 39*(1), 1–37.

Windschitl, M. (2002). Framing constructivism in practice as the negotiation of dilemmas: An analysis of the conceptual, pedagogical, cultural, and political challenges facing teachers. *Review of Educational Research, 72*(2), 131–175. doi:10.3102/00346543072002131

Woodruff, D. J., & Ziomek, R. L. (2004). *High school grade inflation from 1991 to 2003*. (Research Report Series 2004-04). Iowa City, IA: ACT.

Surveys of Teachers' Grading Practices and Perceptions

James H. McMillan

A recently published comprehensive review of grading over the past century (Brookhart et al., 2016) shows that K–12 teachers use a mix of factors, both academic and nonacademic, in determining grades. This long-standing practice has often been derided as inappropriate, and calls have been made to base grades only on academic performance. Research on teachers' perceptions about grading helps us understand these varied practices.

Why Is This Area of Research Important?

Because grading is a staple of education, can have strong influences on students, and has implications for future opportunities, it is important to understand why mixed grading practices have persisted. In this chapter, I review studies of teachers' grading practices and perceptions and suggest implications for research and practice. Understanding perceptions about grading in the context of practice helps to show how grading is done, why it is done in different ways, how it influences student learning and motivation, and why there are varied grading practices (Brown & Harris, 2016). Studies in this area suggest themes and approaches to grading policies and practice that result in a more complete understanding of the well-documented idiosyncratic grading practices of teachers.

The term *grading practices* refers to the ways teachers use information from assessments and other sources of information to determine and report student grades, whether on papers, unit tests, or semester reports. The term *teacher perceptions* denotes the range of teacher thinking about grading and grading practices. Perceptions can include beliefs, attitudes, and understandings—ranging from awareness and recognition to deeper meaning—and can be characterized by having value and even emotional components. Because perceptions are more elusive than practices, they are more difficult to document. However, recent research shows why these perceptions are important for understanding grading practices.

What Significant Studies Have Been Conducted in This Area?

Studies of grading practices and perceptions have been conducted since at least the middle of the 20th century. In this chapter I briefly describe earlier research and more thoroughly review research conducted since 1994. Research on teacher grading practices can be traced to the early studies of grading reliability described in Chapter 1. Starting from this base, studies from the late 20th century were generally critical of teachers' practices. More recent studies have sought to understand teachers' thinking about grading instead of merely criticizing their grading practices.

What Questions Have Been Addressed in This Research?

Studies documenting teachers' varied grading practices grew out of early studies of grading reliability (see Chapter 1), which suggested that because standards for grading were different, any given grade did not have a common or agreed-upon meaning. This led to widespread concern and distrust about the role of teacher judgment in grading (Brookhart, 2013a, 2013b). Later reviews by Crooks (1933), Smith and Dobbin (1960), and Kirschenbaum, Napier, and Simon (1971) ushered in debates about whether grading should be norm-referenced (based on comparing students to one another) or criterion-referenced (based on comparing student work to standards). While high schools tended to stay with norm referencing to accommodate the need for ranking students for college admissions, some at the elementary school level transitioned to what was eventually called mastery learning and then standards-based education.

20th Century Research

Following a period of emphasis on classroom assessment in the 1980s, more systematic investigations of teachers' grading practices and perceptions about grading were published. Brookhart's (1994) review of 10 years of grading literature summarized the findings from 19 studies of teachers' grading practices, opinions, and beliefs. Eleven of the studies involved surveys of mostly high school teachers, ranging in sample size from 84 to 973. Surveys emphasized different aspects of grading. Some focused more on different types of assessments used in grading, whereas others asked teachers about the factors they used to determine grades (typically achievement, effort, improvement, and behavior). Five of the studies used individual and focus group interviews with small numbers of participants, two studies supplemented interviews with observation and document analysis, and two investigations were case studies (one with a single participant).

While the studies Brookhart reviewed were diverse with respect to grade level, location, method, and emphasis, she found five common themes:

1. Measures of academic achievement (e.g., tests, quizzes, papers) were the most important determinants of grades.

2. Teachers emphasized the need for *fair* grading. Fairness was enhanced by using multiple sources of information for grades, being clear about what was assessed and how it would be graded, and by being consistent.

3. It was clear in 12 of the studies that teachers included non-achievement factors to determine grades. These factors included ability, effort, improvement, completion of work, and other student behaviors.

4. There was strong evidence that grading practices were not consistent from one teacher to another, with respect to either purpose or the extent to which nonachievement factors were considered. It was evident that individual teachers emphasize different factors when grading students, reflecting different beliefs and values. Some teachers reported using mostly achievement with few nonachievement factors, while others mixed several factors together.

5. Grading practices tended to vary somewhat by grade level. Although limited by the relatively small number of studies at the elementary level, secondary teachers emphasized achievement products (such as tests) more, while elementary teachers used more informal evidence of learning along with achievement and performance assessments.

Brookhart's review shows that during this 10-year period, there were relatively few empirical studies of grading practices and perceptions. Although overall conclusions were consistent across location (different regions of the United States, England, and Canada), grade levels, and methodology, potential for generalization is limited due to study characteristics. For example, of four large-scale surveys, one was restricted to Virginia teachers, one to science teachers in Canada, and two to teachers in the Midwestern United States. Furthermore, different surveys were used in almost all the studies, making comparisons and syntheses of findings problematic. Nevertheless, Brookhart's review demonstrates that during this period there was an increasing interest in investigating grading practices, with conclusions largely replicating previous research. As Brookhart points out, these findings aligned with policymakers' increasingly intense distrust of teacher judgments about student accomplishments. This distrust was part of the reason for developing student accountability and teacher evaluation systems based on large-scale testing. The findings also align with a period of emphasizing performance-based and portfolio classroom assessment, which resulted in widespread reports of unreliability of teachers' subjective judgments about student work.

Late 20th and 21st Century Research

My search for studies of teachers' grading practices and perceptions identified 38 studies with original data published in scholarly sources between 1994 and 2016 (see Figure 4.1, pp. 90–94). This included 24 empirical studies that were not cited in a recent review (Brookhart, 2013a).

Teachers' Grading Practices. Most studies of teachers' grading practices focus on how teachers determine grades for their students. This was typically accomplished by asking teachers directly about how different factors contributed to final grades for a designated period of instruction (e.g., mid-semester, semester, or year).

In a generalization study of Frary, Cross, and Weber (1993), Cross and Frary (1999) reported that most of the 307 Virginia middle and high school teachers in their sample used "hodgepodge" grading, combining in different ways achievement, effort, behavior, improvement, and attitudes. Nearly 40 percent of the teachers agreed that student conduct and attitude should be considered in determining grades, especially for raising low grades. Cross and Frary extended previous research by asking teachers about actual as well as ideal grading practices, providing confirmation that teachers value the use of nonacademic factors—albeit individually, with little district or school policy as guidance.

McMillan (2001) surveyed 1,483 Virginia middle and high school teachers on the extent to which 19 different elements were used to determine grades. Analysis showed these elements grouped into four meaningful factors: (1) nonachievement items labeled as "academic enablers," including effort, ability, improvement, work habits, attention, and participation; (2) academic achievement based on learning objectives and standards; (3) "external comparisons," including grade distributions of other teachers and comparisons with other students; and (4) use of extra credit. These four components were replicated in a survey study of over 900 elementary students that also found homework to be a fifth significant factor (McMillan, Myran, & Workman, 2002). In these studies, the mean ratings of importance of contributions of the components showed that academic performance and academic enablers were by far the most important in determining grades. This finding was essentially replicated in a study of 513 Canadian secondary teachers (Duncan & Noonan, 2007). Also, the studies showed significant variation among teachers in the same school. That is, the weight teachers gave to separate factors differed greatly within a single elementary or secondary school. In a study of 513 elementary and secondary teachers, Guskey (2009) also reported significant variation among teachers, as did Guskey and Link (2017), using a sample of K–12 teachers from five school districts. The studies also replicated the finding of "hodgepodge" grading. Clearly, both achievement and nonachievement factors were combined to come up with final grades.

FIGURE 4.1 | **Studies of Teachers' Grading Practices and Perceptions**

Studies	Participants	Main Findings
Adrian (2012)	Elementary teachers	• Few teachers thought that nonacademic factors should be included in grading. • Most thought that grades should not be reduced for turning in assignments late.
Bailey (2012)	Secondary teachers	• Teachers used a variety of factors in grading. • Social studies and male teachers emphasized effort more than other groups. • Science teachers emphasized effort least. • Female teachers emphasized student behavior more than male teachers.
Bonner & Chen (2009)	Preservice teacher candidates	• Grading perceptions depended on individual style and focused on equity, consistency, accuracy, and fairness (with nonachievement factors used to make grades higher).
Chen & Bonner (2017)	Elementary and secondary teachers	• Teachers' reasons for using nonachievement factors were thought out and focused on student success, not haphazard.
Cizek, Fitzgerald, & Rachor (1996)	Elementary and secondary teachers	• Teachers synthesized objective and subjective factors to promote high grades. • Few differences based on grade level or years of experience were noted. • Teacher grading practices varied significantly.
Cross & Frary (1999)	Middle and high school teachers	• Achievement, effort, behavior, improvement, and attitudes were combined in various ways to assign grades. • Grading should include noncognitive factors. • Effort, conduct, and achievement should be reported separately from achievement.
Duncan & Noonan (2007)	High school mathematics teachers	• Achievement as well as nonachievement factors were identified as important for grading, with significant variation among teachers in weights given to different factors. • Frame of reference for grading, whether criterion- or norm-referenced, varied.
Frary, Cross, & Weber (1993)	Secondary teachers	• Most teachers believed that nonachievement factors such as ability, effort, and improvement should be used for grading.
Grimes (2010)	Middle school teachers	• Both achievement and nonachievement factors, including improvement, mastery, and effort, should be used for grading.

Studies	Participants	Main Findings
Guskey (2002)	Elementary and secondary teachers	• Significant variation was reported for ideal grade distribution. • Teachers wanted students to obtain the highest grade possible. • The main purpose of grades was to communicate to parents. • Multiple factors were used for grading, including homework, effort, and improvement.
Guskey (2009)	Elementary and secondary teachers	• There was significant variation in grading practices. • Most teachers thought grading was not needed for learning. • Most teachers based grades on established criteria. • Grades were used for communication.
Guskey & Link (2017)	Elementary, middle, and high school teachers	• Teachers varied significantly within grade levels in how much they emphasized achievement and nonachievement "process" factors. • Secondary teachers tended to give more weight to achievement factors. • Elementary teachers tended to give more weight to formative assessment and observation.
Guskey, Swan, & Jung (2010)	Elementary and secondary teachers	• Standards-based grading provided better, clearer, and more easily understood information than traditional grades.
Hay & Macdonald (2008)	Two high school teachers	• Teachers' values and experience influenced grading. • Varied grading practices were reported.
Imperial (2011)	High school teachers	• A wide variety of grading practices was reported. • Teachers considered the primary purpose of grading to be indicating achievement. • About half the teachers used noncognitive factors in their grades.
Kunnath (2016)	High school teachers	• Teachers used both objective achievement results and subjective factors in grading. • Teachers incorporated individual circumstances to promote the highest grades possible. • Grading practices were based on teachers' philosophy of teaching.
Liu (2008a)	Middle and high school teachers	• Six components in grading were identified: (1) importance/value, (2) feedback for instruction and improvement, (3) effort/participation, (4) ability and problem solving, (5) comparisons/extra credit, and (6) grading self-efficacy/ease/confidence/accuracy.

FIGURE 4.1 | **Studies of Teachers' Grading Practices and Perceptions**
—(*continued*)

Studies	Participants	Main Findings
Liu (2008b)	Middle and high school teachers	• Most teachers used effort, ability, and attendance/participation in grading. • Many teachers used classroom behavior. • Few grade-level differences were observed.
Liu, O'Connell, & McCoach (2006)	Secondary teachers	• Three uses of grading were identified: to provide feedback, improve motivation, and provide encouragement.
Llosa (2008)	Elementary teachers	• Teacher interpretations of standards for grading varied. • Teachers approved of using grades for summative purposes. • Teachers did not find using grades for formative purposes to be a good idea.
McMillan (2001)	Middle and high school teachers	• Significant variation in weight was given to different factors. • A high percentage of teachers used nonachievement factors. • Four academic-enabling factors were identified: (1) noncognitive factors, (2) achievement, (3) external comparisons, and (4) use of extra credit.
McMillan & Lawson (2001)	Secondary science teachers	• Most reported use of both cognitive and noncognitive factors in grading, especially effort.
McMillan, Myran, & Workman (2002)	Elementary school teachers	• Five grading factors were identified: (1) improvement and effort, (2) extra credit, (3) achievement, (4) homework, and (5) external comparisons. • Most teachers based grades on effort, improvement, and ability. • Few differences were noted between math and language arts teachers. • The weight given to different factors varied considerably by teacher.
McMillan & Nash (2000)	Elementary and secondary math and English teachers	• Teaching philosophy was a key factor in determining grading criteria. • Teachers used grading to enhance student effort, motivation, and learning.

Studies	Participants	Main Findings
McMunn, Schenck, & McColskey (2003)	Elementary and secondary teachers	• Grading practices were found to be highly idiosyncratic. • Over half the teachers used student participation and homework as factors in their grading. • Teachers understood the need to report academic and nonacademic factors separately.
Randall & Engelhard (2009)	Elementary, middle, and high school teachers	• Achievement was clearly the most important factor for grading. • Effort and behavior were used primarily to provide feedback. • Teachers placed little emphasis on ability.
Randall & Engelhard (2010)	Elementary, middle, and high school teachers	• Achievement was the most important factor teachers considered. • Effort and classroom behavior were grading factors for borderline cases.
Russell & Austin (2010)	Secondary music teachers	• Noncognitive factors weighed as much or more than achievement. • In high school, there was a greater emphasis on attendance. • In middle school, there was a greater emphasis on practice.
Simon, Tierney, Forgette-Giroux, Charland, Noonan, & Duncan (2010)	One high school math teacher	• Grading policies conflicted with professional judgments about what to include in grading.
Sun & Cheng (2013)	English language secondary teachers	• Teachers individualized grades to motivate students. • Teachers used noncognitive factors in their grading, especially for borderline cases, for encouragement, and to promote effort. • Greater emphasis was placed on nonachievement factors than achievement.
Svennberg, Meckbach, & Redelius (2014)	Four physical education teachers	• Four important factors were identified: (1) knowledge/skills, (2) motivation, (3) confidence, and (4) interaction with others.

FIGURE 4.1 | **Studies of Teachers' Grading Practices and Perceptions**
—(*continued*)

Studies	Participants	Main Findings
Swan, Guskey, & Jung (2014)	Elementary and middle school teachers	• Most teachers indicated that standards-based reporting provided more information than traditional formats. • Standards-based reporting resulted in higher-quality use of descriptors (e.g., *exemplary, proficient, progressing, struggling*) that were more accurate and more easily understood.
Tierney, Simon, & Charland (2011)	High school math teachers	• Most teachers stressed improvement, with little emphasis on attitude, motivation, or participation, for fair grading. • Teachers considered it appropriate for grading to be individualized to students. • Effort was considered for borderline grades.
Truog & Friedman (1996)	High school teachers	• Significant variability in grading practices was reported. • Most teachers used both achievement and nonachievement factors in their grading.
Webster (2011)	High school teachers	• Focus was mostly on achievement as defined by standards. • Multiple purposes and inconsistent practices were reported.
Welsh & D'Agostino (2009)	3rd and 5th grade teachers	• Most teachers agreed that grading should be based primarily on achievement. • There was significant variability in using effort and progress.
Wiles (2013)	Middle school teachers	• Most teachers agreed grades should represent achievement on predetermined standards. • Teachers thought the effect of nonachievement factors on grades should be limited.
Wiley (2011)	High school teachers	• There was significant variation in the use of nonachievement factors. • Teachers placed significant emphasis on nonachievement factors for low-ability or low-achieving students.
Yesbeck (2011)	Ten middle school language arts teachers	• Teachers believed both achievement and nonachievement factors should be included in grades.

Source: From "A Century of Grading Research: Meaning and Value in the Most Common Educational Measure," by S. M. Brookhart, T. R. Guskey, A. J. Bowers, J. H. McMillan, J. K. Smith, L. F. Smith, et al., 2016, *Review of Educational Research, 86*(4), pp. 803–848. Copyright 2016 by American Educational Research Association. Adapted with permission.

Other studies conducted with different grade levels also document the extent to which nonacademic factors are included in the determination of grades. Using the Teachers' Perceptions of Grading Practices Scale, Liu (2008b) showed that middle and high school teachers used several factors in grading. Although her sample was small, over 90 percent of the teachers reported using effort in grading, over 60 percent used student ability and attendance/participation, and over 40 percent used classroom behavior. Imperial (2011) used a carefully developed 63-item survey to ascertain grading purposes, practices, and values with 416 Catholic high school teachers from 33 California high schools. He found that approximately 50 percent indicated that grades represent only academic achievement, although 78 percent included homework (with 50 percent of those saying homework counted for 20 percent or more of grades), 57 percent effort, and 70 percent participation. This suggests that teachers' conceptions of "academic achievement," as indicated by grades, includes academic enablers (McMillan, 2001).

In a qualitative interview study of middle school English teachers, Yesbeck (2011) also found clear evidence of "hodgepodge" grading, as did Russell and Austin (2010) in their survey study of 352 secondary music teachers, Deshpande (2015) in a mixed methods study of 188 New York City public middle school teachers, and Guskey (2002) in his study of 94 elementary and 112 secondary teachers. McMillan and Lawson (2001) found that a sample of 213 secondary science teachers included a variety of factors in grading, including ability and effort. Svennberg, Meckbach, and Redelius (2014) interviewed physical education teachers about their grading practices and found that student motivation, confidence, and interaction with others were important grading criteria. Aronson (2008), in a study of 168 middle and high school teachers, also found that the vast majority considered effort in grades and also considered attendance to be an important factor.

Cizek, Fitzgerald, and Rachor (1996) used a survey with 143 elementary and secondary teachers. They found that teachers generally considered and incorporated both objective and subjective factors when assigning grades, synthesizing information to increase the likelihood of achieving high grades. They also found, as McMillan and colleagues (2002), Randall and Engelhard (2009), and Brookhart (1994) did, that high variability was common among teachers within the same school regarding the meaning and purpose of grades. In a focus group with eight teachers, Truog and Friedman (1996) further confirmed the prevalence of "hodgepodge" grading, which they explained as being due in part to a lack of awareness of grading policies and to individual teaching styles. McMillan and Nash (2000), in a qualitative study, found that teaching philosophy and judgments about what is best for student motivation and learning contribute to variability of grading practices, including how much emphasis is placed on effort. Randall and Engelhard (2010) also found that teacher beliefs about what best supports students are important in determining factors used for grading (especially nonacademic factors for borderline grades), as did Sun and Cheng (2013) with a sample of 350 Chinese secondary-level teachers.

In summary, studies of teachers' grading practices over the past 20 years have primarily used surveys to document how teachers use both achievement and nonachievement evidence (primarily effort) and their own professional judgment to determine grades. This finding has been demonstrated with few differences between grade levels and core subjects taught, showing considerable variation among teachers. Teachers grade students in noncore subjects differently, with greater weight placed on nonachievement factors.

Teacher Perceptions About Grading. There are relatively few studies that focus directly on teacher perceptions of grading (e.g., by asking about teachers' attitudes and values). The finding that teachers include effort and other nonachievement factors when determining grades suggests that these factors are perceived as important.

However, since survey results are limited to what is asked, it is hard to draw definitive conclusions about perceptions and beliefs from studies of grading practices. The investigations I report in this section have studied perceptions directly.

Most of the research on teachers' perceptions focuses on what grading means, the reasons for how grading occurs, and the consequences of grading for students. These questions are based on a framework for thinking about the validity of measures developed by Messick (1989).

Sun and Cheng (2013) surveyed 162 secondary-level teachers, asking them to make grading decisions for three different student scenarios, varying students' effort, homework, achievement, improvement, and ability. They also asked the teachers to provide a rationale to explain their choices. The findings showed that teachers believed that good grades served as rewards for successfully completed work, based on effort and quality, completion of homework, and learning progress. The authors suggest that grades are useful for encouragement and attributing success to effort. Teachers also indicated that lower grades may be justified in cases of low effort or poor participation, and that strict, "hard" grading is appropriate for high achievers. This suggests that teachers valued different contributions of nonacademic factors based on variations in student characteristics. That is, "fair" grading is best accomplished, to some extent, by individualization, resulting in variability within classes of students as well as among teachers. Finally, teachers considered consequences—for other students, future success, and students' feelings of competence. The authors conclude that two themes were prevalent: (1) fair grading, and (2) grading in a manner that is beneficial to students. The results also imply that grading is done on an individual student basis, depending on the ability, effort, and participation of each student. The value of grading, then, is as a tool not only to record achievement but also to have a positive effect on motivation and other nonachievement outcomes. Grading is perceived to have value for students on an individual basis, and this is seen at least by some as a benefit rather than as problematic.

Fairness is also a theme in a study by Tierney and colleagues (2011), who examined 77 Canadian high school math teachers' grading in the context of standards-based education using survey and interview methods. Teachers stressed that grading should reflect fair assessment and instructional processes and be consistent with principles of standards-based education policies. Almost all agreed that grades should reflect achievement expectations, and 75 percent also thought grades should be based on improvement (self-referenced). Approximately 25 percent also thought it was appropriate to use norm-referenced information in grading. In contrast to previous studies in the United States, over 80 percent of teachers indicated that they did not consider attitude, motivation, or participation in determining grades. About a third of the teachers considered effort (usually for borderline cases), and many used participation and incomplete assignments. A unique contribution of this study is the inclusion of questions about how final semester grades were calculated. There were significant differences of opinion about whether certain assessments should be dropped, and some teachers were more concerned than others about such dimensions as accuracy and integrity.

Notably, and consistent with what Sun and Cheng (2013) report, teachers in Tierney and colleagues' study relied on their understanding of individual student circumstances and instructional experience to make professional judgments (most teachers relied on professional judgment in addition to a specific grading formula). Professional judgment is also reflected in a qualitative study of four Swedish physical education teachers (Svennberg et al., 2014), in which the researchers found that teachers clearly had some kind of "internalized" grading criteria that included motivation, knowledge and skills, self-confidence, and interaction with others in ways that would facilitate student learning. Hay and Macdonald

(2008) replicated this finding with physical education teachers in Queensland, Australia. In contrast, Simon and colleagues (2010) report a case study of one high school math teacher who indicated that although standardized grading policy conflicted with his professional judgment, it had a significant impact on determining final grades. This reflects the impact of policy in Canada, an important contextual influence.

Guskey (2009) and Guskey and Link (2017) found that elementary and secondary teachers differed in their perspectives about the purposes of grading. Elementary teachers were more likely to view grading as a process of communication with students as well as parents and to differentiate grading for individual students. Secondary teachers believed that grading served a classroom control and management function, emphasizing student behavior and completion of work. Bonner and Chen (2009) also examined teachers' perceptions about grading, using a sample of 222 teacher candidates. They incorporated principles of effective grading reflected in the measurement literature with constructivist views of education to develop and pilot the Survey of Assessment Beliefs, which focused on perceptions rather than practice, for teachers at all grade levels. Using a series of scenarios depicting teachers' grading, the researchers found evidence for four factors: (1) raising grades based on nonachievement factors, (2) varying grades for effort and allowing students to obtain the highest grade possible, (3) using a variety of assessment types, and (4) managing student behavior. Interpretation of the results suggested that perceptions focused on equity, consistency, accuracy, and fairness; academic-enabling factors to obtain the highest grade; and the range of different types of evidence needed for grades. This study is unique in showing the influence of instructional style on teacher perceptions of grading. The researchers replicated their work using the same instrument in a later study (Chen & Bonner, 2017).

Grimes (2010) surveyed 199 middle school teachers' attitudes toward grading and found, consistent with other research, that teachers thought grades should represent both academic and nonacademic indicators. As expected, over 90 percent of the teachers agreed that grades need to indicate academic progress and mastery of content, but over 80 percent also thought grades should indicate effort and should be viewed as feedback to students. Over 70 percent of the teachers used grades to motivate students and agreed that homework and participation should be considered in grading. Grimes found few differences by subject, grade level, or student ability.

The development of the Teachers' Perceptions of Grading Practices Scale (Liu, 2008a; Liu et al., 2006) represents a promising effort to assess teachers' beliefs and attitudes about grading. The survey includes items about importance, usefulness, effort, ability, grading habits, and perceived self-efficacy of the grading process. The usefulness items are particularly relevant to perceptions, including items such as "Grading provides feedback to my students," "High grades can motivate students to learn," and "Grading can encourage good work by students." While only one study of 307 secondary teachers used this instrument to relate perceptions of grading to student motivation, the work demonstrates how research about teachers' grading can progress beyond a simple reporting of practices. Kebles (2016) adapted Liu's scale to assess secondary mathematics teachers' perceptions of grading. Although the sample was small (35 teachers), the results showed respondents varied in the amount of emphasis they gave to effort, improvement, and participation in determining grades.

Another promising approach has been reported by Wiley (2011). She has developed and piloted (with 15 teachers) the Wiley Grading Questionnaire, which includes grading vignettes using Brookhart's (1993) research protocol, survey items developed by McMillan (2001), and additional open-ended and forced-choice items. However, early results do not show the ability to capture the more comprehensive understanding of perceptions that probe beyond nonacademic and academic factors that determine grades.

The limited number of studies on teacher perceptions of grading, for which new instruments are being developed, provide some indication of the rationale behind varied grading practices. Several studies have successfully explored the bases for practices and show that teachers view grades as having fair, individualized, positive effects on students' learning and motivation (and to a lesser extent, classroom control).

Studies Based on Standards-Based Grading. A few studies have explored grading practices and perceptions within the context of standards-based rather than more traditional modes of grading (Adrian, 2012; Guskey et al., 2010; McMunn et al., 2003; Swan et al., 2014; Welsh & D'Agostino, 2009; Wiles, 2013). Overall, these studies suggest a trend in grading practices and beliefs that are congruent with the goals of standards-based grading, including more favorable views about reporting effort, behavior, and homework separately from achievement (Wiles, 2013).

Most of these studies examine teachers' grading beliefs in the context of professional development to move toward standards-based grading. Guskey and colleagues (2010) and Swan and colleagues (2014) produced two research reports that compare teachers' and parents' views of standards-based report cards. They showed that teachers receiving professional development viewed standards-based grades as providing somewhat higher-quality and clearer information about student achievement. Since the standards-based report cards used a rubric to indicate achievement and a separate rating for process goals such as preparation and homework, the results suggest that teachers find a standards-based approach that shows only achievement more effective. However, in these studies, teachers did not seem to understand completely the implications of the new approach for grading (Brookhart, 2013b).

McMunn and colleagues (2003) reported a case study of 241 elementary and secondary teachers who participated in professional development to enhance standards-based grading practices.

Prior to training, teachers reported highly idiosyncratic grading practices within the same school, with over 50 percent including participation and homework. Following training, teachers indicated a greater understanding of the need to separate achievement from nonachievement factors, but their classroom practices did not reflect this change in belief. Adrian (2012) studied reasons 86 elementary teachers gave for grading and what should be included in grading as part of a professional development program. She found only 20 percent of the teachers thought that effort, behavior, and homework should be included in grades, and 88 percent thought that it was not appropriate to reduce grades for late assignments. Wiles (2013) found that while few grading beliefs changed due to professional development for 22 middle school teachers, 78 percent thought grades should represent understanding of predetermined educational standards, and most thought other factors should have a limited effect. Finally, Welsh and D'Agostino (2009) used a sample of 37 3rd and 5th grade teachers to explore how those using a standards-based approach to grading could be described according to what they termed *appraisal style*. Through a series of interviews, they came to the same conclusions as McMunn and colleagues (2003). Teachers understood the importance of grading only on achievement, but there was still great variability about the emphasis given to effort or progress. Similar findings were reported by Llosa (2008) in her summary of two studies that showed tension between grading based on growth for individual students and absolute standards. Webster (2011) used a mixed methods design with 42 teachers to report multiple purposes and inconsistent practices, with a clear desire to focus more on academic achievement as emphasized in standards-based education.

What Are the Implications of These Research Findings for Improvement in Grading Policy and Practice?

Research on teachers' grading practices and perspectives suggests several clear conclusions, some trends over time, and implications for practice and policy. With respect to conclusions, whether teachers' grading practices are described as varied, idiosyncratic, individualized, hodgepodge, mixed, diverse, or "kitchen sink" (see Cizek et al., 1996), the evidence shows that they continue to be highly variable. The empirical support for this conclusion is largely consistent over time—indeed, for over 100 years, across different subjects and all levels of teaching, and using different methodologies. It is a firm finding that probably does not need further documentation. According to Brookhart (2013a), "Teachers at all levels mix effort and behavior into their achievement grades, especially for lower achieving students.... The mixing of effort and behavior into grading practices is robust" (p. 269). Furthermore, we know that variability in practice occurs among teachers at the same school, and even within a single classroom. This dynamic is what now needs further investigation and greater understanding. Why do some teachers weigh some nonachievement factors more heavily than others? Why do teachers in some subjects use nonachievement factors more than teachers in other subjects do? Labeling these varied practices as "hodgepodge" suggests a haphazard mix, whereas the research shows that, on the contrary, grades are informed by what teachers believe is in the best interests of students.

It seems that grading practices, while varied, are best understood when teachers' views toward the purpose, meaning, value, and consequences on student learning and motivation are taken into consideration. That is, a teacher's perceptions about grading provide a rationale and explanation for how grading does much more than document learning—it is, rather, a key element in promoting learning and motivation. This dynamic suggests that a "one-size-fits-all" set of required grading guidelines for all teachers is not in the best interests of student learning, and also that teachers need to fully understand their reasons for using different factors in grading. This may be best accomplished by reflecting on the purposes of grading. A great stimulus for reflection is to use scenarios as case studies.

Beyond documenting academic achievement, what do grades represent? These beliefs need to be clearly articulated and then discussed with others. A collaborative approach to elucidating grading practices will enhance the validity of what is done and provide a stimulus for more in-depth understanding. Too often, teachers' grading is idiosyncratic and isolated, even within the same school. Planned discussions about grading with other teachers will have great value, providing shared insights and experiences that all will benefit from.

Fairness should be a part of these discussions. "Being fair" is clearly a concern of teachers, and there is a need for shared clarity and consistency about how fairness is interpreted. What *is* "fair" grading? What are some examples of different grading practices for students that are most fair to all students? How is fairness related to the purposes of grading?

Student effort, whether documented by participation, homework, behavior, completion of work, or other indicators, is clearly a key element of grading. Whether recorded separately or combined with achievement, effort is recognized by teachers as important to achievement and motivation. Standards-based grading has promoted separate reporting of effort, but progress is not widespread, especially in higher grades. Given recent advances in motivation theory and research, it would be helpful to conduct further studies that probe more deeply into how evaluation of effort as reflected in grading is used for motivation. Although it's clear that most teachers use effort in grading, it is not as clear how and why teachers identify, record, and use effort indicators. Teachers need to address and discuss what effort means and how it is used for grading and motivation (e.g., by suggesting a separate reporting of effort and debating the pros and cons of this approach).

Most teachers want to give students the highest grades possible. This dynamic, "pulling for students," explains why nonachievement, academic-enabling factors have been important in grading, especially the use of effort and improvement: they allow most students to be successful (Bonner, 2016). In this sense, grading may be individualized to some extent in the same classroom. This aspect of grading also needs discussion among teachers. Specifically, it would be helpful to provide a clear rationale for how "pulling for students" is operationalized to better assure fairness and consistency within and across classrooms. Under what circumstances should teachers individualize the weight given to different factors in their grading? Is it fair to bump a grade based on improvement for one student and consider effort for another? What guidelines and principles would help teachers more effectively incorporate nonacademic factors in their grading? These are all questions worth further consideration.

The research suggests some guidelines for grading "borderline" students. Because a grade must represent an accurate indication of student achievement, factors that may have negatively influenced performance (such as student illness) should be taken into consideration. For borderline cases, such grades should receive less weight than other assessments. For students exhibiting a clear learning progression, cumulative assessments should tip the balance toward a higher grade. A particularly egregious example of how grading is unfair in borderline cases is when a missed assignment is calculated as a zero. This is because the zero assumes no knowledge or proficiency and unduly skews the overall score in a negative direction. Finally, it is best to grade individual assignments and assessments more strictly and then bump semester grades higher for borderline students.

Teacher judgment is at the heart of grading and based on each teacher's unique teaching styles, values, and beliefs. While this leads to some level of inconsistency in grading, it probably enhances validity in the sense that variability results in more accurate grades that have a positive influence on learning and motivation. Teachers' professional judgments supplement more objective evidence, yet there is little research that probes the nature of these judgments to better understand how they are formed and supported. This suggests a need for policy that addresses these variations. For example, teachers can be asked to articulate how their values and beliefs about learning and motivation influence their grading practices. Currently, there seems to be an unspoken and unaddressed acceptance of varied practices, rather than a shared discourse about why a practice is used, how fair it is for all students, and how it relates to learning and motivation. Teachers should accept the need to make professional judgments, understand how they are made, and be comfortable in making them. High-quality grading is much more than crunching numbers! In fact, mindless number crunching is recognized as deleterious. Grading involves teachers' qualitative judgments about assignment and test difficulty and about the criteria used to evaluate students' work. Teachers should recognize and rely on these judgments.

The research suggests that grades are often viewed as a form of feedback to students. But is the feedback the teacher intends the feedback students hear? The meaning that students give to grades is what is most important. Teachers need to consult with students about how they interpret grades—what message students receive, what this suggests about their learning, and what the effect of the grade is on motivation.

Recent findings suggest that teachers believe idiosyncratic and individualized grading practices are helpful to students, and the use of "academic enablers" such as effort and participation reflect actual achievement. This perception seems to outweigh concerns about variability in grading. Just as assessment more broadly now emphasizes how tests can enhance as well as document student learning, grading may appropriately be applied by teachers in varied ways because doing so is in the best interests of students. Grading *for* learning may be as important as grading *of* learning when thinking about the purpose of grading and its consequences. Rather than denigrate "hodgepodge" grading, therefore, it may be more useful to better understand it and help teachers use both academic and nonacademic factors in ways that are well thought out, transparent, and fair, to improve student motivation and learning.

References

Adrian, C. A. (2012). *Implementing standards-based grading: Elementary teachers' beliefs, practices and concerns* (Doctoral dissertation). Washington State University, Pullman, Washington. Retrieved from http://research.libraries.wsu.edu/xmlui/handle/2376/4090

Aronson, M. J. (2008). *How teachers' perceptions in the areas of student behavior, attendance and student personality influence their grading practice* (Doctoral dissertation). University of Rochester, New York.

Bailey, M. (2012). *The relationship between secondary school teacher perceptions of grading practices and teacher perceptions of student motivation* (Doctoral dissertation). University of Missouri, St. Louis.

Bonner, S. M. (2016). Teacher perceptions about assessment: Competing narratives. In G. T. L. Brown & L. R. Harris (Eds.), *Handbook of human and social conditions in assessment* (pp. 21–39). New York: Routledge.

Bonner, S. M., & Chen, P. P. (2009). Teacher candidates' perceptions about grading and constructivist teaching. *Educational Assessment, 14*(2), 57–77.

Brookhart, S. M. (1991). Letter: Grading practices and validity. *Educational Measurement: Issues and Practice, 10*(1), 35–36.

Brookhart, S. M. (1993). Teachers' grading practices: Meaning and values. *Journal of Educational Measurement, 30*(2), 123–142.

Brookhart, S. M. (1994). Teachers' grading: Practice and theory. *Applied Measurement in Education, 7,* 279–301.

Brookhart, S. M. (2013a). Grading. In J. H. McMillan (Ed.), *Sage handbook of research on classroom assessment* (pp. 257–271). Thousand Oaks, CA: Sage.

Brookhart, S. M. (2013b). The use of teacher judgment for summative assessment in the USA. *Assessment in Education: Principles, Policy & Practice, 20*(1), 69–90.

Brookhart, S. M., Guskey, T. R., Bowers, A. J., McMillan, J. H., Smith, J. K., Smith, L. F., et al. (2016). A century of grading research: Meaning and value in the most common educational measure. *Review of Educational Research, 86*(4), 803–848.

Brown, G. T. L., & Harris, L. R. (Eds.). (2016). *Handbook of human and social conditions in assessment.* New York: Routledge.

Chen, P. P., & Bonner, S. M. (2017). Teachers' beliefs about grading practices and a constructivist approach to teaching. *Educational Assessment, 22*(1), 18–34. doi:10.1080/10627197.2016.1271703

Cizek, G. J., Fitzgerald, J. M., & Rachor, R. A. (1996). Teachers' assessment practices: Preparation, isolation, and the kitchen sink. *Educational Assessment, 3*(2), 159–179. doi:10.1207/s15326977ea0302_3

Crooks, A. D. (1933). Marks and marking systems: A digest. *The Journal of Educational Research, 27,* 259–272.

Cross, L. H., & Frary, R. B. (1999). Hodgepodge grading: Endorsed by students and teachers alike. *Applied Measurement in Education, 12*(1), 53–73.

Deshpande, A. (2015). *Making the grade: Exploring the variability of grades and teacher beliefs about grading in New York City public middle schools* (Doctoral dissertation). New York University, New York.

Duncan, R. C., & Noonan, B. (2007). Factors affecting teachers' grading and assessment practices. *Alberta Journal of Educational Research, 53*(1), 1–21.

Frary, R. B., Cross, L. H., & Weber, L. J. (1993). Testing and grading practices and opinions of secondary teachers of academic subjects: Implications for instruction in measurement. *Educational Measurement: Issues & Practice, 12*(3), 23–30.

Grimes, T. V. (2010). *Interpreting the meaning of grades: A descriptive analysis of middle school teachers' assessment and grading practices* (Doctoral dissertation). Virginia Commonwealth University, Richmond.

Guskey, T. R. (2002). *Perspectives on grading and reporting: Differences among teachers, students, and parents.* Paper presented at the Annual Meeting of the American Educational Research Association, New Orleans, LA. (ED464113)

Guskey, T. R. (2009). *Bound by tradition: Teachers' views of crucial grading and reporting issues.* Paper presented at the Annual Meeting of the American Educational Research Association, San Francisco. (ED509342)

Guskey, T. R., & Link, L. J. (2017). *Grades represent achievement and "something else": Analysis of the nonachievement factors teachers consider in determining students' grades.* Paper presented at the Annual Meeting of the American Educational Research Association, San Antonio, TX.

Guskey, T. R., Swan, G. M., & Jung, L. A. (2010). *Developing a statewide, standards-based student report card: A review of the Kentucky initiative.* Paper presented at the Annual Meeting of the American Educational Research Association, Denver, CO. (ED509404)

Hay, P. J., & Macdonald, D. (2008). (Mis)appropriations of criterion- and standards-referenced assessment in a performance-based subject. *Assessment in Education: Principles, Policy & Practice, 15*(2), 153–168.

Imperial, P. (2011). *Grading and reporting purposes and practices in Catholic secondary schools and grades' efficacy in accurately communicating student learning* (Doctoral dissertation). University of San Francisco. Retrieved from https://repository.usfca.edu/cgi/viewcontent.cgi?article=1002&context=diss

Kebles, K. E. (2016). *What's in an A? A quantitative study on the grading perceptions of middle school and high school math teachers* (Doctoral dissertation). Wilmington University, Wilmington, DE. Retrieved from http://search.proquest.com/docview/1787831395/

Kelly, F. J. (1914). *Teachers' marks: Their variability and standardization.* No. 66. New York: Teachers College, Columbia University.

Kirschenbaum, H., Napier, R., & Simon, S. B. (1971). *Wad-ja-get? The grading game in American education.* New York: Hart Publishing.

Kunnath, J. P. (2016). *A critical pedagogy perspective of the impact of school poverty level on the teacher grading decision-making process* (Doctoral dissertation). California State University, Fresno, CA.

Liu, X. (2008a). *Assessing measurement invariance of the teachers' perceptions of grading practices scale across cultures.* Paper presented at the Annual Meeting of the Northeastern Educational Research Association, Rocky Hill, CT.

Liu, X. (2008b). *Measuring teachers' perceptions of grading practices: Does school level make a difference?* Paper presented at the Annual Meeting of the Northeastern Educational Research Association, Rocky Hill, CT.

Liu, X., O'Connell, A. A., & McCoach, D. B. (2006). *The initial validation of teachers' perceptions of grading practices.* Paper presented at the Annual Meeting of the American Educational Research Association, San Francisco.

Llosa, L. (2008). Building and supporting a validity argument for a standards-based classroom assessment of English proficiency based on teacher judgments. *Educational Measurement: Issues & Practice, 27*(3), 32–42. doi:10.1111/j.1745-3992.2008.00126.x

McMillan, J. H. (2001). Secondary teachers' classroom assessment and grading practices. *Educational Measurement: Issues and Practice, 20*(1), 20–32. doi:10.1111/j.1745-3992.2001.tb00055.x

McMillan, J. H., & Lawson, S. R. (2001). *Secondary science teachers' classroom assessment and grading practices.* (ED450158)

McMillan, J. H., Myran, S., & Workman, D. (2002). Elementary teachers' classroom assessment and grading practices. *The Journal of Educational Research, 95*(4), 203–213. doi:10.1080/00220670209596593

McMillan, J. H., & Nash, S. (2000, April). *Teacher classroom assessment and grading decision making.* Paper presented at the Annual Meeting of the National Council of Measurement in Education, New Orleans, LA.

McMunn, N., Schenck, P., & McColskey, W. (2003). *Standards-based assessment, grading, and reporting in classrooms: Can district training and support change teacher practice?* Paper presented at the Annual Meeting of the American Educational Research Association, Chicago. (ED 475763)

Messick, S. (1989). Validity. In R. L. Linn (Ed.), *Educational measurement* (3rd ed.) (pp. 13–103). New York: American Council of Education and Macmillan.

Randall, J., & Engelhard, G. (2009). Differences between teachers' grading practices in elementary and middle schools. *The Journal of Educational Research, 102,* 175–185.

Randall, J., & Engelhard, G. (2010). Examining the grading practices of teachers. *Teaching and Teacher Education, 26*(7), 1372–1380. doi:10.1016/j.tate.2010.03.008

Rugg, H. O. (1918). Teachers' marks and the reconstruction of the marking system. *The Elementary School Journal, 18*(9), 701–719.

Russell, J. A., & Austin, J. R. (2010). Assessment practices of secondary music teachers. *Journal of Research in Music Education, 58*(1), 37–54. doi:10.1177/0022429409360062

Simon, M., Tierney, R. D., Forgette-Giroux, R., Charland, J., Noonan, B., & Duncan, R. (2010). A secondary school teacher's description of the process of determining report card grades. *McGill Journal of Education, 45*(3), 535–554.

Smith, A. Z., & Dobbin, J. E. (1960). Marks and marking systems. In C. W. Harris (Ed.), *Encyclopedia of educational research* (3rd ed.) (pp. 783–791). New York: Macmillan.

Starch, D., & Elliot, E. C. (1912). Reliability of the grading of high-school work in English. *School Review, 20,* 442–457.

Starch, D., & Elliot, E. C. (1913a). Reliability of grading work in mathematics. *School Review, 21,* 254–259.

Starch, D., & Elliott, E. C. (1913b). Reliability of grading work in history. *School Review, 21,* 676–681.

Sun, Y., & Cheng, L. (2013). Teachers' grading practices: Meaning and values assigned. *Assessment in Education: Principles, Policy & Practice, 21*(3), 326–343. doi:10.1080/0969594.2013.768207

Svennberg, L., Meckbach, J., & Redelius, K. (2014). Exploring PE teachers' "gut feelings": An attempt to verbalise and discuss teachers' internalised grading criteria. *European Physical Education Review, 20*(2), 199–214. doi:10.1177/1356336X13517437

Swan, G. M., Guskey, T. R., & Jung, L. A. (2014). Parents' and teachers' perceptions of standards-based and traditional report cards. *Educational Assessment, Evaluation and Accountability, 26*(3), 289–299.

Tierney, R. D., Simon, M., & Charland, J. (2011). Being fair: Teachers' interpretations of principles for standards-based grading. *The Educational Forum, 75*(3), 210–227.

Truog, A. L., & Friedman, S. J. (1996). *Evaluating high school teachers' written grading policies from a measurement perspective.* Paper presented at the Annual Meeting of the National Council of Measurement in Education, New York.

Webster, K. L. (2011). *High school grading practices: Teacher leaders' reflections, insights, and recommendations* (Doctoral dissertation). Lewis and Clark College, Edwardsville, IL. Retrieved from http://search.proquest.com/docview/929134496

Welsh, M. E., & D'Agostino, J. (2009). Fostering consistency between standards-based grades and large-scale assessment results. In T. R. Guskey (Ed.), *Practical solutions for serious problems in standards-based grading* (pp. 75–104). Thousand Oaks, CA: Corwin.

Wiles, G. (2013). *A quantitative study exploring grading and assessment practices in the middle school environment* (Doctoral dissertation). Northwest Nazarene University, Nampa, ID. Retrieved from http://search.proquest.com/docview/1462053512

Wiley, C. R. (2011). *Profiles of teacher grading practices: Integrating teacher beliefs, course criteria, and student characteristics* (Doctoral dissertation). University of Arizona, Tempe, AZ. Retrieved from http://search.proquest.com/docview/887719048

Yesbeck, D. M. (2011). *Grading practices: Teachers' considerations of academic and non-academic factors* (Doctoral dissertation). Virginia Commonwealth University, Richmond, VA.

5

Standards-Based Grading

Megan Welsh

Standards-based grading (SBG) is a relatively new and increasingly ubiquitous report card format that extends standards-based instruction and assessment by establishing new methods of communicating with parents and students the degree to which students have met grade-level expectations (Grindberg, 2014). As Guskey and Bailey (2001) explain, SBG reports are differentiated from previous grading practices because they (1) require teachers to report student performance on the key standards that must be attained at each grade level (e.g., adding fractions, computing area) in lieu of content-area grades; and (2) assess grade achievement using a scale similar to the ones used by state or provincial assessments (e.g., using grades of *modest, intermediate, proficient,* or *exemplary* performance). When well implemented, SBG reports should also provide detailed information on the extent to which students have attained the most important skills for a grade level and content area and, separately, report behaviors that support learning, like study skills, homework completion, and engagement.

SBG systems have the potential to improve consistency of grades among teachers and across grades by explicitly separating academic achievement from other aspects of performance. Brookhart (2011) refers to SBG as "learner-focused grading" (p. 10), while McMillan (2009) argues that it will improve the validity, fairness, and motivational aspects of report cards. McMillan argues that SBG ensures fairness by (1) limiting scores to performance on standards and (2) increasing transparency. Specifically, he says, "Students can see the direct link between the criteria and their performance. Learning for greater understanding becomes more important than what rewards follow from successful attainment" (p. 116).

Many guidelines exist to advise practitioners on SBG implementation, but these are largely based on the general research on grading. Empirical research that examines the implementation, design, and validity of SBG reports is just emerging and is the subject of this chapter.

Why Is It Important to Study Standards-Based Grading?

Standards-based grading needs extensive investigation because it is both widely used and under-studied. It should be examined to make sure it helps meet its intended goals and to learn how to improve upon current grading efforts. There are several reasons that a district might adopt SBG: (1) to focus instruction and assessment on a set of key standards, (2) to encourage teachers to operationally define what it looks like for a student to attain course and grade-level expectations, and (3) to improve communication with students and parents. Because there are many purposes associated with SBG, the extent to which it helps districts achieve each of these aims should be studied.

As Scriffiny (2008) explains, SBG can be used to enhance the quality of instruction. Since teachers record students' performance on specific skills, these records can be useful monitoring tools to help teachers individualize instruction. Scriffiny argues that this can lead to SBG creating an impetus for reform, since reflecting on students' achievement will lead teachers to identify changes that need to be made. However, this effect of SBG is unexplored in academic research.

It is important to study how educational practice has changed in response to SBG. Educators should know how and whether implementation affects assessment and grading practices. While several authors have provided advice on this front (Brookhart, 2011; Guskey & Bailey, 2010; O'Connor, 2009), only limited research has been conducted on what teachers actually do in classrooms.

An additional line of inquiry involves learning how teachers conceptualize what it means to achieve course or grade-level standards. Because SBG is exceptionally detailed, teachers must track student progress on several skills within each content area, assessing enough times to accurately gauge student mastery. This can become a record-keeping challenge, but it also allows teachers to reflect on student progress in a new way. Since teachers report what students know using achievement-level descriptors (e.g., *below basic, basic, proficient, advanced*), they must also define what kind of performance is required at each level in transforming assessment results into SBG reports. This is a much more complex task than simply averaging percent correct scores across assessments and assigning scores above 90 percent an *A*. We cannot understand what SBG reports represent without also learning how teachers approach grading.

Given this increased complexity and a research base showing that traditional grades reflect both academic content knowledge and other kinds of performance such as effort, homework completion, and compliance with teachers' directions (Bowers, 2009; Kelly, 2008), research is needed to determine whether SBG infers a false level of precision. Evidence is needed to determine whether grades truly reflect performance on each standard, as opposed to more global skills or the student behaviors that are known to affect traditional grades. This is especially important, as some scholars assert that improvements in the quality of information provided by SBG should lead to instructional improvements and larger educational reforms (Scriffiny, 2008). Put simply, students, parents, teachers, and administrators need to be able to trust the information they use for decision making.

Because they are expressed in achievement levels, SBG reports provide insight into how teachers conceptualize grade-level performance. The standards-based reform movement is predicated upon the notion that educators can accurately interpret the standards and that the standards will be consistently applied across classrooms. However, standards are often intentionally broad, to allow an entire year's worth of curriculum to be encompassed in a relatively short document. There is some evidence to suggest that highly skilled people can legitimately draw different conclusions about what is expected by a standards-based grade (Hill, 2001; D'Agostino, Welsh, & Corson, 2007). Studying differences between classrooms in the consistency between SBG and state standards-based assessment scores and SBG implementation more globally provides some insight into the extent to which teachers consistently interpret the standards. This information not only helps us understand the implementation of standards-based reform, but also could be used to foster rich conversations among teachers about how they approach instruction.

Finally, SBG is like all other report card formats in that it is primarily a communication tool among students, parents, and teachers. As such, it is important to understand not only how teachers conceptualize SBG but also how students and parents interpret these reports. The added cognitive load on teachers may also be felt by parents, who are unaccustomed to thinking outside the letter-grade format. Knowing more about how parents interpret SBG, how they act on this information, and how this differs from the way parents approach traditional report cards can help districts think through the supports they should provide. Investigating student responses to SBG is also needed to understand how it might be used to help students reflect on their performance and act upon feedback.

What Significant Studies Have Been Conducted on Standards-Based Grading?

Compared to other grading methods, SBG is a relatively new phenomenon, having first appeared in practitioner-oriented journals in 1994. That year, staff from the Tucson Unified School District reported on their efforts to implement a rubric-based grading system designed to put grades and state or provincial assessments on the same scale, provide more information to parents about student progress, and improve consistency in grading practices districtwide (Clarridge & Whitaker, 1994). That same year, Wiggins (1994) wrote a theoretical paper asserting that grades should provide information about performance relative to end-of-elementary, -middle, and -high school expectations. He also argued that these performance-level grades should distinguish among the quality of student work, its level of sophistication, and the work habits employed. These basic principles, sometimes referred to as "criterion-referenced grading," separate reports on attainment of standards from reports on behavior and have become hallmarks of SBG (Brookhart, 2011; Guskey & Bailey, 2001, 2010; McMillan, 2009; Scriffiny, 2008; Shippy, Washer, & Perrin, 2013).

This chapter focuses on empirical research on SBG and its implications. The 15 studies described here and in Figures 5.1, 5.2, and 5.3 were published between 1999 and 2013. They present the experiences of students and educators from four countries across a wide array of grade levels and content areas. These studies focused on three areas: (1) descriptions of SBG implementation, (2) teacher and parent perceptions of SBG as a communication tool, and (3) concordance between SBG and state or provincial assessments.

Implementation of SBG

Seven studies (see Figure 5.1, pp. 120–121) have described the implementation of standards-based grading, basing their results on the perceptions of approximately 425 teachers working in four U.S. school districts, one Australian school, and one Canadian province (Cox, 2011; Hay & Macdonald, 2008; Howley, Kusimo, & Parrott, 2001; McMunn, Schenck, & McColskey, 2003; Simon et al., 2010; Tierney, Simon, & Charland, 2011; Welsh & D'Agostino, 2009).

Four of these studies (Cox, 2011; Hay & Macdonald, 2008; Simon et al., 2010; Welsh & D'Agostino, 2009) used interviews with teachers to generate fine-grained descriptions of how teachers interpreted grading expectations set out in official district or province policies, how teachers approached grading, and what tensions existed between grading expectations and teacher practice. As such, they provide insight into what SBG looks like on the ground and how teachers adhere to and ameliorate expectations to arrive at a grade.

Three papers (Howley et al., 2001; McMunn et al., 2003; Tierney et al., 2011) are based on surveys that asked about the extent to which teachers implement various aspects of SBG. McMunn and colleagues (2003) also compared survey responses with classroom observations and student focus groups to gauge the accuracy of survey responses. Howley and colleagues (2001) mention analyzing qualitative data but only briefly describe the data or their analysis.

SBG as a Communication Tool

Two interrelated papers report on teachers' and parents' perceptions of SBG as a communication tool. Using an innovative design, Guskey, Swan, and Jung (2010) and Swan, Guskey, and Jung (2014) administered surveys to teachers and parents during marking periods in which teachers completed both standards-based and traditional report cards. The surveys asked participants to compare SBG with traditional report cards using four criteria: (1) quality of information, (2) quantity of information, (3) clarity, and (4) understandability. Teachers were also asked to compare the amount of time it took to complete the two report card forms. Surveys were also administered to teachers in two nearby districts that were considering implementing SBG to gauge their impression of this reporting format.

Comparing SBG Reports and State or Provincial Assessment Results

Seven papers report on the degree of concordance between SBG and state and provincial assessments. Four examine scores for Swedish 9th graders across many years (Klapp Lekholm, 2011; Klapp Lekholm & Cliffordson, 2008, 2009; Thorsen & Cliffordson, 2012); one reports on elementary students in Ontario, Canada (Ross & Kostuch, 2011); and two are based in the United States (Howley et al., 2001; Welsh et al., 2013).

The Swedish and Canadian papers analyzed data collected from large numbers of students—in some of the Swedish cases, the full population of Swedish 9th graders—and examined the relationship between grades and assessment results after controlling for student demographic characteristics. The Swedish papers use sophisticated statistical techniques to examine factors that affect the relationship between national assessment results and grades. By contrast, Howley and colleagues (2001) ran simplified attempts to examine the relationship between grades and assessment results after controlling for basic student demographics because their sample size was quite small, perhaps too much so for meaningful quantitative analysis.

Welsh and colleagues (2013) provide descriptive data on the consistency of grades and state standards–based assessments but do not control for student demographic characteristics. Instead, they aggregate consistency rates to the classroom level and examine the extent to which consistency between grades and state assessments can be attributed to teacher characteristics, content area, year

Figure 5.1 | Studies of Standards-Based Grading Implementation

Studies	Participants	Main Findings
Cox (2011)	16 U.S. secondary mathematics teachers	• Although a district policy limited the effect of non-achievement factors on grades, teachers varied a great deal in their implementation. High implementers – Substituted end-of-course assessment and high-stakes assessment scores for grades when students performed better on these exams than on others, – Allowed students to retake exams and record the highest score, – Assigned a score of 50 to all failing grades, and – Accepted late work without penalty.
Hay & Macdonald (2008)	2 secondary Australian PE teachers	• Teachers relied on memory instead of formalized assessment practices to grade students, despite a system in which external raters scored students for comparison with teacher-assigned grades.
Howley, Kusimo, & Parrott (2001)	52 U.S. middle school teachers	• Teachers differed in the extent to which noncognitive factors like effort were used to determine grades.
McMunn, Schenck, & McColskey (2003)	241 U.S. teachers, all levels	• Teachers who volunteered to participate in standards-based grading reported changing their grading practices after participating in professional development. • Classroom observations and student focus group data indicated that implementation of standards-based practice was not as widespread as teachers reported.
Simon, Tierney, Fogette-Giroux, Charland, Noonan, & Duncan (2010)	A secondary mathematics teacher in Ontario, Canada	• The teacher dealt with several tensions in grading, including contradictory provincial and school board grading policies, policies that were more appropriate for some content areas than others, and policies inconsistent with the principles of standards-based grading.
Tierney, Simon, & Charland (2011)	77 secondary mathematics teachers in Ontario, Canada	• Even in a system where the principles of standards-based grading are laid out in policy, teachers were not cognizant of all aspects and implemented only a portion of standards-based grading practices. A large minority of teachers considered effort in grading and/or graded students on improvement instead of attainment of standards.

Studies	Participants	Main Findings
Welsh & D'Agostino (2009)	37 U.S. elementary teachers	• Teacher interviews were used to describe standards-based grading practices. These were then quantitatively coded to generate an Appraisal Style score, and vignettes were generated from transcripts to generate examples of each practice. • District challenges in converting to a standards-based system were also described.

Source: From "A Century of Grading Research: Meaning and Value in the Most Common Educational Measure," by S. M. Brookhart, T. R. Guskey, A. J. Bowers, J. H. McMillan, J. K. Smith, L. F. Smith, et al., 2016, *Review of Educational Research, 86*(4), pp. 803–848. Copyright 2016 by American Educational Research Association. Adapted with permission.

examined, and interactions among these factors. (Year examined is an indicator of fluctuations in grading methods as teachers further develop their practice, differences in the students served, and variations in report card format, as different SBG reports were used in each year.)

What Questions Have SBG Studies Addressed?

Implementation studies examined the extent to which teachers adhered to the SBG principles promoted by their school district. This line of inquiry allowed researchers to better understand district or provincial policy with respect to SBG as well as to explore the processes teachers used to generate SBG reports. They explored the following questions:

1. How do the grading practices of "high implementers" of SBG differ from other teachers at the school site? (Cox, 2011)

2. What do districts do to implement SBG and how effective are these efforts? (Cox, 2011; McMunn et al., 2003; Simon et al., 2010; Welsh & D'Agostino, 2009)

3. To what extent do teachers adhere to the SBG principles expected by their school district? (Cox, 2011; Hay & Macdonald, 2008; McMunn et al., 2003; Simon et al., 2010; Tierney et al., 2011; Welsh & D'Agostino, 2009)

4. What aspects of SBG do teachers find problematic or resist? (Simon et al., 2010; Welsh & D'Agostino, 2009)

Papers that addressed the use of SBG as a communication tool examined the extent to which teachers and parents found SBG informative and whether they perceived it to be more informative than traditional report cards. They also explored whether teachers thought improvements in the information provided were worth the extra time it takes to complete an SBG report.

Other studies examined the concordance between state or provincial assessment results and SBG. Most of these studies gauged the extent to which grades capture both academic achievement and other factors not directly related to achievement, such as compliance with teacher instructions, diligence, and other behaviors that support learning (Howley et al., 2001; Klapp Lekholm, 2011; Klapp Lekholm & Cliffordson, 2008, 2009; Thorsen & Cliffordson, 2012). Some studies also examined the effect of student characteristics, school characteristics, and parent characteristics on grades, on assessment results, and on the relationship between grades and assessment results (Klapp Lekholm, 2011; Klapp Lekholm & Cliffordson, 2009).

Finally, researchers gauged the strength of the association between grades and assessment results and whether this relationship varied by subject, sex, or grade level (Ross & Kostuch, 2011; Welsh et al., 2013). The predictive validity of SBG has also been examined, determining the extent to which current report card grades predict future grades (Thorsen & Cliffordson, 2012) and future state or provincial assessment results (Ross & Kostuch, 2011).

What Have the Results of SBG Studies Revealed?

The research conducted thus far has included a wide array of practices under the label of standards-based grading (see the text box on page 125). Because SBG generally refers to grading on specific skills using a criterion-referenced scale, factors unrelated to skill of interest (e.g., completing work on time, using conventions correctly, or following directions for a number-sense grade) should not affect report card performance. This focus on skill-based reporting is a hallmark of SBG; grades only represent attainment of the skill presented on the report card.

Many approaches can be used to grade solely on attainment of reported skills, and the term *standards-based grading* is associated with a variety of strategies that were developed to meet the demands of local contexts while also aligning to standards. For example, McMunn and colleagues (2003) use the following strategies: (1) grading solely based on attainment of standards, (2) being transparent with students about grading criteria, and (3) explicitly using both formative and summative assessment as key SBG implementation indicators. In contrast, Cox (2011) describes (1) the use of common assessments, (2) minimum grading policies (e.g., setting the lowest possible grade received to 50 instead of 0), (3) no penalty for late work, and (4) replacing poor scores with retest scores as all supportive of SBG.

Differences in how SBG is operationally defined will be further discussed below, organized by implementation, communication, and comparison of grades to state or provincial assessment results.

Factors Contributing to Inconsistent Implementation

Several studies reported that teachers varied tremendously in their adherence to district, state, or provincial SBG policy. Policymakers provided directions for how to go about grading instead of developing a report card form and expecting teachers to figure out how to complete it on their own. However, directions were not consistently followed. For example, Hay and Macdonald (2008) studied SBG among physical education teachers, a population with limited exposure to the pressures of standards-based reform. They found that teachers did not use any formal assessment practices at all, despite being told which standards to assess and what level of performance is associated with different grades. Teachers also knew that their grades would be compared with the scores of external raters but still relied only on memory to grade.

A variety of factors that contribute to this kind of inconsistent implementation of SBG have been identified in the literature, including unclear policies, frequent changes in policy, differing interpretations of the standards, resistance to enacting SBG, and inconsistent fidelity of implementation of SBG practices. These are discussed below.

Unclear Policies. Confusing policies can contribute to inconsistent practice. Simon and colleagues (2010) noted discrepancies between provincial and district board of education grading policies that forced teachers to adopt one approach or the other. A second study in Ontario (Tierney et al., 2011) reported that few teachers were aware of and implementing provincial or district grading policies. While teachers tended to embrace statements consistent with the principle of criterion-referenced grading and believed that grades should clearly communicate student achievement, the information presented by grades was of questionable quality because standards-based grading practices were not consistently implemented.

Policy Change. Welsh and D'Agostino (2009) also found that changes in a district's policies over time can lead to inconsistencies among teachers. In that study, the district initially required teachers to take student progress into account in grading but later decided that grades should be expressed only in terms of end-of-year expectations. Some teachers continued to implement the original system and did not seem to know that policy had changed.

The Wide Array of Practices Associated with SBG in the Literature

- Grading on achievement, not effort
- Identifying a key set of standards to report on
- Aligning report cards to state standards (not curricular objectives)
- Using the same achievement-level indicators that appear on state or provincial assessments
- Organizing gradebooks by standard instead of by content area
- Reporting nonacademic performance separately
- Ensuring transparency in grading criteria
- Using a variety of assessment formats
- Weighting end-of-marking-period assessments heaviest
- Using common assessments
- Implementing minimum grading policies
- Accepting late work with no penalty
- Allowing students to retest and replace low scores with retest scores
- Transforming percent-correct grades to achievement levels
- Using scoring rubrics
- Developing teacher-created assessments to better align with standards
- Grading on product, progress, and/or process
- Assessing frequently
- Providing extended time on assessments
- Grading independent work
- Assigning grades only after instructional units are completed
- Involving students in grading
- Grading using a holistic review of student performance

Source: From "A Century of Grading Research: Meaning and Value in the Most Common Educational Measure," by S. M. Brookhart, T. R. Guskey, A. J. Bowers, J. H. McMillan, J. K. Smith, L. F. Smith, et al., 2016, *Review of Educational Research, 86*(4), pp. 803–848. Copyright 2016 by American Educational Research Association. Adapted with permission.

Standards Interpretation. Interpretation of the standards themselves can also lead to inconsistencies. Welsh and D'Agostino (2009) observed that even among teachers who use a common assessment, differences in scoring can lead to substantial differences in how a grade should be interpreted. For example, some 3rd grade teachers required students to solve combinations by making lists or stating the total number of combinations that could be generated. Others only gave full marks if students explained how the number of combinations could be determined from a multiplication sentence.

Resistance to Enacting Policies. Other teachers disagreed with SBG policy and actively resisted it. Simon and colleagues (2010) interviewed one teacher who believed SBG to be problematic for mathematics. The teacher said that reporting only on performance as of the end of the marking period did not make sense, because course content changes and does not involve incremental improvement on related skills. The teacher followed policies that required transforming percentage grades to achievement levels without considering the qualitative difference in performance associated with each score. The teacher also admitted that she found it difficult to determine how to address nonacademic variables such as effort, homework, and late assignments in calculating final grades.

Welsh and D'Agostino (2009) also noted areas in which teachers disagreed with and ignored district grading policies. For example, some teachers believed that grading homework and assigning zeroes to missing work is necessary to provide sufficient motivation. Teachers also argued that students could not learn the material if they did not practice.

Inconsistency of Implementation Fidelity. There were also instances in which teachers believed they had implemented SBG, but additional evidence suggested that they were overly optimistic about the extensiveness of implementation. For example, McMunn and colleagues (2003) surveyed teachers who reported that they implemented SBG by creating new grading systems, using a variety of assessment formats, allowing students to retake tests, providing extended time on assessments, and using portfolios. Because of these efforts, teachers believed that students knew how they were being graded, and that the reforms had both improved achievement and motivated students. However, student focus groups and classroom observations indicated that standards-based practices were less widespread than the teachers claimed.

SBG practices are not easily standardized. Teachers may continue "hodgepodge grading" (Brookhart, 1991) approaches despite greater clarity regarding expected content and the kinds of performance that grades are expected to reflect. While training and efforts to align grading policies across the various levels of the education system seem like obvious first steps, the evidence thus far indicates that these approaches are not sufficient. The studies reviewed here provide valuable insight into needed improvements. For example, teachers clearly struggle with separating academic achievement from behaviors that support learning. This is important not only to grading, but also to teaching philosophy—some teachers may believe that the only way to learn is through diligence and that grades should therefore reward hard work (Bonner & Chen, 2009). As such, at least some comingling of SBG grades with behavior may be unavoidable.

While the fundamental goal of SBG is clear—to grade students on specific skills using achievement-level descriptors—the practices used to generate these grades differ widely across educational systems and among teachers (Guskey, 2016). In some places, SBG is reduced to specific combination of practices instead of hewing to the larger goal of reporting on the attainment of specific skills (Simon et al., 2010). Little empirical research compares the quality of information provided by various grading techniques, but there is strong evidence that no measure is perfect (Brookhart & Nitko, 2015). To address this fact, teachers might reflect on the following questions before finalizing report cards: (1) What evidence have I collected with respect to this specific standard? (2) What are the strengths and limitations of the evidence? and (3) Based on the evidence I have, does this grade accurately reflect this student's performance?

Communication

SBG reports serve as an important tool for communicating student progress to students, parents, and other educators (Guskey & Bailey, 2010; O'Connor, 2009). The studies reviewed here both address this role and present the potential to improve communication with SBG. They also acknowledge that SBG reports sometimes present new communication challenges. Figure 5.2 summarizes the results of papers focused on communication.

FIGURE 5.2 | **Studies of Standards-Based Grading as a Communication Tool**

Studies	Participants	Main Findings
Guskey, Swan, & Jung (2010) Swan, Guskey, & Jung (2014)	115 parents and 24 teachers, whose students received both standards-based and traditional report cards in the same marking period, and 383 teachers considering adopting standards-based report cards, all in the United States	• Both teachers who had adopted or were considering adopting standards-based grading and parents preferred standards-based over traditional report cards, reporting that they (1) provide higher-quality information, (2) provide more information, (3) are clearer, and (4) are more easily understood than traditional report cards. • Teachers who were implementing both methods also reported that although standards-based grades took more time to generate, the effort was worthwhile due to improvements in the quality of information provided.

Source: From "A Century of Grading Research: Meaning and Value in the Most Common Educational Measure," by S. M. Brookhart, T. R. Guskey, A. J. Bowers, J. H. McMillan, J. K. Smith, L. F. Smith, et al., 2016, *Review of Educational Research, 86*(4), pp. 803–848. Copyright 2016 by American Educational Research Association. Adapted with permission.

Recent studies have found that both teachers and parents prefer SBG over traditional report cards because they believe that they communicate higher-quality information than traditional ones. Swan and colleagues (2014) and Guskey and colleagues (2011) report results from a common data-collection effort in which teachers and parents were asked to compare the amount, quality, and clarity of information provided by an SBG report and a traditional report card. The papers also addressed overall ease of understanding for each format, collecting survey data from 115 parents whose children received both traditional and standards-based report cards in the same marking period, the 24 teachers who completed the report cards, and 383 teachers considering adoption of standards-based report cards who reviewed both formats. They found that all groups preferred the SBG reports over traditional report cards, with teachers who were considering adopting SBG the most favorably disposed. Teachers implementing SBG said that they took longer to complete than traditional report cards, but that the additional time was worthwhile due to the improved quality of information.

Previous studies reported that both teachers and parents had concerns about the quality of information provided by SBG reports. Welsh and D'Agostino (2009) mentioned that one district faced resistance from both teachers and parents in implementing SBG. Teacher challenges were largely associated with figuring out how to grade and what aspects of performance to grade, with some teachers admitting that they convert percent-correct scores to achievement-level descriptors using the same system used to generate letter grades. According to teachers and news reports, parents struggled with interpreting the achievement-level descriptors that replaced letter grades and with understanding how performance on specific standards translated to a global picture of student performance (Sparks, 2002; Welsh & D'Agostino, 2009).

There is an extensive set of practitioner-oriented papers that report on the use of SBG as a communication tool. These papers are not a major focus of this chapter because they were not designed to yield information that can be generalized across settings. However, two of these works may be useful in that they provide some context for the results described above. The first paper, Guskey (2004), explores what kinds of achievement-level descriptors (e.g., *novice, apprentice, proficient,* or *distinguished*) are easiest for parents to interpret and found that parents attempted to interpret each label in terms of letter grades. Clarridge and Whitaker (1994) piloted an SBG system and concluded that successful implementation requires a multipronged approach, including (1) efforts to ensure that both parents and teachers understand the curriculum so they can accurately interpret report cards; (2) substantial district support for SBGs, including workshops and trainings for both parents and teachers; and (3) clear communication and marketing to parents. In short, SBG interpretation is complex. Parents are unlikely to understand report cards unless they are familiar with both the standards and the curriculum and are explicitly taught how to interpret grades.

The research evaluated thus far indicates that SBG has the potential to bolster communication with parents and students about learning expectations and the progress made toward them. However, success relies on the ability of teachers to develop, administer, and score high-quality standards-based assessments and to effectively use this information to generate accurate grades. In addition, parents need assistance in interpreting SBG reports, as both achievement-level descriptors and the standards themselves can be confusing. It can also be difficult to take a set of standards-specific grades and generalize to glean a global picture of student performance.

Comparing SBG Grades and State or Provincial Assessment Results

Because both SBG and state assessments are purported to be standards-based, we might expect SBG and standards-based assessments to yield consistent results. However, like traditional report card grades, most research has found that SBG is only moderately related with state or provincial assessments, indicating that unique aspects of performance are captured in each measure.

Two U.S. studies and five international studies find moderate relationships between SBG and other measures of student achievement (see Figure 5.3). Of the two U.S. studies, one is based on a small sample size and found that a composite that combined state assessment results across subjects was strongly associated with grade point average (r^2 = 0.50; Howley et al., 2001). The other focused on one school district but had a larger sample size and examined consistency subject by subject (Welsh et al., 2013). That study found weak relationships when consistency estimates required an exact match between SBG and assessment results (κ = 0.12 to κ = 0.32) and moderate ones when consistency was defined as assigning students the same rank order (τ = 0.32 to τ = 0.50).

Welsh and colleagues (2013) also found that the SBG–test score gap varied by content area. Specifically, teachers tended to assign lower grades than test scores in mathematics and higher grades than test scores in reading and writing. The interaction of teacher and year also explained a lot of the variation in the gap, suggesting that teachers changed their grading practice over time or that they graded differently depending on report card format (reporting formats changed considerably between years in the district studied).

Ross and Kostuch (2011) examined the correspondence between grades and assessment results for a large sample of Canadian elementary school students. They also found a moderate correlation between grades and assessment results, with greater consistency observed in mathematics than in reading or writing (r = 0.47 on average). In contrast to the findings of Welsh and colleagues (2013), grades tended to be higher than assessment results, with some exceptions in writing. Ross and Kostuch also examined the effect of grade level and sex on the strength of SBG–test score relationship but did not find that demographics had an effect. They did find that grades predicted future test performance.

The remaining four studies all examined data from Swedish high school students and examined the relationships among subject-specific grades and assessment results (Klapp Lekholm, 2011; Klapp Lekholm & Cliffordson, 2008, 2009; Thorsen & Cliffordson,

FIGURE 5.3 | Studies of the Consistency Between Standards-Based Grades and Assessment Results

Studies	Participants	Main Findings
Howley, Kusimo, & Parrott (2001)	52 U.S. middle school girls	• Half of the variation in grade point average could be explained by assessment results, but the relationship between grades and assessment results varied by school.
Klapp Lekholm & Cliffordson (2008) Klapp Lekholm & Cliffordson (2009) Klapp Lekholm (2011) Thorsen & Cliffordson (2012)	1,800–300,000 Swedish 9th graders, depending on the study	• While grades and assessment results of the same subject were found to be related, a common grading dimension also existed after controlling for content area, suggesting that classroom performance is judged similarly after accounting for differences in knowledge of each content area. • Grading effects (but not assessment results) were related to student affect and interacted with student sex. Students with more educated parents also performed better on each content area but worse on the common grading dimension. • Both grades and 9th grade assessment results predicted future GPA, with the strongest relationship observed for content-area knowledge.
Ross & Kostuch (2011)	15,942 elementary students from Ontario, Canada	• Moderate correlations were observed between grades and assessment results. • The magnitude of the SBG–test score relationship did not vary by sex or grade, but was stronger in mathematics than in reading or writing. • Grades tended to be higher than assessment results, except in writing.
Welsh, D'Agostino, & Kaniskan (2013)	Student-level grades and assessment results from approximately 80 U.S. classrooms over two years (data on approximately 2,800 students); 37 of these teachers were interviewed, yielding Appraisal Style scores.	• Teachers tended to grade more rigorously in mathematics and less rigorously in reading and writing. • Appraisal Style and implementation of high-quality, standards-based grading were moderately correlated with convergence rates.

Source: From "A Century of Grading Research: Meaning and Value in the Most Common Educational Measure," by S. M. Brookhart, T. R. Guskey, A. J. Bowers, J. H. McMillan, J. K. Smith, L. F. Smith, et al., *Review of Educational Research, 86*(4), pp. 803–848. Copyright 2016 by American Educational Research Association. Adapted with permission.

2012). The studies used structural equation modeling to estimate the extent to which the same information is provided by grades and assessments as opposed to providing unique information. The researchers found that, although grades and assessment results that reflect the same subject area produce consistent information, they also identified what they referred to as a "common grading dimension," suggesting that grades also reflect student performance on factors beyond subject-area knowledge. The studies do not explore which skills compose the common grading dimension. However, it is important to note that there are commonalities in what grades measure beyond subject-specific performance.

These scholars also examined the effect of student demographics, student affect, and school characteristics on subject-specific performance and on the common grading dimension. Here I present the effect of student demographics first, followed by student affect and school characteristics.

Klapp Lekholm and Cliffordson (2008) conducted the first study in the series, which found that grades are more strongly related to subject-specific performance (λ = 0.90 to 0.93) than are assessment results (λ = 0.74 to 0.89). This indicates that grades provide important information about content knowledge. The researchers also estimated the extent to which socioeconomic status (SES) as measured by parental education levels and students' sex explain these findings. They found that greater parental education was associated with lower scores on the common grading dimension (λ = -0.33), with this negative effect magnified for boys ($\lambda girls$ = -0.26, $\lambda boys$ = -0.54). This suggests that parental education and sex play a role in the extent to which factors beyond subject-area performance, like effort, affect grades. After taking academic performance into account, students whose parents attended college tend to have lower grades than those whose parents did not attend college. In addition, the effect of parental education on grades is greater for boys than for girls, with boys whose parents attended college receiving lower grades on average after taking academic achievement into account. This seems to indicate that teachers may be less tolerant of poor performance on the behavioral aspects of grades (e.g., submitting work late, missing assignments, etc.) for students of higher SES and for high-SES boys in particular.

Thorsen and Cliffordson (2012) conducted a similar study but checked for the robustness of findings across three successive cohorts of students, confirming that a common grading dimension and subject-specific factors were found in all three cohorts. In addition, they examined the extent to which 9th grade performance predicted end-of-high school GPA. They found that Swedish and mathematics assessment results were two to three times as strongly related (λ = 0.33 to λ = 0.43) to high school GPA than was the common grading factor (λ = 0.15 to λ = 0.16). English assessment results were least predictive (λ = 0.01 to λ = 0.03). In addition, the relationship between the 9th grade common grading factor and end-of-high school GPA is different for boys and girls and for students of low and high socioeconomic status, indicating that girls exhibit higher performance on the common grading factor and on end-of-high school GPA and that low-SES students perform better on the common grading factor and worse on end-of-high school grades than do high-SES students. In short, the validity of grades seems to differ across student demographic groups.

Klapp Lekholm and Cliffordson (2009) extended this work by examining the role affect has on subject-specific performance and on the common grading dimension. They found that affect is predictive of grades but that different kinds of affect influence boys' and girls' grades. Self-perceptions of ability to read, write, and speak Swedish; parental engagement; and interest in school were related to girls' performance. In contrast, self-perception of mathematics ability, ability to cope in school, and adjustment to or contentment with school predicted boys' performance. Finally, Klapp Lekholm (2011) studied whether school-level factors might also influence student performance, but found that school-level characteristics were not predictive once students' SES was taken into account.

In summary, studies of the relationship between SBG and assessment results reveal both that grades and assessment results are correlated and that grades capture additional characteristics that are not gauged by tests. Grades and assessment results are more likely to rank-order students similarly than to come to identical student performance-level ratings. In addition, while SBG is predictive of future school performance and of future test performance, these relationships vary by students' sex, affect, and SES. These finding are consistent with the review of SBG implementation and indicate that teachers may struggle to generate grades that reflect only achievement in relation to standards. Differential results by content area suggests that teachers are better able to assess performance in relation to the standards in some subject areas than in others. Alternately, SBGs may over- or underemphasize specific skills when compared to large-scale assessments, or may define achievement-level performance differently. Whatever the cause, both SBGs and traditional grades are only moderately related to large-scale assessment results (Brookhart et al., 2016).

What Are the Implications of These Research Findings for Improvement in Grading Policy and Practice?

SBG spans both policy and practice in that school districts often develop both SBG reports and guidelines for parents and teachers that outline how grades should be developed and interpreted. In practice, these guidelines are sometimes broad and sometimes specify the exact grading practices teachers should implement. Given the many somewhat contradictory practices associated with SBG, it is important that policies define SBG for a particular context and outline the kinds of grading practices that are expected.

SBG is often adopted to improve consistency on three fronts: (1) between the capabilities addressed on report cards and those expected by the standards, (2) among teachers in their grading methods, and (3) between grades and students' assessment results. This often involves changing practice to remove nonacademic factors from subject-specific grades, to grade performance as of the end of the marking period, and to share information about grading practices and expectations with parents and students so that they understand what grades represent. Successful implementation of SBG requires both changes to policy (through report card formats) and to the assessment and grading practices used to communicate student progress.

Grading Policy

Because the current evidence base for SBG is sparse, additional research is needed to evaluate the effect of current policies on the quality of grades and on the quality of education provided to students. It is important for policymakers both to seek out the latest research and to actively support research efforts.

The evidence base that does exist reveals that while SBG and assessment results are related, they reflect different aspects of a skill and therefore should not be expected to perfectly match. This is because SBG reports at a different level of granularity than a state test. SBG also reflects the results of multiple assessments administered at different times and uses a variety of methods to gauge performance. Therefore, while some policymakers may hope that SBG implementation will increase the consistency of report card grades and assessment results, perfect consistency is not a realistic goal.

At the same time, SBG has the potential to support standards-based reform, especially when coupled with regular opportunities for teachers to discuss (1) the kinds of performance they view as meeting grade-level expectations, (2) the standards their students find particularly challenging or easy, and (3) the strategies they use to teach and assess these standards. These kinds of discussions are crucial to increasing the consistency of grades across classrooms and relative to state tests. They also might increase buy-in for reform efforts by helping teachers identify needed instructional changes. Regular teacher meeting time to discuss standards-based assessment and instruction as well as how to convert assessment scores to report card grades is essential to standards-based grading.

To successfully situate SBG within larger standards-based reform efforts, training on the curriculum, grading, and communication is needed at all levels of the system, including among administrators, teachers, parents, and students. Both implementing and interpreting SBG require a nuanced understanding of the standards and of grade-level expectations in addition to knowledge of assessment and grading. It would therefore behoove educators to follow Guskey and Bailey's (2010) advice to use SBG as an opportunity to educate parents and students about learning goals, student progress, and the grading process itself so that they can act as partners in the educational process. Continuous training is required to account for staff turnover, for changes in the SBG system as people learn from and improve their processes, and for the fact that new families are constantly moving into school districts.

Grading Practice

SBG seems to rarely be implemented as intended. Teachers either do not faithfully implement the practices outlined in district or provincial grading policy, or incorporate factors that are tangential to the reported skill in grades. The most prevalent finding may be that educators include behaviors that support learning in academic content-area grades—a common theme across all kinds of grading. While policymakers may adopt SBG to address this issue, it seems clear that changing the report card format alone will not be enough. The effectiveness of explicit training on separating behavior from achievement in grading is unclear, as many teachers consider grades to be a key motivator for getting students to practice. In addition, grade variations between the sexes suggest that compliant behavior (such as following directions) is not yet disentangled from measures of academic performance, irrespective of report card format.

Given the intractability of this issue, it might be wise to focus on other aspects of practice. For example, it may be helpful to train teachers to include students in the SBG process as a vehicle for enhancing motivation. O'Connor (2009) devotes a chapter of his book to methods for involving students in grading. He emphasizes the importance of ensuring that students understand how their grades will be determined and suggests that student-teacher communication about this is an important formative tool to help students learn.

Other SBG strategies, such as grading on performance as of the end of the marking period and allowing students to retest, are also important, as they improve student persistence. Knowing that poor performance can be corrected and lead to improved grades encourages students to stick with difficult topics and teaches them how to learn. While multiple assessments of a skill help to capture a variety of aspects of student performance, including the results from assessments administered before mastery is expected results in giving students who arrived at school already having mastered the skill a higher grade than those who learned the skill at school (Cox, 2011; Guskey, 2009; Marzano & Heflebower, 2011; Melograno, 2007; Shippy et al., 2013).

These practices represent a small sample of the wide array of strategies associated with SBG. It is ultimately up to school districts or provinces to decide which approaches to emphasize and which standards and grading scale to include on the report card. Given the volume of recommended approaches, targeted information on exactly what it looks like to implement SBG in a specific locale is needed. It is not enough to decide to transition to SBG and assume that educators, parents, and students will understand what is expected. Coaching on how to implement the specific requirements of a given district's SBG system is recommended. Such support might focus on two or three of the most central and most attainable strategies. This would help ensure high-quality implementation of a few practices as opposed to limited implementation of an extensive grading reform.

Because improved communication is also a key goal of SBG, giving teachers strategies for communication about grades is advised. Several practitioner-oriented papers (Cizek, 2000; Wiggins, 1994) recommend that teachers share student work samples, anchor papers, and rubrics with parents to provide detailed information about the expected level of performance and children's standing with respect to that expectation. As a parent, I can attest to the value of these examples, especially when teachers focus on one or two key examples and take the time to explain what they see as the strengths and limitations of my child's performance.

It seems especially important to have clear lines of communication about expectations for the quality of work, given research that found students spend more time practicing skills outside school and do better on academic tests when their teachers grade them more rigorously than the state test does (Figlio & Lucas, 2004). Figlio and Lucas also found that the relationship between teachers and parents is better when teachers are less rigorous graders; that is, setting high expectations is likely to result in decreased parent satisfaction and in greater attention to academics. Parental dissatisfaction may be greater when there is inconsistency in the expectations set within a school, highlighting again the importance of communication among teachers about standards, assessment, and grades.

To help teachers reflect on the extent to which their approach to grading is particularly lenient or rigorous, school districts or provinces might share classroom-, school-, and district-level information about the consistency between end-of-year grades and state assessment results. It is unlikely that teachers have reflected either on the consistency of their grades with state or provincial policy expectations (as enacted in assessment results) or on the extent to which they are particularly rigorous or lenient in comparison with other teachers. Such an approach may also be useful in deepening teachers' understanding of the standards.

Teachers might also discuss how they organize for grading in collaborative meetings. Ensuring that all competencies are assessed and recorded in a way that supports grading can be daunting (Welsh & D'Agostino, 2009). Teachers come up with clever strategies for addressing these kinds of problems and often divide up the work associated with implementing a new approach. Teachers might (1) identify which common assessment items address each SBG competency, (2) generate stand-alone assessments that focus on specific topics, (3) create a new gradebook format, or (4) develop rubrics or scoring guidelines aligned to a new grading scale. The workload associated with these tasks is substantial, and the importance of building time to implement SBG into teachers' workdays cannot be understated.

Some studies also suggest that some content areas are easier to grade within an SBG framework than others. Fields like mathematics involve instruction on distinct skills at different points in the school year, which makes it easy to identify points at which a skill should be mastered and assessed for a grade. In contrast, language arts tends to involve development of complex, integrated skills over the course of a student's education, making both the expected mastery point and grades on distinct skills for reporting purposes more challenging. While these differences are substantial and important, they are not insurmountable. In fact, the more teachers work through these issues and identify and communicate what kinds of performance are expected at what points in the school year, the greater the student opportunity to work to meet these goals. Teachers might benefit from opportunities to collaborate across department and grade levels in developing their grading methods.

The research suggests SBG is a promising reporting strategy that requires teachers to reflect both on student performance and on their own conceptions of what it means to meet grade-level expectations. SBG also challenges teachers to distinguish academic achievement from student behaviors that support learning, allowing for improved reflection upon and communication about student progress. While there are a variety of SBG-related strategies that districts or provinces might enact, the overarching goal of clearly and accurately communicating what students know and can do must remain at the forefront. Only those SBG practices that lead to close monitoring of student progress and to greater understanding of the standards on the part of teachers, parents, and students should be embraced. Although more research is needed, teachers are often the best innovators, so structuring opportunities to learn from them is our wisest step forward.

References

Bonner, S. M., & Chen, P. P. (2009). Teacher candidates' perceptions about grading and constructivist teaching. *Educational Assessment, 14*(2), 57–77.

Bowers, A. J. (2009). Reconsidering grades as data for decision making: More than just academic knowledge. *Journal of Educational Administration, 47*(5), 609–629. doi:10.1108/09578230910981080

Brookhart, S. M. (1991). Grading practices and validity. *Educational Measurement: Issues and Practice, 10*(1), 35–36. doi:10.1111/j.1745-3992.1991.tb00182.x

Brookhart, S. M. (2011). Starting the conversation about grading. *Educational Leadership, 69*(3), 10–14.

Brookhart, S. M., Guskey, T. R., Bowers, A. J., McMillan, J. H., Smith, J. K., Smith, L. F., et al. (2016). A century of grading research: Meaning and value in the most common educational measure. *Review of Educational Research, 86,* 803–848. doi:10.3102/0034654316672069

Brookhart, S. M., & Nitko, A. J. (2015). *Educational assessment of students* (7th ed.). London: Pearson.

Chen, P. P., & Bonner, S. M. (2017). Teachers' beliefs about grading practices and a constructivist approach to teaching. *Educational Assessment, 22*(1), 18–34.

Cizek, G. J. (2000). Pockets of resistance in the assessment revolution. *Educational Measurement: Issues and Practice, 19*(2), 16–23. doi:10.1111/j.1745-3992.2000.tb00026.x

Clarridge, P. B., & Whitaker, E. M. (1994). Implementing a new elementary progress report. *Educational Leadership, 52*(2), 7–9.

Cox, K. B. (2011). Putting classroom grading on the table, a reform in progress. *American Secondary Education, 40*(1), 67–87.

D'Agostino, J. V., Welsh, M. E., & Corson, N. M. (2007). Instructional sensitivity of a state's standards-based assessment. *Educational Assessment, 12*(1), 1–22.

Figlio, D. N., & Lucas, M. E. (2004). Do high grading standards affect student performance? *Journal of Public Economics, 88,* 1815–1834.

Grindberg, E. (2014, April 7). Ditching letter grades for a "window" into the classroom. *CNN.* Retrieved from http://www.cnn.com/2014/04/07/living/report-card-changes-standards-based-grading-schools/

Guskey, T. R. (2004). The communication challenge of standards-based reporting. *Phi Delta Kappan, 86*(4), 326–329. doi:10.1177/003172170408600419

Guskey, T. R. (2009). Grading policies that work against standards... and how to fix them. In T. R. Guskey (Ed.), *Practical solutions for serious problems in standards-based grading* (pp. 9–26). Thousand Oaks, CA: Corwin.

Guskey, T. R. (2016, October 14). Standards-based learning: Why do educators make it so complex? [Blog post]. *EdWeek.* Retrieved from http://blogs.edweek.org/edweek/finding_common_ground/2016/10/standards-based_learning_why_do_educators_make_it_so_complex.html

Guskey, T. R., & Bailey, J. M. (2001). *Developing grading and reporting systems for student learning.* Thousand Oaks, CA: Corwin.

Guskey, T. R., & Bailey, J. M. (2010). *Developing standards-based report cards.* Thousand Oaks, CA: Corwin.

Guskey, T. R., Swan, G., & Jung, L. (2010, April). *Developing a statewide, standards-based student report card: A review of the Kentucky initiative.* Paper presentation at the 2014 Annual Meeting of the American Educational Research Association, Philadelphia.

Hay, P. J., & Macdonald, D. (2008). (Mis)appropriations of criterion- and standards-referenced assessment in a performance-based subject. *Assessment in Education: Principles, Policy & Practice, 15*(2), 153–168.

Hill, H. C. (2001). Policy is not enough: Language and the interpretation of state standards. *American Educational Research Journal, 38*(2), 289–318.

Howley, A., Kusimo, P. S., & Parrott, L. (2001). Grading and the ethos of effort. *Learning Environments Research, 3*(3), 229–246. doi:10.1023/A:1011469327430

Kelly, S. (2008). What types of students' efforts are rewarded with high marks? *Sociology of Education, 81*(1), 32–52.

Klapp Lekholm, A. (2011). Effects of school characteristics on grades in compulsory school. *Scandinavian Journal of Educational Research, 55*(6), 587–608. doi:10.1080/00313831.2011.555923

Klapp Lekholm, A., & Cliffordson, C. (2008). Discrepancies between school grades and test scores at individual and school level: Effects of gender and family background. *Educational Research and Evaluation, 14*(2), 181–199. doi:10.1080/13803610801956663

Klapp Lekholm, A., & Cliffordson, C. (2009). Effects of student characteristics on grades in compulsory school. *Educational Research and Evaluation, 15*(1), 1–23. doi:10.1080/13803610802470425

Marzano, R. J., & Heflebower, T. (2011). Grades that show what students know. *Educational Leadership, 69*(3), 34–39.

McMillan, J. H. (2009). Synthesis of issues and implications for practice. In T. R. Guskey (Ed.), *Practical solutions for serious problems in standards-based grading* (pp. 105–120). Thousand Oaks, CA: Corwin.

McMunn, N., Schenck, P., & McColskey, W. (2003, April). *Standards-based assessment, grading, and reporting in classrooms: Can district training and support change teacher practice?* Paper presented at the Annual Meeting of the American Educational Research Association, Chicago.

Melograno, V. J. (2007). Grading and report cards for standards-based physical education. *Journal of Physical Education, Recreation and Dance, 78*(6), 45–53. doi:10.1080/07303084.2007.10598041

O'Connor, K. (2009). *How to grade for learning: Linking grades to standards.* (3rd ed.). Glenview, IL: Pearson Professional Development.

Ross, J. A., & Kostuch, L. (2011). Consistency of report card grades and external assessments in a Canadian province. *Educational Assessment, Evaluation and Accountability, 23*(2), 159–180. doi:10.1007/s11092-011-9117-3

Scriffiny, P. L. (2008). Seven reasons for standards-based grading. *Educational Leadership, 66*(2), 70–74.

Shippy, N., Washer, B. A., & Perrin, B. (2013). Teaching with the end in mind: The role of standards-based grading. *Journal of Family and Consumer Sciences, 105*(2), 14–16.

Simon, M., Tierney, R. D., Forgette-Giroux, R., Charland, J., Noonan, B., & Duncan, R. (2010). A secondary school teacher's description of the process of determining report card grades. *McGill Journal of Education, 45*(3), 535–554. doi:10.7202/1003576ar

Sparks, C. (2002, October, 10). Parents tutored on new report cards. *Arizona Daily Star,* p. F5.

Swan, G. M., Guskey, T. R., & Jung, L. A. (2014). Parents' and teachers' perceptions of standards-based and traditional report cards. *Educational Assessment, Evaluation and Accountability, 26*(3), 289–299. doi:10.1007/s11092-014-9191-4

Thorsen, C., & Cliffordson, C. (2012). Teachers' grade assignment and the predictive validity of criterion-referenced grades. *Educational Research and Evaluation, 18*(2), 153–172. doi:10.1080/13803611.2012.659929

Tierney, R. D., Simon, M., & Charland, J. (2011). Being fair: Teachers' interpretations of principles for standards-based grading. *The Educational Forum, 75*(3), 210–227. doi:10.1080/00131725.2011.577669

Welsh, M. E., & D'Agostino, J. (2009). Fostering consistency between standards-based grades and large-scale assessment results. In T. R. Guskey (Ed.), *Practical solutions for serious problems in standards-based grading* (pp. 75–104). Thousand Oaks, CA: Corwin.

Welsh, M. E., D'Agostino, J. V., & Kaniskan, R. (2013). Grading as a reform effort: Do standards-based grades converge with test scores? *Educational Measurement: Issues and Practice, 32*(2), 26–36. doi:10.1111/emip.12009

Wiggins, G. (1994). Toward better report cards. *Educational Leadership, 52*(2), 28–37.

6

Grading Students with Learning Differences

Lee Ann Jung

Although there has been much research on grading in general over the past 100 years, there is a significant gap in the research base for grading students with learning differences or disabilities. Until recently, relatively little information has been available in the special education research and practice journals to guide schools in how to approach grading for students who are behind grade level, particularly for those who qualify for an individualized education program (IEP). Because of the sparseness of suggestions from the field, most teachers have made informal adaptations to the grading process for students with IEPs (Gottlieb, 2006; Polloway et al., 1994; Silva, Munk, & Bursuck, 2005).

One reason for the gap in the research on grading students with IEPs could be attributed to the age of the field of special education. The Education for All Handicapped Children Act—or the Individuals with Disabilities Education Act, as it is now known—was first brought into legislation as PL 94-142 in 1975. There have been many studies on measuring the progress of students with disabilities on IEP goals. In fact, some of the most sophisticated work on measurement of learning and behavior has come from the field of special education. But the connections between using these practices to measure progress on goals and grading are thin.

Why Is This Area of Research Important?

While the measurement field has forged ahead in developing grading practices and procedures, in some ways the field of special education and students who are behind grade level have been left behind. The field has developed sophisticated procedures for competency and standards-based grading with a variety of recommendations that converge into a theme: grades should be an accurate reflection of what students know and can do; these grades should indicate what students know and can do at the present time; students' behavior should not be included as an indicator of academic achievement; and feedback must accompany the grade if it is to support the purpose of improving instruction so students show growth. Grading students who have disabilities or are behind grade level poses the greatest challenge in all of grading.

Developing more precise procedures for grading and providing feedback to students who have learning differences and disabilities is an area ripe for research and additional development. Arguably, the students in our schools who need the *best* information on how they are performing and what to do next are the students who are behind grade level. Important decisions on instruction and intervention hinge upon our having accurate, meaningful, and timely information about the performance of this group of students. Furthermore, the 2017 U.S. Supreme Court decision *Endrew v. Douglas County School District* (2017) compels us to improve the quality of progress monitoring and reporting for this population.

What Questions Have Been Addressed in This Research?

The research on grading and special education began in 1983 (Carpenter, Grantham, & Hardister, 1983) and led to an initial position statement on grading exceptional learners (Carpenter, 1985) and procedural recommendations (Bradley & Calvin, 1998). Soon after this research began, studies began examining how teachers were approaching the grading process for this population, finding that teachers were informally adapting the grades for students with disabilities (Bursuck et al., 1996; Polloway et al., 1994). Almost every teacher was making adaptations that included changes like adding points for behavior, changing the grading scale, grading solely on progress, and weighting easier assignments more heavily.

Next, the research turned to examining the fairness of these procedures for modifying grades for students with disabilities, and the findings were clear: parents, students, and teachers found that the grading adaptations that teachers were using were fraught with problems and seen by most as unfair (Bursuck, Munk, & Olson, 1999; Engelberg & Evans, 1986; Michael & Trippi, 1987; Pollard & Rojewski, 1993; Rojewski, Pollard, & Meers, 1991). In fact, there was no grading adaptation that students without disabilities viewed as fair (Bursuck et al., 1999). Teachers reported that the commonly used letter, number, and percentage grades were not useful for students with disabilities (Bursuck et al., 1996). Teachers were concerned about fairness and objectivity of grades and felt that their students may interpret grades as a proxy of their self-worth. This led researchers and thought leaders to recommend different variations of grading adaptations, including personalized grading plans (Munk & Bursuck, 2001; Silva et al., 2005).

What Have the Results of Those Studies Revealed?

Educators of all levels have consistently reported a lack of training and preparation for the task of grading students with disabilities. Although the studies demonstrate that educators and students alike find grading adaptations to be unfair, this was the solution employed by the vast majority of teachers. The practice did not always result in higher grades for students with disabilities, and, in fact, Donahue and Zigmond (1990) found students with disabilities were only narrowly passing. Unfortunately, students with disabilities were less likely to feel they had the ability to improve their grades, and poor grades were believed to affect students' feelings of self-worth. Figure 6.1 (pp. 150–151) includes a summary of findings for key studies of grading students with disabilities.

What Are the Implications of These Research Findings for Improvement in Grading Policy and Practice?

The results of the studies indicate that, without question, educators need explicit guidance on how to grade students with disabilities. With so few recommendations in the literature, procedures are needed to address what is probably the greatest challenge in grading that teachers of all levels face. One requirement that is necessary to any procedures for grading students with disabilities is the Individuals with Disabilities Education Improvement Act (IDEIA; 2004) provision that students and their families must receive information on how they are performing on the level of work they are able to complete. This portion of the law had traditionally been met by sending progress notes to families on IEP goals. The literature on grading students with disabilities reveals a struggle in defining procedures that accomplished this requirement within a schoolwide report card.

Through an iterative process of working with teachers in schools on issues of both practicality and fairness and an examination of the requirements of IDEIA, and in response to the movement toward standards-based grades, I developed the Inclusive Grading Model (Jung, 2009) as a recommendation for assigning grades to any student who is behind grade level. This model rests upon educators understanding clearly the distinction between accommodations and modifications and how they affect our measurement of learning (Jung, 2017). Jung and Guskey combined the existing work on standards-based grading with this new model on grading exceptional learners to make comprehensive recommendations for teachers, leaders, and school policymakers (e.g., Jung & Guskey, 2007, 2012).

In 2017, I modified the decision-making model to include a key assessment step that had been missing in the earlier model. The revised Differentiated Assessment and Grading Model (DiAGraM) pays particular attention to identifying the precise measurement used for modified expectations (Jung, 2018). The DiAGraM model is designed to support any student who needs support, not only those who qualify for IEPs. To implement the model only for students who have IEPs places them at risk of disclosing disability status on transcripts, which is in violation of IDEIA requirements for confidentiality. Figure 6.2 (p. 153) includes two examples of using the DiAGraM process. The steps of the model are as follows and are illustrated in Figure 6.3 (p. 154).

1. Does the student require any accommodations (support for a skill other than the one being measured) to meet grade-level expectations? If so, measure the student's performance according to grade-level criteria, because with the accommodation, the disability is not manifested in the skill.

2. Does the student require any modifications? The student is not on track to be at grade level with this skill; expectations

FIGURE 6.1 | **Summary of Studies for Grading
Students with Disabilities**

Studies	Participants	Main Findings
Bursuck, Munk, & Olson (1999)	High school students	• No grading adaptations were viewed as fair by a majority of students without disabilities. Most students believed that grading scales should be the same for all students, without variations, and that adaptations to the grading scale would diminish the motivation of higher-achieving students. • Students with disabilities were more likely to favor giving students a higher grade for showing improvement, changing the grading weights of certain class requirements, and using a different grading scale.
Bursuck et al. (1996)	Elementary and secondary regular education teachers	• Respondents indicated that letter/number/percentage grades were not particularly useful for students with disabilities. • Many teachers used supplements to traditional grading systems to provide a more comprehensive view of progress than traditional systems portray.
Donahue & Zigmond (1990)	High school students with learning disabilities	• Although approximately 60–75 percent of the students with learning disabilities received passing grades in their inclusive classes, they consistently achieved grade point averages of 0.99.
Engelberg & Evans (1986)	Students with and without disabilities	• High-achieving students were less likely than lower-achieving ones to see grades as an expected and necessary part of school life or as a source of feedback. • Lower-achieving students were less likely to believe they were capable of positively affecting their grades than average students, and average students were less likely to believe that they could affect scores than gifted students. • Students with disabilities were more likely to believe that grades reflected learning than students in gifted programs.
Michael & Trippi (1987)	General and special education teachers	• Educators believed that grading for students with disabilities should reflect criterion-referenced procedures rather than norm-referenced procedures and effort as well as achievement.
Munk & Bursuck (2001)	General and special education teachers and their students with learning disabilities	• The most common adaptation to grades in the personalized grading plans (PGPs) was to change the weight of assignments and tasks.

Studies	Participants	Main Findings
		• Most PGPs included altered grading scales, despite previous research indicating that these were considered unfair and unhelpful by students and teachers, respectively. • Parents and teachers indicated that they were pleased with the outcomes of the PGP, and students expressed that they were motivated to work harder with these programs in place, whether or not the grade improved. • Overall, satisfaction with student grades may be dependent not upon increasing student grades but upon how accurately students, parents, and teachers implement their responsibilities as part of the plan.
Pollard & Rojewski (1993)	Secondary vocational educators	• More than 92 percent of teachers experienced problems or frustration when grading students with special needs. • Teachers expressed a lack of involvement in the IEP process as their biggest concern. • Teachers also had concerns with issues of fairness but reported a lack of training or preparation in grading students with disabilities.
Polloway et al. (1994)	District superintendents	• Having modified grading policies in place did not guarantee that students with disabilities received higher scores. • Only 12 percent of grading systems required collaboration between special and regular educators in the assignment of grades. • Narrative grading components were included in 45.1 percent of elementary schools and 18 percent of high schools. Pass-fail options were in 25 percent of school systems.
Rojewski, Pollard, & Meers (1991)	Secondary vocational teachers	• Teachers believed that successful grading techniques were individualized, flexible, and collaborative, and based on prestated standards; used multiple measures of evaluation; and focused on the strengths of student performance to parents and students. • Teachers were concerned with ensuring that grades were fair and objective, feeling that students often generalized from the grades to indicate their overall self-worth and potential. • Teachers also noted that they believed college-bound students and their parents were more concerned with the actual letter grade, whereas students with disabilities and their parents were more focused on actual learning. All vocational educators indicated that they had not received training on grading.

must be revised because the student's disability is manifested in the skill.

3. For skills requiring modification, determine the *comparably rigorous* expectation. This should be achievable in one year and should be an appropriately challenging goal. For students who qualify, this becomes the IEP goal.

4. For skills requiring modification, determine the growth plan, including intervention strategies and exactly how you will measure progress and provide feedback on classroom assessments.

5. Report progress using the school grading scale *on the modified expectation* on the report card and transcript, with a notation that the expectation was modified.

Once schools implement the DiAGraM, other questions arise. School boards and leaders will need to make decisions about course credit and GPA for students requiring modifications. Further research is needed to determine the specific effects of the model on transition planning, family participation, and family understanding of grades. Additional research is needed to explore the effects of the model on student motivation. Although previous research (Donahue & Zigmond, 1990) indicates that artificially inflating a student's grade without clear connections to what the student accomplished can decrease a student's motivation to engage in learning, it is only theoretical at this point that the DiAGraM can correct this complex issue.

The newest recommendations for assessing and grading students with learning differences are in line with IDEIA and follow a conceptual framework that responds to the literature and more than a decade of applied work with educators. Still, much work is left to do in this relatively young field.

FIGURE 6.2 | **Example Applications of the DiAGraM Process**

Support Needed	Expectation Used	Assessment Strategy	Reporting Procedure
Accommodation	**Use the grade-level criteria.**	**Assess the student's performance using the accommodation with no additional changes.**	**No change is needed to the report card or transcript grades.**
Example: Student needs to complete social studies assignments orally instead of in writing.	*Example: Grade-level criteria are used for all assignments.*	*Example: The student completes the social studies assignments orally, but the responses are assessed and scored according to the same criteria used for students who completed the assignment in writing.*	*Example: The student's social studies grade is reported without any change or notation on the report card and transcript.*
Modification	**Determine a modified, achievable, comparably rigorous expectation.**	**Determine the intervention and specific scale of measure for use on classroom assessment tasks. Everyone on the team uses the same intervention and measurement scale for this skill.**	**Grades reflect performance on the modified expectation. Note the grade was based on a modified expectation on report card and transcript.**
Example: Student is behind in reading fluency and needs a lower-level reading requirement.	*Example: Team determines that reading 2nd grade material at 80 words per minute (rather than 4th grade material at 150 words per minute) is achievable and comparably rigorous.*	*Example: The student receives reading fluency intervention and is assessed on words per minute reading of 2nd grade content. Everyone on the team uses the same reading intervention strategies and assesses words per minute read of 2nd grade material. If the student achieves 80 words per minute, the student receives the score that coincides with mastering the expectation.*	*Example: The student's reading fluency grade is reported according to the modified expectation and an asterisk or other notation is added to the report card and transcript to denote the grade was based on a modified expectation. If the school uses a 4-point scale, and the student achieved 80 words per minute by the end of the year, the student would receive a 4* on the report card and transcript.*

FIGURE 6.3 | **Differentiated Assessment and Grading Model (DiAGraM)**

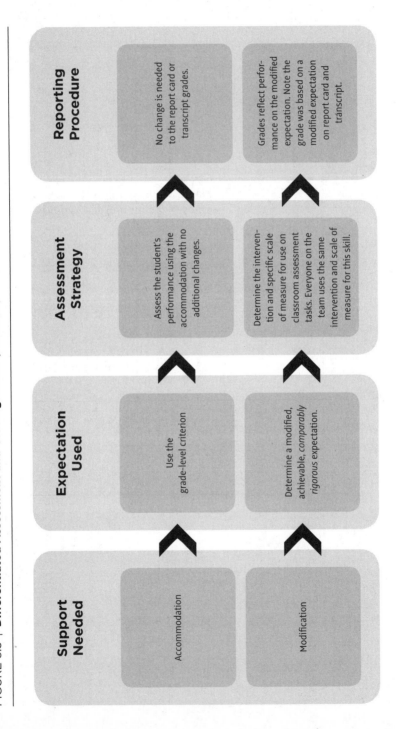

References

Bradley, D. F., & Calvin, M. B. (1998). Grading modified assignments. *Teaching Exceptional Children, 31*(2), 24.

Bursuck, W. D., Munk, D. D., & Olson, M. M. (1999). The fairness of report card grading adaptations: What do students with and without learning disabilities think? *Remedial and Special Education, 20*(2), 84–105. doi: 10.1177/074193259902000205

Bursuck, W., Polloway, E. A., Plante, L., Epstein, M. H., Jayanthi, M., & McConeghy, J. (1996). Report card grading and adaptations: A national survey of classroom practices. *Exceptional Children, 62*(4), 301–318.

Carpenter, D. (1985). Grading handicapped pupils: Review and position statement. *Remedial and Special Education, 6*(4), 54–59. doi: 10.1177/074193258500600409

Carpenter, D., Grantham, L. B., & Hardister, M. P. (1983). Grading mainstreamed handicapped pupils: What are the issues? *The Journal of Special Education, 17*(2), 183–188. doi:10.1177/002246698301700209

Christiansen, J., & Vogel, J. R. (1998). A decision model for grading students with disabilities. *Teaching Exceptional Children, 31*(2), 30.

Donahue, K., & Zigmond, N. (1990). Academic grades of ninth-grade urban learning disabled students and low-achieving peers. *Exceptionality, 1*(1), 17–27.

Education for all Handicapped Children Act of 1975, PL 94-142, United States Code, 20, sections 1401 *et seq.*

Endrew v. Douglas County School District, 580 U. S. (2017).

Engelberg, R. A., & Evans, E. D. (1986). Perceptions and attitudes about school grading practices among intellectually gifted, learning-disabled, and normal elementary school pupils. *The Journal of Special Education, 20*(1), 91–101.

Gottlieb, M. (2006). *Assessing English language learners: Bridges from language proficiency to academic achievement.* Thousand Oaks, CA: Corwin.

Individuals with Disabilities Education Improvement Act of 2004, PL 108-446, 20 U.S.C. §§1400 *et seq.*

Jung, L. A. (2009). The challenges of grading and reporting in special education: An inclusive grading model. In T. R. Guskey (Ed.), *Practical solutions for serious problems in standards-based grading* (pp. 27–40). Thousand Oaks, CA: Corwin.

Jung, L. A. (2015). *A practical guide to planning interventions and monitoring progress*. Bloomington, IN: Solution Tree Press.

Jung, L. A. (2017, May 17). *A differentiated assessment and grading model for students with learning differences*. Retrieved from https://www.leadinclusion.org/single-post/2017/05/17/Differentiated-Assessment-and-Grading-Model-DiAGraM

Jung, L. A. (2018). *From goals to growth: Intervention and support in every classroom*. Alexandria, VA: ASCD.

Jung, L. A., & Guskey, T. R. (2007). Standards-based grading and reporting: A model for special education. *Teaching Exceptional Children, 40*(2), 48–53.

Jung, L. A., & Guskey, T. R. (2012). *Grading exceptional and struggling learners*. Thousand Oaks, CA: Corwin.

Michael, R. J., & Trippi, J. A. (1987). Educators' views of procedures for grading mainstreamed handicapped children. *Education, 107*(3), 276.

Munk, D. D., & Bursuck, W. D. (2001). Preliminary findings on personalized grading plans for middle school students with learning disabilities. *Exceptional Children, 67*(2), 211–234.

Pollard, R., & Rojewski, J. (1993). An examination of problems associated with grading students with special needs. *Journal of Instructional Psychology, 20*(2), 154–161.

Polloway, E. A., Epstein, M. H., Bursuck, W. D., Roderique, T. W., McConeghy, J. L., & Jayanthi, M. (1994). Classroom grading: A national survey of policies. *Remedial and Special Education, 15*, 162–170.

Rojewski, J. W., Pollard, R. R., & Meers, G. D. (1991). Grading mainstreamed special needs students: Determining practices and attitudes of secondary vocational educators using a qualitative approach. *Remedial and Special Education, 12*(1), 7–15. doi:10.1177/074193259101200105

Silva, M., Munk, D. D., & Bursuck, W. D. (2005). Grading adaptations for students with disabilities. *Intervention in School & Clinic, 41*(2), 87–98.

7

Leadership for Grading Reform

Laura J. Link

Many school leaders have shied away from addressing improvements in grading because of the longheld traditions and difficulties associated with the practice (Cizek, 1996; Guskey, 2015). Recent studies show these difficulties are compounded for school leaders when their learning climate, access to training, and ability to effectively communicate are less than favorable (Gogerty, 2016; Greene, 2015; Sebastian & Allensworth, 2012). Despite these challenges, school leaders are uniquely positioned to affect school change, teachers' classroom practices, and most important, student achievement (Davis, Darling-Hammond, LaPointe, & Meyerson, 2005; Davis, Gooden, & Bowers, 2017; Leithwood & Jantzi, 2005; Sebastian & Allensworth, 2012). School leaders play a critical role in grading reform, even though available research evidence shows they rarely take on the challenge (Guskey, 2015).

Why Is This Area of Research Important?

School leaders are ultimately responsible for students' grades. Although teachers assign grades for students' work, it is school leaders who are legally accountable for those grades when challenged (McElligott & Brookhart, 2009). Additionally, educational leadership standards call for school leaders to develop and guide systems of assessment for student learning, which include teachers' grading practices. School principals in particular are accountable for the day-to-day technical guidance of teachers' grading work. Modern teacher evaluations require principals to address the entire continuum of teachers' instructional practices, from lesson planning to grading and reporting student outcomes. Despite these accountabilities, school leaders are faced with deeply rooted grading traditions that often limit grading reform.

School Leaders, Grading, and the Law

Taking significant action with any school reform can be difficult. Leading reform in an area that has been largely unchanged for a century can be especially daunting, even to the most courageous school leader. Yet under the law, school leaders' responsibilities regarding grading are inescapable. As McElligott and Brookhart (2009) note, "while a local board of education has the penultimate authority, in most cases it is a duty that the school board delegates to others" (p. 58). In most school systems, those delegates are typically superintendents and school principals. In the state of North Carolina, for example, the principal has the explicit duty to grade and classify students (North Carolina Elementary and Secondary Statutes, 2017).

In most cases, however, local boards do not outline provisions that grant role-specific responsibilities. More typically, they leave superintendents and principals responsible for directing districts' and schools' grading policies and procedures. A few states, such as Tennessee, require local school districts to use a uniform grading system for 9th to 12th grade students (Tennessee Education

Statutes, 2018). Other states, such as Florida, require a specific letter grade system for all students and a uniform method of averaging grades for credits (Florida Education Statutes, 2016). But in most states, school leaders have sizable latitude to devise grading policies and systems that are subsequently enforced by local school boards.

Due to the delegation of power from local school boards to superintendents and principals, it is important for school leaders to be intentional in devising grading policies that are fair, accurate, and legally defensible (Chartier, 2003; McElligott & Brookhart, 2009). It is not uncommon for students and their parents to bring concerns about grades to court. Under the 14th Amendment of the U.S. Constitution, students' rights to due process are protected from any state actor, such as a school board member, superintendent, principal, or teacher, who may deprive students of those rights. So when a student challenges a grading decision, school leaders are typically involved, or even charged, in the suit.

Courts have characteristically sided with school districts when they have consistently enforced the application of grading policies, especially if the policies lay out explicit grading provisions and expectations (Axelrod v. Phillips Acad., 1999; Campbell v. Bd. of Educ., 1980; Edinburg Cosol. Indep. Sch. Dist. v. Smith, 2016; Katzman v. Cumberland Valley Sch. Dist., 1984; Raymon v. Alvord Indep. School Dist., 1981; Simmons v. Pittsburg Unified Sch. Dist., 2014). In the absence of explicit grading policies, courts have come to varying conclusions on student grade reductions (Lane v. Belgrade Sch. Dist., 2007; Katzman v. Cumberland Valley Sch. Dist., 1984; New Braunfels Indep. Sch. Dist. v. Armke, 1983) and grading confidentiality cases (Norris v. Board of Educ., 1992; Owasso Ind. Sch. Dist. v. Falvo, 2002).

It is also important to note that courts expect schools to have a legally recognized interest "in ensuring that its students receive a *fair* grade" (Keen v. Penson, 1992). As Chartier (2003) notes, "fairness issues arise with particular force when they include subjective grading decisions" (p. 37). More specifically, in the case of *Knight v. Board of Education* (1976), the court ruled that grades are expected to serve as sources of information about academic performance rather than moral character (Chartier, 2003). Similarly, in *Smith v. Sch. City of Hobart* (1993), a federal judge ruled that grade reductions for nonacademic reasons resulted in "clear misrepresentation of the student's scholastic achievement":

> Misrepresentation of achievement is equally improper... and illegal whether the achievement is misrepresented by upgrading or downgrading, if either is done for reasons that are irrelevant to the achievement being graded. For example, one would hardly deem acceptable an upgrading in a mathematics course for achievement on the playing field. (pp. 397–398)

The issue of fairness becomes particularly problematic when students are subjected to arbitrary grading and the district has few or no grading policies in place. Without explicit policy provisions and subsequent protections, school districts and leaders are at risk of court challenges by students and their families.

Brookhart's (1994) review of 19 empirical studies of teachers' grading practices, opinions, and beliefs revealed that although teachers desire to grade fairly, they also tend to include nonacademic information in determining students' grades, like ability, effort, improvement, and work completion. This mixing of academic and nonacademic factors, combined with variation in grading practices across grade levels, causes policymakers to increasingly distrust teachers' judgment about student achievement (Brookhart, 1994). Over the past 20 years, numerous other empirical studies have documented how "teachers use both cognitive and noncognitive evidence" to determine grades (Brookhart et al., 2016, p. 16).

While some researchers claim this grading mix is necessary to determine fair grades (Chen & Bonner, 2017; McMillan, Myran, & Workman, 2002), others believe teacher subjectivity blurs the meaning of grades and makes it challenging for school leaders to decide what are fair grades for students. Without explicit grading policies, school districts and leaders are vulnerable to litigation challenging the notion of fair grading.

The issue of accuracy also gets entangled in teachers' grading decisions. Courts and transcript readers have relied on grade accuracy to mean "the extent that it permits someone to estimate the extent of a student's knowledge and skills in a given area" (Chartier, 2003, p. 41). According to this definition, including factors such as ability, effort, improvement, or work completion in grades may not be legally defensible.

Bartlett (1987) cites the *Katzman v. Cumberland Valley Sch. Dist.* (1984) case, which ruled that academic grades cannot be enhanced or reduced based on "actions unrelated to academic performance" (p. 164). Academic grades were determined to communicate evidence of student achievement and nothing else. As a result, Bartlett strongly advises school leaders to find other means to solve behavioral issues than in the gradebook.

Accountability for Grading in Leadership Standards and Job Descriptions

Besides state law, accountability for grading practices can also be found in educational leadership standards and job descriptions for school leaders. According to the *Professional Standards for Educational Leaders* (National Policy Board for Educational Administration, 2015), effective school leaders must "develop and support intellectually rigorous and coherent systems of curriculum, instruction, and assessment" (p. 12). Because grades come from assessment evidence of student learning, developing and supporting teachers' grading practices is expected of effective school leaders. Some may contend that because grading is not explicitly written into the standards, it is not in the purview of school leaders. But it has been well argued in the literature that decisions about teachers' work, including grades, is a primary duty of school administrators (Bowers, 2008; Coburn & Talbert, 2006). School board members are expected to ensure the system is accountable for student achievement. Superintendents share accountability for student achievement and assessment with school board members, especially with regard to setting assessment policies. Job descriptions for principal roles generally include the greatest specificity with regard to instructional leadership and assessment responsibility (Fullan, 2001, 2014; Green, 2010; Robbins & Alvy, 2004).

Although responsibility for grading is seldom explicitly mentioned, nearly every principal's job description calls for attention to the improvement of teachers' classroom instruction as a means to improve student learning. To that end, principals are responsible for the entire instructional continuum that includes both the *inputs* (curriculum, lesson planning, teaching, and formative assessment) and *outputs* (summative assessment, grading and reporting student work) of instruction. According to the Wallace Foundation (2013), improving instruction and managing data were two of five key practices identified as fostering student achievement and school improvement. According to the foundation's report, "effective [school] leaders view data as a means to not only pinpoint problems, but to understand their nature and causes," calling for a more intimate relationship with classroom data, including gradebook data (p. 15). Effective principals can gain a technical closeness with grade data through monitoring, asking useful questions, and promoting collaborative inquiry among teachers (Fullan, 2014; Green, 2010).

Accountability for Grading in Teacher Evaluations

In 1996, Charlotte Danielson published *Enhancing Professional Practice: A Framework for Teaching*, which serves as the reference point for many contemporary teacher evaluation models, including the widely used TAP program (National Institute for Excellence in Teaching, 2016). Danielson's framework addresses all phases of teaching, from planning to reporting achievement (Marzano, Frontier, & Livingston, 2011). While assessment of student learning remains an integral part of Danielson's most current version of the model, *The Framework for Teaching Evaluation Instrument* (2011), grades and grading student work are not explicitly included. Under "Professional Responsibilities," however, Danielson emphasizes maintaining accurate records of student learning, including records of learning progress and assignment completion. This suggests that grades are an expected and evaluated part of teachers' work.

School Leaders, Grading Traditions, and Lack of Training

If school leaders are accountable for teachers' grading under the law, in standards for leadership practice, and within teacher evaluations, why do so few take action to address the problems associated with existing grading practices? In many instances, school leaders are simply unaware of the problems. They may not know that there is great variation in the evidence teachers use to assign grades, or that the use of percentage or averaging grades are more illusions of precision than objective measures of student performance. School leaders may not realize that adding more categories to a grading system, such as pluses or minuses, diminishes the reliability of grades, or that computerized gradebook algorithms do not generate more accurate, fair, or objective grades for students (Guskey, 2015; Guskey & Bailey, 2001). In many cases, school leaders who recognize the need for grading changes are working against hidden histories and deeply rooted traditions in both operational and instructional processes of schools (Robbins & Alvy, 2004). These histories and traditions influence how people interact, solve problems, cope with tragedies, celebrate success, and do their work, including classroom grading. Guskey (2015) laments that teachers' grading practices involve "some of education's deepest and longheld traditions" (p. 2) and challenges school leaders to be bold and courageous in addressing grading reform. According to Brookhart and colleagues (2016), these problems were noted in empirical research conducted in the 19th century, specifically Edgeworth's 1888 study.

School leaders advocating change often find that teachers have little training on grading and do not give much thought to their grading practices. Many teachers apply the same practices they experienced as students or mechanically follow school or district grading norms or policies. School leaders rarely search for the reasons behind teachers' grading practices and offer little guidance to teachers (Brookhart et al., 2016; Brookhart & Nitko, 2008; Stiggins, 2002, 2008).

The majority of teachers grade in isolation and are left to make grading decisions using their own professional judgment without the intervention or guidance of school leaders. This could be because principals and other school leaders have little pre- or inservice training on effective grading practices (Impara & Plake, 1996; Stiggins, 1991). Because nearly all principals were once teachers, they likely experienced the same hands-off approach to grading they are affording their own teachers (Gates, Ringel, Santibanez, Ross, & Chung, 2003).

School Leaders and Empirical Research on Grading

Hundreds of peer-reviewed scholarly articles are available to school leaders on the topic of grading reform. In addition, an array of practitioner journals, blogs, newsletters, and social media sites offer viewpoints and information on grading issues. These non-scholarly sources provide introductions, rouse interest, and prompt professional reflection with regard to grading. It is vital, however, that school leaders' bases for altering grading practices rely not on conjecture or forcefully argued opinions (Guskey, 2015) but on close examination of the research evidence about what works best.

A Brief History of School Leaders and Grading

School leadership can be traced back to colonial times. From the colonial period through the early 1800s, the responsibility for schools rested with various members of the community, mostly composed of clergy and merchants, who oversaw lone teachers with no pedagogical training (Tracy, 1995). This period is often called the "inspection stage" of school leadership (more commonly referred to as school supervision) because of the monitoring role assigned to the community leaders. Even though these community members had no pedagogical training themselves, they viewed their role as one of improving instruction by helping the teacher make needed instructional changes (Tanner & Tanner, 1987). These community members would form "visiting committees" that would observe a teacher's lesson and methodologies, much like a school principal would conduct a classroom observation today. The visiting committee assessed the classroom environment and curriculum being taught, judged the appropriateness of the teacher's methods of instruction, and assessed student progress by collecting information on students' end-of-year exams. These assessments included any written information or grades provided by the teacher. Moreover, it was assumed not only that the visiting or supervisory committee had a right to intervene in all classroom processes, but also that they *should* intervene, as they were expected to set the "criteria for effective instruction," which was "defined in terms of desired outcomes" (Tracy, 1995, p. 321). Teachers took the instructional feedback seriously or faced dismissal.

During the mid-1800s, new administrative positions such as superintendent, principal, and head teachers were created in cities and eventually spread to rural areas. As populations expanded, the need for more professional expertise and oversight of several schools in a given geographic region increased. School districts emerged with administrative hierarchies to manage what went on in schools, much like what's in place today. Still, as Blumberg (1985) noted in his examination of 1840s school leadership, "the quality and methodology of teaching was of foremost concern" (p. 62), no matter the school leadership role. This concern for effective methodologies included teachers' grading practices.

The expansion of school leaders' roles through the 1800s brought increased attention to teachers' grading practices. In a paper read before the Southern Indiana Teachers' Association, Jessie Robertson (1884) noted:

> Our present system of grading has an evil tendency. While it may stimulate the pupils to greater effort, it is a most unworthy incentive to labor. The eagerness to receive a high grade, which often leads to dishonesty, testifies that the grade itself, rather than the merit it represents, is of greater value. Besides these evil effects on the pupils it demands too much of the teacher's time, precious time which could be employed so much more profitably. (p. 6)

Not all school leaders, however, viewed student tests and grading as a poor use of time. In *The Teacher's Test of His Pupil's Work* (1893), Principal Inch wrote:

> It is a mistake to hold that testing takes time from teaching. If properly handled, these tests teach by the corrections marked on the exercises which should be returned... and the teacher who does not require and examine a fair number of these tests, is doing slipshod, indefinite work. (Barto, 1893, p. 256)

To Inch, graded corrections on tests were to be used for communication with students. The more frequent the test, the more information students had for self-reflection and improvement—and the more information teachers had to help students improve. This thinking is similar to our use of assessment *for* learning and formative assessment today, although modern scholars draw a distinction between assessment and grading (Black & Wiliam, 1998). Today, the primary purpose of assessments is to inform and be used during the instructional process, whereas grades come after the instructional process and represent students' level of achievement (Guskey, 2015). Inch blurred the two while highlighting the communicative value of grades.

Other early school leaders saw the need to separate assessments from grades, and some argued for the elimination of grades altogether. In an article written in the March edition of *The Journal of Education* (1893) titled "Examinations and Promotions in Elementary Schools," Colonel Parker described how student examinations were to be used for teacher and student growth but also noted that they were problematic for this purpose: "No figures can mark the intrinsic in education" (p. 151), he wrote, explaining that grades should not form the basis of student grade-level promotions as they "excited rivalry" among pupils. Instead, Parker encouraged grade-level promotions when teachers and school leaders were confident "the child can do the work of that grade" (p. 151). In an 1894 article, Orville Bright cautioned that "there is great danger in [students'] graded work becoming monotonous" (p. 148), and in an 1898 address to the New England Superintendents' Association, George Martin called for the emancipation from unjust grading and tests used for the sorting, ranking, and promoting of pupils (Winship, 1898).

Martin's call for emancipation from grades may have been influenced by the earliest empirical research on grading: Edgeworth's 1888 research proving that grades had multiple sources of error and were consequently unreliable. Starch and Elliott's (1912, 1913a, 1913b) classic studies supported Edgeworth's findings that grading efforts were unreliable among teachers and across subject areas. In an attempt to solve grading issues and other educational problems of this era, from around 1900 through the 1920s, school leaders looked to scientific principles of business management for help. School leaders began to view measurement as the ultimate tool for a more scientific approach to schooling (Marzano et al., 2011). In particular,

William Wetzel (1929) proposed measures of student learning to determine the effectiveness of a teacher or school that would require a scientific supervisory approach for school leaders. In their search for reliable measures of student learning, school leaders emphasized classroom data, including grades, with which to make decisions about future actions. To make grading measures more reliable during this time, grading systems with fewer and broader categories emerged, such as the *A–F* scale (Brookhart et al., 2016). Grading on the curve became increasingly popular, as this approach seemed to minimize the subjective nature of scoring.

Still, the application of more scientific methods led to problems for school leaders. The effectiveness of teachers' grading practices was difficult to measure, and the reliance on quantitative measures of student achievement was thought to prompt lower-level thinking (Tracy, 1995). As a result, throughout the 1930s and 1940s, school leaders shifted from a scientific perspective focusing on achievement measures to a human relations perspective that focused on individuals within the organization. The Great Depression brought awareness of societal inequities, the development of the social sciences, and social psychology asserting that correct methods depended on circumstances. As a result, school leaders deemphasized attention to objective measurement goals and focused on individual development by creating supportive learning environments for teachers and students. This shift in focus didn't affect the *A–F* grading scale brought about by the earlier scientific approach, as more than 80 percent of U.S. schools had adopted this scale by the 1940s (Brookhart et al., 2016).

By the late 1950s, investigations into how student learning is affected by grades with and without teacher comments emerged (Page, 1958). Results showed that if teachers provide individualized comments alongside quantitative grades on students' work, grades can have a beneficial effect on student learning. Thus, school leaders zeroed in on the interactive grading patterns between students and teachers, drawing from more scientific leadership approaches found in the early 1900s. In the 1950s, teachers began to analyze their own classroom grading data, but many did not have the technical skills needed to do so effectively. By the 1960s, school leaders relied on clinical supervisory models. Through clinical supervision, school leaders borrowed from the human relations phase of the 1930s and 1940s to systematically observe and analyze teachers' instructional, assessment, and grading patterns together. School leaders relied on sustained cycles of improvement through precise observation- and evidence-based conversations with teachers about all aspects of the instructional continuum, including classroom grading data. The school leader was now "required to be highly skilled in data collection, providing feedback, and relating to people" (Tracy, 1995, p. 324). The same holds true today.

By the mid-1980s, researchers and theorists in school leadership began to articulate alternative perspectives to the more prescriptive clinical supervisory models of the 1960s and 1970s (Marzano et al., 2011). Glatthorn (1984); Levine (1989); Glickman, Gordon, and Ross-Gordon (1998); and others shifted school leaders' attention to adult learning and developmental issues, which set the stage for an emphasis on teacher evaluation, as previously discussed. During this time, grading researchers reported the wide variability found in teachers' grading practices (Brookhart, 1993, 1994; Cizek, Fitzgerald, & Rachor, 1996; McMillan et al., 2002), while others noted school leaders' inaction with regard to grading reform, despite the variabilities found (Allison & Friedman, 1995; Pardini, 1997). Contemporary grading researchers have added to our knowledge base on effective standards-based grading practices, offered practical solutions toward successful change, and strongly encouraged school leaders to take action as a result (Guskey, 2009, 2015; Guskey & Bailey, 2001). To date, most school leaders have resisted the call for grading reform.

What Significant Studies Have Been Conducted in This Area?

Reviewing the research on school leaders and grading led to 21 studies published in scholarly sources from 1981 to 2016. Fifteen of the 21 studies were conducted in the last 10 years, and most involved reviews of school leaders' perceptions of contemporary grading practices. Several investigations identified the factors school leaders and other school stakeholders perceive as necessary to successfully transition away from traditional grading and reporting systems. The six earlier studies focused primarily on school leaders' desire for grading consistency. A summary of all 21 studies is provided in Figure 7.1 (pp. 172–175).

What Questions Have Been Addressed in This Research?

Most of the studies are paired with more than one question, as study investigations were often multidimensional. The six major questions explored in these studies are as follows:

1. Do school leaders have an understanding of effective grading and reporting practices? (Akins, 2016; Greene, 2015; Michael & Trippi, 1987; Morrow, Casteel, & Isom 1986; Nagy & Moorhead, 1989; Olson, 2013; Patrick, 2015; Williams, 2014)

2. What are the obstacles to implementing effective grading and reporting practices? (Bauer, 2015; Bloom, 2011; Gibbs, Andrews, & Barnes, 2016; Greene, 2015; Schiffman, 2016)

3. What are the enablers to implementing effective grading and reporting practices? (Bauer, 2015; Brazouski, 2015; Carter, 2016; Cox, 2011; Gogerty, 2016; Greene, 2015; Kain, 1996; Mehring, Parks, Walter, & Banikowski, 1991; Patrick, 2015; Schiffman, 2016; Sebastian & Allensworth, 2012; Williams, 2014)

4. Can grades help school leaders make building- and district-level decisions? (Bloom, 2011; Bowers, 2008; Williams, 2014)

5. Are there certain leadership styles or approaches that can enable the use of effective grading and reporting practices? (Bloom, 2011; Brazouski, 2015; Carter, 2016; Cox, 2011; Gogerty, 2016; Patrick, 2015; Schiffman, 2016; Williams, 2014)

6. Can district leaders enable the use of effective grading and reporting practices? (Bowers, 2008; Brazouski, 2015; Gogerty, 2016)

What Have the Results of Those Studies Revealed?

The major finding from these studies of the relationship between school leadership and grading is the vital importance of the principal. The principal's leadership can enable or deter successful implementation of more effective school grading practices. District leaders and parents can be instrumental in grading reform, but their influence is comparatively minimal. The majority of these studies equate effective grading practices with the use of standards-based grading, which calls for the evaluation of student progress aligned to specific learning criteria. According to Guskey (2009), standards-based grading prompts teachers to

> identify what they want their students to learn, what evidence best reflects that learning, and what criteria they will use to judge that evidence. Grades based on specific learning criteria and standards have direct meaning and serve well the communication purposes for which they are intended. (p. 12)

With a standards-based grading approach, grades are not based on a student's relative standing among classmates, which positions students to compete with one another. Standards-based grading is success- rather than punishment-oriented. In a traditional approach

FIGURE 7.1 | **Studies of School Leaders and Grading**

Studies	Participants	Main Findings
Akins (2006)	High school principals	• Principals understood but rarely applied effective grading and reporting practices. • Principals of schools with over 600 students favored applying effective grading and reporting practices over those leading schools with fewer students. • Principals with 11+ years leadership experience favored applying effective grading practices over those with less experience. • Principals utilizing standards-based report cards and traditional report cards conveyed similar attitudes toward effective grading practices.
Bauer (2015)	Middle school principals	• Principals perceived culture and climate as the most significant obstacles to implementing standards-based grading. • Principals prioritized implementation time when shifting from traditional to standards-based grading practices. • Principals perceived parents as an important stakeholder group when shifting to standards-based grading practices.
Bloom (2011)	Elementary students, teachers, parents, and principals	• Principals' communication and decision making were found to negatively affect teachers' grading practices and students' grades.
Bowers (2008)	High school students	• Grades provided multidimensional information for school leaders. • Leaders used grades for decision making.
Brazouski (2015)	High school teachers, principals, and district-level leaders	• Building-level leadership played a prominent role in enabling successful standards-based grading implementation. • District-level leadership played a prominent role in enabling successful standards-based grading initiation. • Both building- and district-level leadership played a prominent role in sustaining standards-based grading practices. • Principal-driven systems of collaboration, continuous and effective communication, and a culture of trust played a prominent role in enabling successful standards-based grading implementation.

Carter (2016)	Middle and high school principals	• Nine essential leadership practices were identified during transitions from traditional to standards-based grading systems.
Cox (2011)	High school teachers	• Nondirective leadership approaches to grading reform led teachers to choose course-alike grading agreements.
Gibbs, Andrews, & Barnes (2016)	High school students, teachers, parents, and principals	• Principal-mandated changes to grading polices had a limited effect.
Goehring (1981)	Middle and high school principals, guidance counselors, and teachers	• Principals favored emphasizing teacher tasks related to grading during preservice teacher training. • High school principals more strongly favored emphasizing teacher tasks related to grading during preservice teacher training over middle school principals.
Gogerty (2016)	High school teachers, principals, and district leaders	• Teachers identified collaboration, training, and mandated use of standards-based report cards as successful factors in making the shift to standards-based practices. • All respondents identified implementation time and teachers playing an active role as factors in successfully shifting to standards-based practices. • Principals were underutilized in the change process.
Greene (2015)	Middle school teachers and principals	• Principal perceptions affected overall implementation of standards-based grading. • Teachers and principals reported that lack of training in standards-based practices affected anticipated implementation results, and principals agreed that standards-based grading more clearly communicated students' learning strengths and weaknesses. • Teachers and principals agreed that communicating with parents is essential when implementing standards-based practices.
Kain (1996)	High school teachers and principals	• Grading used as a central theme for collaboration and problem solving offered a promising approach to school reform.
Mehring, Parks, Walter, & Banikowski (1991)	Elementary teachers and principals	• Interpretation of report card grades varied widely among teachers and principals. • Direct training on grading practices resulted in high levels of consistency in teachers' and principals' interpretations of what report card grades represent.

FIGURE 7.1 | **Studies of School Leaders and Grading—(*continued*)**

Studies	Participants	Main Findings
Michael & Trippi (1987)	Elementary, middle, and high school teachers and principals	• Teachers and principals did not favor norm-based grading but did favor criterion-based grading.
Morrow, Casteel, & Isom (1986)	Elementary, middle, and high school teachers and principals	• Principals and teachers at all levels perceived grading as a top-five concern. • Elementary and high school principals ranked grading concerns higher than middle school principals.
Nagy & Moorhead (1989)	High school principals	• Principals desired grading consistency. • Principals differed in how large a role they felt they should play in ensuring grading consistency. • Principals differed in their views of parents' grading complaints.
Olson (2013)	Middle and high school teachers and principals	• Principals and teachers did not agree on what constituted sound grading practices. • Principals were more concerned with grading consistency than teachers.
Patrick (2015)	Middle school students, parents, teachers, and principals	• All respondents agreed that standards-based grading practices promoted student learning. • All respondents agreed that parent communication is essential to supporting grading reform. • Principals differed in the standards-based grading practices they thought should be implemented. • Teachers reported that training was essential for successfully reforming grading practices.
Schiffman (2016)	High school teachers, one principal, and one district-level leader	• Respondents agreed there were challenges to implementing standards-based grading practices. • Respondents considered implementation time for standards-based grading to be a primary challenge. • Respondents identified communication with parents and school stakeholders as a necessary factor to success when implementing standards-based grading. • Respondents agreed that teachers were more focused on standards now that standards-based grading is the expectation.
Sebastian & Allensworth (2012)	High school teachers	• Teachers favored principals that create safe and college-focused school learning climates. • Respondents identified learning climate as influencing higher student grades.

Williams (2014)	Elementary teachers and principals	• Teachers and principals agreed that standards-based report cards clearly and effectively communicate students' progress toward standards. • Teachers and principals agreed that implementing standards-based report cards improve one's ability to assess student learning and increase reporting proficiency. • Teachers and principals agreed that parent communication is important to help transition from traditional to standards-based report cards. • Teachers reported a need for strong leadership to help successfully transition from traditional to standards-based report cards.

to grading, if students fail to turn in an assignment or turn it in late, the assignment grade is reduced or not scored at all. In standards-based grading, by contrast, they receive an "incomplete" and additional effort is required (Guskey, 2009). And because teachers draw from various sources of evidence to determine students' grades (e.g., exams, effort, work habits, attendance, behavior, homework, progress), standards-based grading separates assessments of achievement from other criteria, such as progress and effort, so grades are more meaningful. The overall intent is to ensure that grades communicate more accurately and fairly what students are accomplishing in school (Guskey, 2002).

To better understand how principals influence successful implementation of effective grading and reporting practices, researchers have addressed the following questions:

1. Do school leaders have an understanding of research-based grading and reporting practices? School leaders, especially principals, have been shown to have a basic understanding of effective, research-based grading and reporting practices. Akins (2016) surveyed 247 high school principals on their understanding of and agreement with grading literature that emphasized the need for accuracy, fairness, specificity, timeliness, standards-based approaches, formative assessments, and identification of inherent problems with traditional grading systems. Of the principals surveyed, 95 percent responded favorably to the use of these research-based grading practices over traditional practices. Interestingly, the more experienced principals at larger schools (over 600 students) reported more favorable reactions to research-based practices than did their less experienced counterparts in smaller schools (under 600 students). Olson's (2013) study showed similar findings: 524 middle and high school principals reported understanding of "sound" research-based grading practices, even though principals and teachers did not agree on what these practices were. Morrow and colleagues (1986) conducted a survey with 459 elementary, middle, and high school principals, and as in the other studies, these principals were able to identify and prioritize grading concerns found in traditional grading systems. Middle school principals placed the least emphasis on grading concerns when compared with elementary and high school principals. Michael and Trippi (1987) conducted an earlier study with 27 elementary, middle, and high school teachers and principals in which both groups favored grading practices that rely on subject-specific learning criteria over traditional practices based on norm-based criteria. Other studies show principals understanding the need for grading consistency (Nagy & Moorhead, 1989), standards-based grading (Greene, 2015; Patrick, 2015), and standards-based reporting (Williams, 2014).

2. What are the obstacles to implementing effective grading and reporting practices? Bauer (2015) investigated obstacles at all phases of the standards-based grading transition process. Notably, the 175 middle school principals involved in the study identified *school culture and climate* as the most significant obstacle to implementing standards-based grading. Some principals reported that the learning culture of their school lacked a common purpose for grading, while others reported that their climate was more teacher-focused than student-focused and that grading was therefore viewed as a personal act of teachers rather than as a primary means to communicate to parents and other stakeholders. For these reasons, culture and climate became impediments to implementing standards-based grading reforms. In Greene's (2015) study, middle school teachers and principals identified lack of training in standards-based practices as negatively affecting implementation results. Without specific training, inconsistent application of standards-based practices was more likely, which limited implementation results for those involved in the study. This same study revealed that principals' perceptions can affect overall implementation of standards-based practices, exposing a need for a principal's positive outlook and disposition throughout the transition process. Other studies illuminate lack of principal communication (Bloom, 2011), insufficient implementation time (Schiffman, 2016), and principal-mandated changes to grading policies as obstacles to successful grading and reporting practices (Gibbs et al., 2016).

3. What are the enablers to implementing effective grading and reporting practices? Several studies found specific enablers that helped schools and districts successfully implement effective grading and reporting practices. Seven out of the 12 studies that provide answers to this question point to *principal communication* as a significant enabler (Bauer, 2015; Brazouski, 2015; Carter, 2016; Greene, 2015; Patrick, 2015; Schiffman, 2016; Williams, 2014). All seven studies note that clear, ongoing, purpose-driven communication from the principal makes for shared understanding and promotes greater alignment among all stakeholders. Teachers are viewed as primary grading stakeholders needing frequent guidance and feedback from the principal (Carter, 2016). However, parents cannot be overlooked: Five studies specifically identified principals' *communication with parents* as a key enabler to successfully implementing effective grading and reporting practices, especially since contemporary practices such as standards-based report cards depart from traditional practices more familiar to parents. In Williams's

(2014) study, both elementary teachers and principals across two school districts highlight how intentional parent communication can promote standards-based report card success. Principals in one district conducted parent meetings that included training on the standards-based report card, with an emphasis on both the technical aspects of the report card and the "whys" behind its use (Williams, 2014). Teachers and principals indicate that during the parent meetings, principals were able to help parents understand the large amount of information associated with standards-based reporting and were able to answer parental concerns proactively. The district that did not conduct parent meetings reported higher levels of parental confusion with reading the standards-based report cards and greater difficulty with helping parents understand why there are no letter grades on the standards-based report cards (Williams, 2014).

Six studies identify *teacher collaboration* as a significant enabler to helping schools and districts successfully implement effective grading and reporting practices (Brazouski, 2015; Carter, 2016; Cox, 2011; Gogerty, 2016; Kain, 1996; Patrick, 2015). In Gogerty's (2016) study, high school teachers favorably highlighted their principal's support of teacher-team collaboration to successfully address implementation concerns together. The middle school teachers in Patrick's (2015) study pointed to their principal encouraging them to make grading decisions together as a necessary support when reforming grading practices. Carter (2016) found that principals collaborating with teachers is an essential leadership practice when schools are making the transition to standards-based grading practices, and that collaboration among principals is a necessary first step. Brazouski (2015) identified principal-driven systems of collaboration (e.g., professional learning communities) and district-driven systems of collaboration (e.g., offering grading-specific training to principals and teachers) as important to successful implementation. In his study, Brazouski noted that both principal- and district-driven systems of collaboration are essential for sustaining change, but that district collaboration was found to be more influential during the initial phases of implementation, whereas principal-driven collaboration is needed throughout all phases of standard-based grading implementation. Other studies reveal that course-alike grading agreements can emerge through teacher collaboration (Cox, 2011), and grading as a central theme for collaboration is a promising approach to whole-school reform (Kain, 1996).

Five studies found *direct training* on grading to be a significant enabler helping schools and districts successfully implement effective grading and reporting practices (Carter, 2016; Gogerty, 2016; Greene, 2015; Mehring et al., 1991; Patrick, 2015). Most prominently, Mehring and colleagues (1991) investigated 397 elementary teachers' and principals' interpretations of report card grades and found that specific training on grading practices can achieve high levels of grading agreements between teachers and principals. Goehring (1981) conducted a study that included 83 middle and high school principals that determined principals favor training that places an emphasis on teacher tasks related to grading, although principals in this study identified preservice as the appropriate time for such training. Carter (2016) found training on research-based grading practices to be essential in schools making the transition to standards-based grading practices. The 148 middle school teachers in Patrick's (2015) study perceived grading-specific professional development as key to reforming grading practices. Teachers surveyed in Greene's (2015) study reported lack of training as a concern and identified the need for more direct training on grading to help reach their standards-based grading and reporting goals.

Three studies found ample *time to implement* to be a significant enabler to helping schools and districts successfully implement effective grading and reporting practices (Bauer, 2015; Gogerty, 2016; Patrick, 2015). Bauer (2015) discovered a significant difference in teachers' grading implementation after teachers have been utilizing standards-based grading practices over time. Schools implementing standards-based grading practices for one to three years showed more aligned teacher grading practices than those in schools not currently implementing standards-based grading. There was an even greater difference in teachers' grading practice alignment discovered between schools implementing standards-based grading for four or more years and those that are not implementing at all. Teachers in Patrick's (2015) study reported a need for time to implement grading changes correctly, although there was no indication as to what would constitute sufficient time. Gogerty (2016) found teachers responding favorably to the 30 hours allotted for training that covered the "how and why" of standards-based grading, as well as an additional 16 hours for aligning teachers' curriculum, instruction, and assessments to the new standards-based grading practices.

4. Can grades help school leaders make building- and district-level decisions? Yes. Bowers (2008) found that grades provide two significant dimensions of information for school leaders: assessment of academic knowledge and assessment of a student's ability to negotiate the social processes of school. Bowers's (2008) analysis of 195 high school students' grades suggests that grades have been overlooked by school leaders and should be revisited as key sources of decision-making data. Bloom (2011) presents a case study analysis that involves grading discrepancies found between two teachers at the same school, each teaching one of a set of identical twins. She investigated the leadership practices of two elementary principals and their responses to the "Case of the Failing Twin." In her investigation, Bloom found that principals can resolve issues of instructional and assessment inequities among teachers if they use grades as a source for decision making. Additionally, she found that principals who do not use grades as a source for decision making can negatively affect teachers' grading practices and students' grades. In her study, Williams (2014) showed that elementary teachers and principals agreed that standards-based grades can be used to accurately assess and make more informed decisions about student learning.

5. Are there certain leadership styles or approaches that can enable the use of effective grading and reporting practices? Yes. In fact, there seems to be one school leader approach that stands out from the rest. Seven studies identified that principals who use a nondirective, collaborative approach with teachers, parents, district leaders, and other school stakeholders can enable the use of effective grading and reporting practices (Brazouski, 2015; Carter, 2016; Cox, 2011; Gogerty, 2016; Patrick, 2015; Schiffman, 2016; Williams, 2014). Another study (Gibbs et al., 2016) identified the negative and limiting effects of principals using a directive approach to grade reform. Brazouski (2015) reported a need for principals' "shared control" when transitioning to standards-based grading. When investigating high school teachers', principals', and district-level leaders' perceptions of standards-based grading implementation, Brazouski (2015) identified "collaboration" as a theme of necessary leadership practice. Foremost, a successful transition to standards-based grading involves the principal's ability to allocate time for team building, build opportunities for shared adult learning, and entrust and empower teachers to develop and deliver activity and application strategies toward standards-based grading. Shared decision making and problem solving between principal and teachers was found to be essential when making the transition to standard-based practices. Additionally, Brazouski (2015) identified district leaders collaborating with principals throughout the implementation process as another necessary school leader approach. District leaders serving as coaches to principals, supporting site-based standards-based grading activities, and providing supportive communication when stakeholder concerns arose were important to the successful implementation of standards-based grading practices. Williams (2014) confirmed similar findings with regard to collaboration with district leaders. Patrick (2015) found that teachers rated "making grading decisions together as a faculty" with the guidance (not mandate) of the principal as the highest factor necessary for successful grading reform. Gogerty (2016) noted that the more support teachers had from school leaders, the more teachers reported successful standards-based grading implementation results. Carter (2016) found building "guiding coalitions" (p. 88) with teachers, parents, and other school stakeholders early in the process to be an essential leadership practice when schools are making the transition to standards-based grading practices. Schiffman's (2016) study established two-way communication between principals and parents as key to enabling effective grading and reporting practices. Cox (2011) discovered that nondirective school leader approaches led teachers to choose grading reforms aligned to effective practice. Moreover, Gibbs and colleagues (2016) found that when principals do utilize a directive approach with grading policies, there can be unintended negative consequences on teachers' grading practices that limit and even undermine the potential effect of the mandated grading policies. However, Gogerty (2016) did find that when principals used a directive approach when mandating teachers' use of a standards-based reporting system, teachers changed their grading practices to ones more closely aligned with effective standards-based grading practices.

6. Can district leaders enable the use of effective grading and reporting practices? Yes. As discussed earlier, district leaders can enable the use of effective grading and reporting practices, although their influence is secondary to that of school principals. Three studies in particular affirm this understanding (Bowers, 2008; Brazouski, 2015; Gogerty, 2016). Bowers (2008) found that district-level leaders can and should use grades as useful decision-making data. Brazouski (2015) noted the importance of district-level leaders' role during the initial implementation phase and the sustaining phase when enacting standards-based grading change, and Gogerty (2016) identified district-led training as a key support for teachers when they are shifting to standards-based grading practices.

What Are the Implications of These Research Findings for Improvement in Grading Policy and Practice?

School leaders, particularly school principals, have a uniquely powerful influence on the successful implementation of grading reforms. Teachers need the guidance, support, and trust of school leaders to be successful in their efforts. Parents need principals to be the source of ongoing communication about the reasons for change in grading systems. District leaders can serve as positive influencers as well. But without the school principal's direct involvement and overt support, grading reforms won't be realized.

Knowing that school principals are ultimately accountable for grading reform and that they are best positioned to lead, what should they do next? The 21 studies reviewed in this chapter provide important direction.

It is imperative that principals look to sound research before taking action. We have long lamented our frustration with innumerable educational initiatives that yield only limited and short-lived results. Too often we purchase and adopt programs under the promise of improvement and fill teachers' plates with expectations of student results without first checking to determine if sound empirical evidence supports our efforts. Ensuring best practice dictates a more informed approach.

Before buying a new car, we typically consult *Consumer Reports,* take multiple test drives, and check under the hood to ensure the car is mechanically sound. Before investing in a program or initiative, school leaders similarly need to take the time to investigate its credibility. With online access to research reports and scholarly articles, school leaders can readily retrieve research-based evidence to determine best practice.

Nonnegotiables for School Leaders and Grading Reform

Besides encouraging principals to take the lead, the research findings about school leaders and grading offer sound guidance on how best to proceed with improving grading practices. These critical themes emerge so consistently in the studies reviewed, it seems appropriate to label them *nonnegotiables*.

Communication. A major finding from these studies is that principals must regularly and purposefully communicate with teachers and parents about changes in grading. Both of these stakeholder groups need intentional communication at all phases of the reform process. In the initial phase, clear and consistent articulation of the purpose for the grading reform is most needed. In the implementation phase, communication that reinforces the purpose, along with messages that promote shared understanding, are essential. In the sustaining phase, communication that highlights purpose, shared understanding, and evidence of success is key.

Carter (2016) identified *frequent communication* from principals to teachers as a top leadership action necessary for leading changes to standards-based grading. In Williams's study (2014), *parent communication* was determined significant to ensure the successful transition from traditional to standards-based report cards. Both findings suggest that principals must prioritize and persist in grading reform messaging even when it may appear to be overkill.

Principals must saturate channels of teacher and parent communication and, in doing so, rely on multiple media to socialize their messages and receive input. Reliance on one or two forms of communication may not be enough. Instead, principals must consider how teachers and parents prefer to receive messages and provide feedback, which are often varied. Some teachers prefer face-to-face communication in faculty or grade-level meetings, while others desire regular e-mail communication, internal newsletters, or even participation in anonymous surveys. Parents may prefer communication through one-on-one conferencing, whole-group meetings, external newsletters, phone calls, texts, or even classes geared especially for them (Williams, 2014). Essentially, *all* methods of two-way communication should be used to maximize opportunities to reach *all* teachers and parents throughout *all* phases of the grading reform process.

Like teachers, school principals must use multiple means to communicate what is to be learned and consider the key stakeholders in the learning process. Moreover, since principal communication is such a significant enabler to grading reform, principals shouldn't be afraid to repeat purpose and direction over time. Instead, they should embrace the repetition as necessary for shared understanding and clarity.

Collaboration. Several studies found that *teacher collaboration* was a significant enabler to helping schools and districts implement effective grading and reporting practices. More specifically, the majority of studies highlight the necessity of principals and teachers working interdependently and sharing in decision making to successfully enact grading changes. Glickman, Gordon, and Ross-Gordon (2014) describe typical behaviors found in collaborative principal-to-teacher relationships. These include *clarifying* (identifying the problem as seen by teachers), *listening* (understanding teachers' perception of the problem), *reflecting* (verifying teachers' perception of the problem), *presenting* (providing the principal's perception of the problem), *problem solving* (exchanging possible solutions), *encouraging* (accepting conflict), *negotiating* (finding an acceptable solution), and *standardizing* (agreeing on details of the plan). Effectively using these behaviors presumes that both principals and teachers understand they have equally important roles in the grading reform process.

Although school principals and teachers may be growing in their knowledge of effective grading practices together, both must commit to solving the problems found in traditional grading systems. It is this shared commitment that allows principals and teachers to assume responsibility and trust the collaborative process. It is important, therefore, to note that teacher collaboration involves more than the mechanical procedures of democracy. Principals cannot present the illusion of collaborative behaviors, such as *listening* or *problem solving*, then choose to influence or not act on teacher decisions. This misuse of collaboration will erode teachers' trust and their commitment to the grading reform process.

Collaboration does not mean principals take a laissez-faire approach to grading reform decisions and implementation. In seven of the reviewed studies, it was found that a nondirective, collaborative leadership approach enabled the use of effective grading and reporting practices. Still, principals remained actively involved throughout the grading reform process. Nondirective principals share control with teachers. At the same time, they work with district leaders to acquire training and resources, cull and share grading data with teachers, clarify the purpose of grades, remove obstacles, monitor and communicate progress, support and encourage teachers' shifts in practice, and work directly with parents. A nondirective leadership approach does not mean principals abdicate responsibility. Nondirective principals share responsibility with teachers and realize moving their school toward more effective grading practices requires collaborative effort.

Training. Principals' communication and collaboration must be anchored by direct training on effective grading practices. Although teachers' grading practices are frequently inconsistent, five studies in this analysis reveal that greater levels of consistency can be achieved if specific training is provided to those directly involved in the grading reform process. Direct training can help resolve disagreements between principals and teachers on what constitutes the proper criteria for determining student achievement (Mehring et al., 1991). In particular, Carter (2016) identified training on research-based grading practices as the necessary first step for school leaders desiring a successful transition to standards-based grading.

Training plays an important role in the grading reform process. Both Brazouski (2015) and Gogerty (2016) found that district leaders can positively support teachers' shifts in grading practices by providing training on research-based grading, especially during the initial phase of the reform process. Carter (2016) further identified training principals as a necessary prerequisite to training teachers.

District leaders are in key positions to enable and provide the resources for training principals and teachers on effective, research-based grading practices. Specifically, district leaders must take the time to determine which resources are supported by evidence from sound research. Before offering training, district leaders must vet the scholarship associated with the training effort. Otherwise, efforts to successfully reform grading practices can be undermined and risk failure.

Time. In addition to the time required for research-based training, school leaders must provide ample time for implementing effective grading practices. While only three studies considered the significance of time on grading reform, many other studies highlight time to implement as an implication of their findings. For example, the studies that found principal communication as a significant enabler discuss the importance of the principal's communication over time, not just during the initial phase of the reform process. Similarly, studies that analyzed teacher collaboration note that collaboration is to be intentional throughout all phases of the reform process, implying that time plays an important role in the successful transition to more effective grading practices.

Although the amount of time necessary to achieve a successful transition is not certain, a few studies provide important insights. Bauer's (2015) study indicates that schools need up to three years implementing standards-based grading to evidence more aligned teacher grading practices. Teachers often need sustained support to transfer their learning into practice and to achieve results. Gogerty's (2016) study confirmed that teachers need 30+ hours of direct training on standards-based grading to see successful applications in the classroom.

Conclusion

The studies reviewed in this chapter convincingly show that among school leaders, principals are the most critical actors in the grading reform process. For improvements in grading policies and practices to occur, principals must remove existing obstacles to change and ignite the enablers to implementing effective grading practices.

To help create positive change, principals must rely on (1) communication, (2) collaboration, (3) training, and (4) time to guide their work. District leaders have a crucial role in supporting principals in grading reform efforts as well. The evidence reviewed here shows that grading practices can be improved, but only when principals lead the effort, communicate to all stakeholders the need for change and the benefits it will bring, and offer sustained support for teachers throughout the implementation process.

References

Akins, J. A. (2016). *Secondary principals' perceptions of grading and grade reporting practices* (Unpublished doctoral dissertation). Southwest Baptist University, Bolivar, MO.

Allison, E., & Friedman, S. J. (1995). Reforming report cards. *Executive Educator, 17*(1), 38–39.

Axelrod v. Phillips Acad., 46F. Supp. 2d 72, 82 (D. Mass. 1999).

Bartlett, L. (1987). Academic evaluation and student discipline don't mix: A critical review. *Journal of Law & Education, 16,* 155–165.

Barto, L. M. (1893). Current educational literature. *The School Review, 1*(4), 253–261.

Bauer, P. (2015). *Middle school principals' perceptions of obstacles to implementing standards-based grading* (Unpublished doctoral dissertation). Southwest Baptist University, Bolivar, MO.

Black, P., & Wiliam, D. (1998). Assessment and classroom learning. *Assessment in Education: Principles, Policy & Practice, 5*(1), 7–74.

Bloom, C. M. (2011). Leadership effectiveness and instructional supervision: The case of the failing twin. *Journal of Case Studies in Education, 1*, 1–14.

Blumberg, A. (1985). Where we came from: Notes on supervision in the 1840s. *Journal of Curriculum and Supervision, 1*(1), 56–65.

Bowers, A. J. (2008). Reconsidering grades as data for decision making: More than just academic knowledge. *Journal of Educational Administration, 47*(5), 609–629.

Brazouski, A. E. (2015). *A phenomenological case study of leadership impacting the implementation of standards-based grading in a public high school* (Unpublished doctoral dissertation). Cardinal Stritch University, Milwaukee, WI.

Bright, O. (1894). Five minute speeches. *The Journal of Education, 39*(10), 147–149.

Brookhart, S. M. (1993). Teachers' grading practices: Meaning and values. *Journal of Educational Measurement, 30*, 123–142.

Brookhart, S. M. (1994). Teachers' grading: Practice and theory. *Applied Measurement in Education, 7,* 279–301.

Brookhart, S. M., Guskey, T. R., Bowers, A. J., McMillan, J. H., Smith, J. K., Smith, L. F., et al. (2016). A century of grading research: Meaning and value in the most common educational measure. *Review of Educational Research, 86*(4), 803–848.

Brookhart, S. M., & Nitko, A. J. (2008). *Assessment and grading in classrooms.* Upper Saddle River, NJ: Pearson Education.

Campbell v. Bd. of Educ., 475 A.2d 289 (Conn. 1980).

Carter, A. B. (2016). *Best practices for leading a transition to standards-based grading in secondary schools* (Unpublished doctoral dissertation). Walden University, Minneapolis, MN.

Chartier, G. (2003). Truth-telling, incommensurability, and the ethics of grading. *B.Y.U. Education and Law Journal, 1,* 37–81.

Chen, P. P., & Bonner, S. M. (2017). Teachers' beliefs about grading practices and a constructivist approach to teaching. *Educational Assessment, 22*(1), 18–34.

Cizek, G. J. (1996). Grades: The final frontier in assessment reform. *NASSP Bulletin, 80,* 103–110.

Cizek, G. J., Fitzgerald, J. M., & Rachor, B. A. (1996). Teachers' assessment practices: Preparation, isolation, and the kitchen sink. *Educational Assessment, 3*(2), 159–179.

Coburn, C. E., & Talbert, J. E. (2006). Conceptions of evidence use in school districts: Mapping the terrain. *American Journal of Education, 112*(4), 469–495.

Cox, K. B. (2011). Putting classroom grading on the table: A reform in progress. *American Secondary Education, 40*(1), 67–87.

Danielson, C. (1996). *Enhancing professional practice: A framework for teaching.* Alexandria, VA: ASCD.

Danielson, C. (2011). *Enhancing professional practice: A framework for teaching* (3rd ed.). Alexandria, VA: ASCD.

Davis, S., Darling-Hammond, L., LaPointe, M., & Meyerson, D. (2005). *School leadership study: Developing successful principals.* Commissioned by the Wallace Foundation. Stanford, CA: Stanford Educational Leadership Institute.

Davis, B. W., Gooden, M. A., & Bowers, A. J. (2017). Pathways to the principalship: An event history analysis of the careers of teachers with principal certification. *American Educational Research Journal, 54*(2), 207–240.

Edgeworth, F. Y. (1888). The statistics of examinations. *Journal of the Royal Statistical Society, 51,* 599–635.

Edinburg Consol. Indep. Sch. Dist. v. Smith, 2016 Tex. App. (Tex. App. Corpus Christi May 26, 2016).

Florida Education Statutes. (2016). K–20 Education CODE 1003.437; 1003.4295(3).

Fullan, M. (2001). *Leading in a culture of change.* San Francisco: Jossey-Bass.

Fullan, M. (2014). *The principal: Three keys to maximizing impact.* San Francisco: Jossey-Bass.

Gates, S. M., Ringel, J. S., Santibanez, L., Ross, K. E., & Chung, C. H. (2003). *Who is leading our schools?: An overview of school administrators and their careers.* Santa Monica, CA: RAND Corporation.

Gibbs, J., Andrews, C., & Barnes, C. (2016). *Standards-based grading: Moving forward equality of opportunity and advancement of learning for all students* (Unpublished doctoral dissertation). Western Carolina University, Cullowhee, NC.

Glatthorn, A. (1984). *Differentiated supervision.* Alexandria, VA: ASCD.

Glickman, C., Gordon, S., & Ross-Gordon, J. (1998). *Supervision of instruction: A developmental approach* (4th ed.). Boston: Allyn & Bacon.

Glickman, C., Gordon, S., & Ross-Gordon, J. (2014). *Supervision of instruction: A developmental approach* (9th ed.). Boston: Allyn & Bacon.

Goehring, H. J. (1981). *Perceptions of secondary school professional personnel in relation to teacher training in pupil evaluation procedures.* Flat Rock, NC: Blue Ridge Technical College.

Gogerty, J. (2016). *The influence of district support during implementation of high school standards-based grading practices* (Unpublished doctoral dissertation). Drake University, Des Moines, IA.

Green, R. L. (2010). *The four dimensions of principal leadership: A framework for leading 21st century schools.* Boston: Allyn & Bacon.

Greene, G. L. (2015). *An analysis of the comparison between classroom grades earned with a standards-based grading system and grade-level assessment scores as measured by the Missouri assessment program.* (Unpublished doctoral dissertation). Lindenwood University, St. Charles, MO.

Guskey, T. R. (2002). *How's my kid doing? A parents' guide to grades, marks and report cards.* San Francisco: Jossey-Bass.

Guskey, T. R. (2009). Grading policies that work against standards... and how to fix them. In T. R. Guskey (Ed.), *Practical solutions for serious problems in standards-based grading* (pp. 9–26). Thousand Oaks, CA: Corwin.

Guskey, T. R. (2015). *On your mark: Challenging the conventions of grading and reporting.* Bloomington, IN: Solution Tree Press.

Guskey, T. R., & Bailey, J. M. (2001). *Developing grading and reporting systems for student learning.* Thousand Oaks, CA: Corwin.

Impara, J. C., & Plake, B. S. (1996). Professional development in student assessment for educational administrators: An instructional approach. *Educational Measurement: Issues and Practice, 15*(2), 14–20.

Kain, D. L. (1996). Looking beneath the surface: Teacher collaboration through the lens of grading practices. *Teachers College Record, 97*(4), 569–587.

Katzman v. Cumberland Valley Sch. Dist., 479 A. 2d 671 (Pa. Commonw. Ct. 1984).

Keen v. Penson, 970 F. 2d 252, 258 (7th Cir. 1992).

Knight v. Bd. of Educ., 38 Ill. App. 3d 603 (Ill. App. Ct. 1976).

Lane v. Belgrade Sch. Dist. No. 44, 2007 Mont. Dist. (Mont. Dist. Ct. December 14, 2007).

Leithwood, K., & Jantzi, D. (2005). Transformational leadership. In B. Davies (Ed.), *The essentials of school leadership* (pp. 31–43). Thousand Oaks, CA: Sage.

Levine, S. (1989). *Adult growth in schools.* Boston: Allyn & Bacon.

Marzano, R. J., Frontier, T., & Livingston, D. (2011). *Effective supervision: Supporting the art and science of teaching.* Alexandria, VA: ASCD.

McElligott, J., & Brookhart, S. M. (2009). Legal issues of grading in the era of high-stakes accountability. In T. R. Guskey (Ed.), *Practical solutions for serious problems in standards-based grading* (pp. 57–74). Thousand Oaks, CA: Corwin.

McMillan, J. H., Myran, S., & Workman, D. (2002). Elementary teachers' classroom assessment and grading practices. *The Journal of Educational Research, 95,* 203–213.

Mehring, T., Parks, C., Walter, K., & Banikowski, A. (1991). Report cards: What do they mean during the elementary years. *Reading Improvement, 28*(3), 162–168.

Michael, R. J., & Trippi, J. A. (1987). *Educators' views of procedures for grading mainstreamed handicapped children.* New Paltz, NY: State University of New York.

Morrow, J. E., Casteel, C. P., & Isom, B. A. (1986, November). *Educational reform: Perceptions of practitioners.* Paper presented at the National Council of States on Inservice Education in Nashville, TN.

Nagy, P., & Moorhead, R. (1989, March). *Administrator response to classroom testing data: A problem-solving perspective.* Paper presented at the Annual Meeting of the National Council on Measurement in Education, San Francisco.

National Institute for Excellence in Teaching. (2016). *Examining the evidence for the impact of TAP: The system for teacher and student advancement.* Santa Monica, CA: Author.

National Policy Board for Educational Administration. (2015). *Professional standards for educational leaders, 2015.* Reston, VA: Author.

New Braunfels Indep. Sch. Dist. v. Armke, 658 S.W.2d 330 (Tex. App. 1983).

Norris v. Board of Educ., 797 F. Supp. 1452, 77 ed. Law Rep. 255, (S.D. Ind. 1992).

North Carolina Elementary & Secondary Statutes, N.C. Gen. Stat. §115C-288(a) (1955, 2005, 2017).

Olson, M. (2013). *Making the grade: Do Nebraska teachers and administrators working in public schools in 7th–12th grade settings agree about what constitutes sound grading practice?* (Unpublished doctoral dissertation). University of Nebraska, Lincoln, NE.

Owasso Ind. Sch. Dist. v. Falvo, 534 U.S. 426 (2002).

Page, E. B. (1958). Teacher comments and student performance: A seventy-four classroom experiment in school motivation. *Journal of Educational Psychology, 49*(2), 173–181.

Pardini, P. (1997). Report card reform. *School Administrator, 54*(11), 19–20, 22–25.

Parker, C. (1893). Examinations and promotions in elementary schools. *The Journal of Education, 37*(10), 154–156.

Patrick, C. M. (2015). *Educational stakeholders' perceptions during grading reform in one middle school* (Unpublished doctoral dissertation). Lindenwood University, St. Charles, MO.

Raymon v. Alvord Indep. School Dist., 639 F.2d 257 (1981).

Robbins, P., & Alvy, H. (2004). *The new principal's fieldbook: Strategies for success.* Alexandria, VA: ASCD.

Robertson, J. (1884). The circle of education methods. *Education Weekly, 2*(15), 4–6.

Schiffman, M. P. (2016). *Standards-based grading: Educators' perception of the effects on teaching, student motivation, and assessment at the high school level* (Unpublished doctoral dissertation). Western Illinois University, Macomb, IL.

Sebastian, J., & Allensworth, A. (2012). The influence of principal leadership on classroom instruction and student learning: A study of mediated pathways to learning. *Educational Administration Quarterly, 48*(4), 626–663.

Simmons v. Pittsburg Unified Sch. Dist., 2014 U.S. Dist. (N.D. Cal. June 11, 2014).

Smith v. Sch. City of Hobart, 811 F. Supp. 391, 397–98 (1993).

Starch, D., & Elliott, E. C. (1912). Reliability of the grading of high-school work in English. *School Review, 20,* 442–457.

Starch, D., & Elliott, E. C. (1913a). Reliability of grading work in mathematics. *School Review, 21,* 254–259.

Starch, D., & Elliott, E. C. (1913b). Reliability of grading work in history. *School Review, 21,* 676–681.

Stiggins, R. J. (1991). Assessment literacy. *Phi Delta Kappan, 7*(7), 534–539.

Stiggins, R. J. (2002). Assessment crisis: The absence of assessment *for* learning. *Phi Delta Kappan, 83*(10), 758–765.

Stiggins, R. J. (2008). *An introduction to student-involved assessment for learning* (5th ed.). Upper Saddle River, NJ: Merrill, Prentice Hall.

Tanner, D., & Tanner, L. (1987). *Supervision in education.* New York: Macmillan.

Tennessee Education Statutes. (2018). Rule 0520-01-03.05.

Tracy, S. (1995). How historical concepts of supervision relate to supervisory practices today. *The Clearing House, 68*(5), 320–324.

Wallace Foundation. (2013). *The school principal as leader: Guiding schools to better teaching and learning.* New York: Author.

Wetzel, W. (1929). Scientific supervision and curriculum building. *The School Review, 37*(2), 179–192.

Williams, A. E. (2014). *Teacher and administrator perceptions of standards-based report cards* (Unpublished doctoral dissertation). Widener University, Chester, PA.

Winship, A. E. (1898). Mr. Martin's great speech. *The Journal of Education, 48*(23), 388–389.

8

Grading in Higher Education

Jeffrey K. Smith and Lisa F. Smith

In 2004, Princeton University adopted a grading policy designed "to provide common grading standards across academic departments and to give students clear signals from their teachers about the difference between good work and their very best work" (Princeton University, 2014, p. 1). The policy recommended that departments cap the number of *A*s awarded at 35 percent. The decision was not well received. In 2014, Princeton abandoned those recommendations and returned its grading policy to the discretion of individual departments. The university's report on grading lamented that students had been misinterpreting the grading targets as quotas. But if only 35 percent could receive an *A,* or if 35 percent were set as a target for the maximum (or even typical) numbers of *A*s, it is difficult *not* to see that as a quota. Princeton is populated with students who have received *A*s all of their lives, so what does receiving an *A* there mean? Is it the same as an *A* at a local state college? What, exactly, is the nature of the communication of a given grade at any institution?

The Princeton report seeks to answer the questions that universities have struggled with over the past 100 years: What are grades? Why do we have them? How should they be constructed? What is the best grading system? Are grades reliable and valid? Do we suffer from grade inflation? Do grades influence learning? Do grades influence student evaluation of instructional quality? Most of these same questions also exist at the high school and probably at the elementary school level.

Why Is This Area of Research Important?

College-level grading practices and issues can inform our understanding of what happens in the K–12 sector. It would also be useful for K–12 educators to have a solid understanding of the kinds of grading practices their students will experience when they reach college. So we take a rather far-ranging and asymmetrical journey through the often irregular and inconsistent world of grading in university-level education. We will begin in lands far away, and then head to long ago, and finally end up with practices that occur in U.S. universities today, examining how they are similar to and different from grading practices in K–12 education.

What Significant Studies Have Been Conducted in This Area?

There has been substantial research conducted in grading in higher education, particularly regarding the relationship between grades and course evaluations. There has also been significant research on grade inflation, but less on differences among countries in grading or on the history of grading. Figure 8.1 (pp. 198–199) presents a summary of the more prominent research in the field to date.

What Questions Have Been Addressed in This Research?

We focus on four key issues in this chapter:

- Grading practices in other countries,
- The history of grading practices,
- Grade inflation, and
- The relationship between grading and course evaluations by students.

The first three issues correspond directly to the K–12 sector in education, and the fourth is probably becoming increasingly important, less in terms of students and course evaluations and more in terms of parental and community response to grading practices in schools. There has also been some work done on how professors generate the grades in their classes, but that work is not extensive.

What Have the Results of Those Studies Revealed?

In this section, we examine the studies listed in Figure 8.1 along with ancillary studies. We also explore some atypical sources to examine the questions under consideration, focusing on university websites to see what kinds of grading practices occur internationally.

University Grading Practices in Other Countries

Grading practices at the university level should not seem all that strange to educators. After all, as students we all went through university and experienced those practices, and if our stories to one another are any indicator, the practices were pretty much the same across the board. But that logic doesn't hold true if one ventures "across the pond." Let us take a long trip and end up on the other side of the globe, in our adopted homeland of New Zealand.

FIGURE 8.1 | **Grading in Higher Education**

Studies	Participants	Main Findings
Abrami, Dickens, Perry, & Leventhal (1980)	Over 400 students in two university introductory psychology courses	• Being assigned grades according to an artificially set standard did not influence student achievement but did have some effect on their rating of the quality of instruction.
Brumfield (2005)	419 institutions that belonged to a college registrars organization	• Almost all colleges gave grades, and there was wide variation in how they did so.
Centra & Creech (1976)	University teachers across over 9,000 courses	• Student ratings of course quality had a small (0.20) correlation with the grades that students expected to receive. There was low reliability in the ratings.
Collins & Nickel (1974)	Over 500 colleges and universities	• There was very little consistency in college grading practices, and a wide variety of atypical approaches to grading were used.
Feldman (1997)	A meta-analysis of 31 studies on course evaluations	• Correlations between the anticipated grade in the course and the course evaluation ranged between 0.10 and 0.30.
Ginexi (2003)	136 undergraduate students in a general psychology course	• The grades that students anticipated receiving were related to higher evaluations of the teacher and to comprehensibility of assigned readings, but not to any other question on the course evaluation survey.
Holmes (1972)	Roughly 100 students in an undergraduate psychology course	• Students who received grades that were unexpectedly lower than they had anticipated gave lower course evaluations than other students. The low grades were artificially manipulated in the study.
Jacoby (1910)	College astronomy professors	• There was very little disagreement on grades for five high-quality exams.
Kasten & Young (1983)	77 students in five different educational administration courses	• Students were randomly chosen to receive one of three different purposes for the course evaluation (personnel decision, instructor's personal use, or no purpose given). There were no differences in the ratings.
Kulick & Wright (2008)	400 students	• Achieving a normal distribution of test score results did not indicate that the test was effective or of high quality.

Lauterbach (1928)	Teachers grading handwritten and typed papers	• This early study resulted in mixed results regarding the reliability of grading student essay work.
Maurer (2006)	17 classes taught by the same instructor over time	• Students' expected grades were predictive of course evaluation, but the stated purpose of the course evaluation was not prediction.
Mayo (1970)	Students in an undergraduate measurement course	• Students rated the mastery learning approach more highly than merely reading material and attending lectures.
Nicolson (1917)	64 colleges supported by the Carnegie Foundation	• Most of the colleges utilized a five-point grading system (e.g., A–F).
Rojstaczer & Healy (2012)	A large number of previous studies on grade inflation	• Grade inflation was seen in the later 1960s and early 1970s due to the war in Vietnam, and again in the last 25 years due to a shift in attitude about students and a desire by faculty to get good course evaluations.
Salmons (1993)	Over 400 university students	• Students' evaluations of the quality of the course were related to whether they were anticipating a high or low grade.
Smith & Smith (2009)	Over 200 university students in an introductory-level course	• Students were randomly assigned to one of three different approaches to grading in the course. Students preferred an approach with many possible points over two 100-point based systems.
Starch & Elliott (1913)	College freshman English instructors	• Instructor disagreement was large, and largest for the two poorest papers. • Sources of variability in grades included variation between graders, difficulty in making judgments, and judgments that were too close to call.

Source: From "A Century of Grading Research: Meaning and Value in the Most Common Educational Measure," by S. M. Brookhart, T. R. Guskey, A. J. Bowers, J. H. McMillan, J. K. Smith, L. F. Smith, et al., 2016, *Review of Educational Research, 86*(4), pp. 803–848. Copyright 2016 by American Educational Research Association. Adapted with permission.

As university professors with quite a few years of experience when we arrived, we were shocked at the differences in grading practices and expectations. To begin, there are university policies on grading, and they are both elaborate and specific. In the United States, we often see grades assigned using one of two approaches that translate numbers (i.e., percentages) to letters. One system sets the scores as follows: 90–100 = *A,* 80–89 = *B,* 70–79 = *C,* 60–69 = *D,* and 59 and below = *F.* The other sets them as 93–100 = *A,* 85–92 = *B,* 77–84 = *C,* 70–76 = *D,* and 69 and below = *F.* Pluses and minuses are liberally sprinkled throughout. How one gets to those numbers also varies dramatically from one course to the next. Most professors are free to invent their own systems of grading, and a survey by Brumfield (2005) suggested that professors gladly take advantage of this freedom. Although the grading system will almost invariably be presented in the course syllabus (see Smith & Lipnevich, 2009), what will be included in that system, and how the results will be tallied, will be under the purview of the individual faculty member.

In contrast, almost all grading at the university level (in English-speaking countries outside the United States, "colleges" are typically high schools or residence halls at universities) is done with the same system. A score of 80 and above receives an *A* (80–84 is an *A–* and 90 and above is an *A+*), 65–79 = *B,* and 50–64 = *C.* A score below 50 is a fail, with there being two levels, *D* (40–49), and *F* (below 40). It may seem that this is an extremely lenient scale that would result in an inordinately large number of high grades, but that is not the case. In fact, grade inflation is not a problem. One of the reasons for this is that multiple-choice testing is rare in New Zealand courses and is seen mostly in courses taught by Americans. Essay examinations are the norm in most of the Commonwealth nations. Furthermore, grades are often discussed in departmental meetings, and adjustments are made by consensus for students with unique mitigating circumstances. This contrasts to the typical situation in the United States, where grades are the exclusive purview of the person teaching the course.

The History of Grading Practices in Higher Education

Depending upon how one defines grading, its roots can be traced hundreds or thousands of years back (if one wishes to include the Chinese civil service examinations; see Franke, 1960). Winter (1993) noted that a norm-referenced approach to grading was developed at Cambridge University in the 16th century using a straightforward approach of having 25 percent of the grades at the top, 50 percent in the middle, and 25 percent at the bottom. Across the Atlantic, and influenced by European models, U.S. universities invented a variety of systems for grading students, as well as developing rankings of them. A student's final standing in a course was often based on progress, conduct, attentiveness, effort, class attendance, and chapel attendance in addition to academic achievement (Cureton, 1971; Rugg, 1918; Schneider & Hutt, 2014). Grades were widely used in higher education at the turn of the 20th century, but they were arrived at rather haphazardly (Schneider & Hutt, 2014). This lack of consistency was, to a degree, brought to a head by the singular work of Starch and Elliott (1912, 1913), who showed that the lack of reliability in teacher grading was disconcerting in mathematics and staggering in English. Rugg (1918) detailed the pervasiveness of the problem and called for a complete revision of how grading was done, with a focus on making it more scientific.

The time was ripe for a different approach to the assignment of grades. Into the void stepped the new science of statistics, with its passion for quantifying every imaginable human characteristic (Pearson, 1930). To the modern eye, it can be difficult to understand the logic of the times. The scholars working on the issue of grading did not question that students would be normally distributed along some scale of performance—that was simply a scientific reality. If one were to be scientific about grading students, this assumption was simply given. Understand that Francis Galton, the pioneer of the new field of statistics, was the cousin of Charles Darwin. Humans were a species and subject to the same laws of nature as Darwin's finches. Rugg (1918) argued:

> Now the term inherited capacity practically defines itself. By it
> we mean the "start in life"; the sum total of nervous possibilities
> which the infant has at birth and to which, therefore, nothing that

the individual himself can do will contribute in any way whatso-
ever. (p. 706)

The issue at hand was not how to fairly reward students for their
learning, but how to realize the normal distribution, and how not to
give a false sense of precision in the scale that was developed (Galton & Galton, 1998). A scale running from 0 to 100 yielded far too
many scores; it was agreed that the measurements were simply not
that precise. Instead, Rugg (1918) argued for transforming numeri-
cal scores into an *A–F* system or a similar approach. (Note that in the
United Kingdom, a "mark" is a score that runs from 0 to 100 and a
"grade" runs from *A* to *F.*)

The question then became how to transform marks into grades.
And that was the problem at Princeton described in the beginning
of this chapter, and which persists today across all levels. We prefer
to employ a criterion-referenced approach to assigning those marks,
whereas in the previous century, reference to the normal distribution was preferred (Brookhart et al., 2016).

Meyer (1908) argued for three broad categories of grades,
with further subdivisions at the two extremes. He started with the
notion of a high group that consisted of 25 percent of the students,
a medium group of 50 percent of the students, and a low group of 25
percent of the students. He believed that a further differentiation
could be found in both the high and the low groups. He argued that
3 percent should receive *excellent,* 22 percent *superior,* 50 percent
medium, 22 percent *inferior,* and 3 percent *failures.* In one of his
more interesting contentions, he held that any student selected at
random from a class was as likely as not to be in the middle group,
so that group should contain 50 percent of the students. Where
he came up with the notion that the middle group should contain
50 percent is not explained. It is interesting to note that the terms
chosen by Meyer for the middle three grades are fundamentally
norm-referenced in nature, whereas the two extreme grades receive

criterion-referenced terms: *superior, medium,* and *inferior* all imply a comparison to others, whereas *excellent* and *failure* do not.

Early research suggests that grades should simply be a method for ranking students, not necessarily for making decisions based on those grades (see Meyer, 1908; Rugg, 1918). Although Meyer argued that 3 percent should fail a typical course (and he fears that people would see this as too lenient), he was less certain about what to do with the "inferior" group, stating that grades should solely represent a student's rank in the class. Roughly 100 years ago, these researchers were attempting to bring what they believed was science to the task of grading, and to ensure that the precision of the ranking system developed did not result in an inappropriate sense of how accurately students could be measured. There was little to no concern about how this system might affect student performance, sense of self-efficacy, or motivation.

Hindsight is an exact science, but in looking back at these practices, they certainly seem to be harsh. To only have 3 percent *A*s in a class seems stingy, not to mention engendering competition among students for those *A*s. Early scholars believed that the proper approach to grading was to generate final marks for students on a 0–100 scale, then to rank-order students on that scale, and then transform the ranking into an *A–F* categorization using a fixed percentage of *A*s, *B*s, *C*s, and *F*s. The motivation was not so much to make sure that not too many *A*s were being given out as to try to reflect performance in the course in a norm-referenced fashion (Guskey, 2000; Kulick & Wright, 2008). And in fact, in a normal distribution, the central 50 percent of the scores tend not to be all that far apart from one another, whereas scores at the extremes are further apart. Thus, the top 3 percent are typically well ahead of the next grouping of 22 percent. Whether having students in competition for grades is justifiable remains in question.

The takeaway here is that historically, the challenge to grading was seen as basically twofold: how to get a set of grades that were representative of ability and that produced the normal curve that the science of the time predicted would occur, and how to transform those scores into a smaller set of categorizations so that a false sense of precision was not communicated. Although one would hope that we are still concerned with grades reflecting course achievement, our focus has shifted far from reproducing a normal curve or worrying about how many levels of grades should exist.

Grade Inflation in Higher Education

For the first half of the 20th century, the discussion presented above represented the dominant approach to university-level grading. This picture changed dramatically in the 1960s. Perhaps the biggest influence on university-level grading was the war in Vietnam (Rojstaczer & Healy, 2012). Male college students could get a four-year military draft deferment if they were students in good standing; if they failed out of college, they immediately became eligible for the draft. This placed university-level instructors in a difficult situation. Failing a student had real consequence. Even awarding a B− versus a C+ could mean that an overall grade point average could be high enough for a student to stay in school. And so, grades increased; some would argue that they inflated.

A second influence was two-pronged. The first prong was a shift in thinking about what educators wanted to achieve in their classes and how they might go about doing that. The work of Benjamin Bloom on mastery learning theory led this change in thinking (Bloom, 1971; Mayo, 1970). The second prong was Glaser's (1963) revolutionary notion of the difference between norm-referenced testing and criterion-referenced testing. Glaser argued that we have two options in trying to make sense out of a test score. We can relate it either to how well other students in the class performed (or the country, if a standardized national test), or to some standard level of expected performance. The first would be referring the score to a norming group, and the second would be referring the score to a standard. For example, a score of 73 on a test may be the highest (or lowest) score in a class. By knowing where it sits in the class overall, the student gets a sense of how well he or she did. If a student's score on a national standardized measure is in the 83rd percentile, the student also knows how good a score that was in comparison to others who took the same measure. Those are both examples of norm referencing.

The second approach to making sense out of a score is to refer it to a standard or criterion. The driver's license examination is a good example of a criterion-referenced test. It doesn't matter how well anybody else did; if your mark is above a certain level, you pass. Another example is using a rubric to mark an essay. A-level performance is determined by teacher expectations, and all students who meet the rubric criteria for an A receive one.

Combining Glaser's (1963) notion of norm-referenced versus criterion-referenced marking, Scriven's (1967) idea of formative and summative evaluation, and Carroll's (1963) model of school learning, Bloom (1971) developed an approach to instruction that believed all (or nearly all) students could learn what only the best students were currently learning (see Guskey, 1997, for a good explication of the mastery learning approach). This approach fit the tenor of the times exceptionally well. Even though mastery learning was probably adopted more overseas than in the United States, Bloom's underlying argument that we should strive to have as many of our students as possible achieve at a high level gained wide acceptance throughout education.

After the war in Vietnam ended, grades appear to have declined somewhat, but that trend then reversed again, and the past 25 years has seen a dramatic increase in grades once more (Rojstaczer & Healy, 2012). Whether this is due to colleges vying for students, faculty vying for good course evaluations (Love & Kotchen, 2010), or just some natural sort of inflation is hard to determine.

This leads us back to where this section started: should Princeton limit the *A*s handed out to a "target" of 35 percent? Certainly Meyer (1908) would be offended, as he thought 3 percent was plenty. But the 35 percent approach brings up two critical issues for consideration. First, fundamentally, how is 35 percent different from 3 percent? If we do not want to consign 97 percent of the class to having no chance for an *A*, then how much better is it of us to only want to consign 65 percent to not having a chance at an *A*? Although an old joke in the measurement community is "Scratch a criterion and you'll discover a norm," should we not set standards and let all students compete for them? Should grades at Princeton perhaps not be higher than the norm? These are some of the very best students in the world, ones who have had amazing success at the secondary level. Why should it surprise us that many perform at a level that even Meyer would consider to be "excellent"?

This is, we think, an issue not in danger of imminent resolution. It is good for the debate and the research that enhances it to continue. For excellent reviews of the history of grading in the United States, we recommend the Cureton (1971) and Schneider and Hutt (2014) articles.

Grading and Course Evaluation in Higher Education

In higher education, student course evaluations are the primary mechanism through which the quality of professors' teaching is assessed. Although other approaches are sometimes used, such as observations by other faculty, the end-of-course student evaluation is still pretty much the gold standard in higher education assessment of instructional quality. In many institutions of higher education, student course evaluations are a serious component of promotion considerations. (For good general discussions of course evaluation in higher education, see Centra, 1993; McKeachie, 1979; Marsh, 1987; or Spooren, Brockx, & Mortelmans, 2013.) Given that student course evaluations *do* play a role in promotion, faculty are naturally concerned about how to receive strong evaluations. It has long been suspected that the easiest route to high course evaluations is to give high grades (Abrami, Dickens, Perry, & Leventhal, 1980; Holmes, 1972). This would be the higher education version of "one hand washes the other." It is sometimes referred to in the research literature as the grade-leniency theory (Love & Kotchen, 2010; McKenzie, 1975) and is so prevalent in faculty lounges across the United States that it is rarely questioned (Ginexi, 2003; Marsh, 1987; Salmons, 1993). But is the conventional wisdom on the relationship between grades and course evaluations backed up by rigorous research? Is there a relationship between the two, and if so, how strong is it?

Before looking at the literature on the strength of the relationship, we might ask why such a relationship should exist in the first place. There are two popular hypotheses that have been argued for here. One is salaciously called "the revenge theory." Ginexi (2003) posited that students who feel that they are going to get a low grade can "get back" at the professor by giving a low course evaluation. It is an idea with some intuitive appeal. Maurer (2006) argued that the revenge theory is particularly popular among faculty members who do not receive high course evaluations. Ginexi (2003) also proposed the cognitive dissonance hypothesis. The argument here is that if a student feels he or she is going to get a low grade, then two attributions for that low grade are possible. The first is that the student either is not very good at the subject matter or did not work hard. This attribution places the locus of responsibility on the student. The alternative is that the course was not well taught or that the professor held some animus toward the student. If the fault lies with the faculty member, it follows that a student would think a low course evaluation is justified. Research by Maurer (2006) and Kasten and Young (1983) found little support for the revenge theory and argued that the cognitive dissonance model provided a stronger explanation of the relationship between grades and course evaluations.

But does that relationship even exist? Two meta-analyses found that the correlation between anticipated course grades and course evaluations are on the order of 0.10 to 0.30 (Centra & Creech, 1976; Feldman, 1997). This means that the percentage of variance in course evaluations that can be attributed to anticipated grades is something on the order of 1 percent to 10 percent. In nonstatistical terms, anticipated grades didn't really influence student evaluations of course quality much, and may simply reflect a student's honest assessment (Smith & Smith, 2009).

What Are the Implications of These Research Findings for Improvement in Grading Policy and Practice?

The purpose of grading and the assumptions that underlie it have changed over the past century. This causes us to think about the purpose behind our grading practices today. Is it worthwhile to seriously question why we grade the way we do and what an optimal approach to grading would be? Are our current grading practices aligned to our educational goals? Consider Bloom's (1971) mastery learning approach. Bloom argued that almost all children could achieve at a very high level if we changed our approach to instruction. Whether this is possible is one question, but we might also ask, "Would we be happy with a system of grading/instruction that regularly gave 95 percent *A*s?" Such a system would make grades almost useless for determining differentially how well students were doing. If 95 percent are earning *A*s, would we then think that our standards are too low? There are no correct answers here (that we know of), only a need for serious discussions about grading approaches, expectations, and communications with parents and students.

Grade inflation clearly exists in the university educational sector. But does it also exist in K–12 education, and if so, is it causing any harm? Although grade inflation is greatly lamented in higher education, there is little evidence that it is doing harm. If grades are increasing because students are achieving more than they used to, then most would conclude that there is no problem here. But if grades are increasing because it is easier to give high grades rather than low ones, or if teachers are overeager to please students (and parents), then maybe there is a problem. As our approach to assessment in education moves from summative to formative, two things can be expected: one is that students will learn more, and the other is that the nature of the relationship between assessment and grading may change. A stronger focus on formative assessment in the classroom changes the nature of summative assessment and grading (Guskey, 2000). The role of the teacher as advocate (as reflected by formative assessment) and the role of the teacher as judge (as reflected by summative assessment) stand in opposition to one another and require thoughtful reconciliation on the part of the teacher.

Given that grade inflation exists in higher education and that higher grades do not seem to be strongly related to course evaluations, is any concern over grade inflation justified? It seems to us that it probably is. It would be easy to say that one should simply set standards and stick to them, but that is easier said than done. To begin, students and parents have a right to know what the basis is for grading and receive assurance that the grading system is valid and fair. So validity and fairness should be the first stop in looking at grading systems (see Guskey, 2008). Then, it is critical to make sure that the system for grading has been fully and clearly communicated to students and parents (Smith, Smith, & De Lisi, 2001). Unless the grading system is understood, it is not possible for students to take responsibility for their grades. After all, grades are not teachers' to give; they are students' to earn.

Grades and grading will probably always be a source of concern and some level of anxiety for students and teachers alike. But perhaps it's worth looking the tiger in the eye, addressing our fears, and thinking hard about whether we have the right approach to grading at all levels of education. Perhaps we do; but perhaps we can improve. We should not be afraid to question our practice and look for a potentially more fruitful approach.

References

Abrami, P. C., Dickens, W. J., Perry, R. P., & Leventhal, L. (1980). Do teacher standards for assigning grades affect student evaluations of instruction? *Journal of Educational Psychology, 72,* 107–118.

Bloom, B. S. (1971). *Mastery learning: Theory and practice.* New York: Holt, Rinehart, & Winston.

Brookhart, S. M., Guskey, T. R., Bowers, A. J., McMillan, J. H., Smith, J. K., Smith, L. F., et al. (2016). A century of grading research: Meaning and value in the most common educational measure. *Review of Educational Research, 86,* 803–848.

Brumfield, C. (2005). *Current trends in grades and grading practices in higher education: Results of the 2004 AACRAO survey.* Retrieved from ERIC database. (ED489795)

Carroll, J. (1963). A model of school learning. *Teachers College Record, 64,* 723–733.

Centra, J. A. (1993). *Reflective faculty evaluation.* San Francisco: Jossey-Bass.

Centra, J. A., & Creech, F. R. (1976). The relationship between students, teachers, and course characteristics and student ratings of teacher effectiveness. *New Directions for Teaching and Learning, 43.*

Collins, J. R., & Nickel, K. N. (1974). *A study of grading practices in institutions of higher education.* Retrieved from ERIC database. (ED097846)

Cureton, L. W. (1971). *The history of grading practices.* NCME measurement in education: A series of special reports of the National Council on Measurement in Education. East Lansing, MI: National Council on Measurement in Education.

European Commission. (2009). *ECTS user's guide.* Luxembourg: Office for Official Publications of the European Communities.

Feldman, K. A. (1997). Identifying exemplary teachers and teaching: Evidence from student ratings. In R. P. Perry & J. C. Smart (Eds.), *Effective teaching in higher education: Research and practice* (pp. 93–143). New York: Agathon Press.

Franke, W. (1960). The reform and abolition of the traditional Chinese examination system. *Chinese Economic and Political Studies. Special Series.* Cambridge, MA: East Asian Research Center.

Galton, D. J., & Galton, C. J. (1998). Francis Galton and eugenics today. *Journal of Medical Ethics, 24,* 99–105.

Ginexi, E. M. (2003). General psychology course evaluations: Differential survey response by expected grade. *Teaching of Psychology, 30,* 248–251.

Glaser, R. (1963). Instructional technology and the measurement of learning outcomes: Some questions. *American Psychologist, 18*(8), 51.

Guskey, T. R. (1997). *Implementing mastery learning* (2nd ed.). Belmont, CA: Wadsworth.

Guskey, T. R. (2000). Grading policies that work against standards... and how to fix them. *IASSP Bulletin, 84*(620), 20–29.

Guskey, T. R. (Ed.). (2008). *Practical solutions for serious problems in standards-based grading.* Thousand Oaks, CA: Corwin.

Holmes, D. S. (1972). Effects of grades and disconfirmed grade expectancies on students' evaluations of their instructor. *Journal of Educational Psychology, 63,* 130–133.

Hughes, P. (1913). College marking systems. *Journal of Educational Psychology,* 4, 298–299.

Jacoby, H. (1910). Note on the marking system in the astronomical course at Columbia College, 1909–1910. *Science, 31*(804), 819–820. doi:10.1126/science.31.804.819

Kasten, K. L., & Young, I. P. (1983). Bias and the intended use of student evaluations of university faculty. *Instructional Science, 12,* 161–169.

Kulick, G., & Wright, R. (2008). The impact of grading on the curve: A simulation analysis. *International Journal for the Scholarship of Teaching and Learning, 2*(2), 5.

Lauterbach, C. E. (1928). Some factors affecting teachers' marks. *Journal of Educational Psychology, 19,* 266–271.

Love, D. A., & Kotchen, M. J. (2010). Grades, course evaluations, and academic incentives. *Eastern Economic Journal, 36,* 151–163.

Marsh, H. W. (1984). Students' evaluations of university teaching: Dimensionality, reliability, validity, potential biases, and utility. *Journal of Educational Psychology, 76*(5), 707.

Marsh, H. W. (1987). Students' evaluations of university teaching: Research findings, methodological issues, and directions for future research. *International Journal of Educational Research, 11,* 253–288.

Maurer, T. W. (2006). Cognitive dissonance or revenge? Student grades and course evaluations. *Teaching of Psychology, 33*(3), 176–179.

Mayo, S. T. (1970). *Trends in the teaching of the first course in measurement.* Paper presented at the National Council on Measurement in Education symposium, Chicago. Retrieved from ERIC database. (ED047007)

McKeachie, W. J. (1979). Student ratings of faculty: A reprise. *Academe, 65,* 384–397.

McKeachie, W. J. (1997). Student ratings: Validity of use. *American Psychologist, 52,* 1218–1225.

McKenzie, R. B. (1975). The economic effects of grade inflation on instructor evaluations: A theoretical approach. *Journal of Economic Education, 6*(2), 99–105.

Meyer, M. (1908). The grading of students. *Science, 28,* 243–252.

Nicolson, F. W. (1917). Standardizing the marking system. *Educational Review, 54,* 225–237.

Nuffic. (2013). *Grading systems in the Netherlands, the United States, and the United Kingdom.* The Hague, Netherlands: Netherlands Organisation for International Cooperation in Higher Education.

Pearson, K. (1930). *Life of Francis Galton.* London: Cambridge University Press.

Princeton University. (2014). *Report from the Ad Hoc Committee to Review Policies Regarding Assessment and Grading.* Princeton, NJ: Author.

Rojstaczer, S., & Healy, C. (2012). Where *A* is ordinary: The evolution of American college and university grading, 1940–2009. *Teachers College Record, 114*(7), 1–23.

Rugg, H. O. (1918). Teachers' marks and the reconstruction of the marking system. *Elementary School Journal, 18,* 701–719.

Salmons, S. D. (1993). The relationship between students' grades and their evaluation of instructor performance. *Applied H.R.M. Research, 4,* 102–114.

Schneider, J., & Hutt, E. (2014). Making the grade: A history of the *A–F* marking scheme. *Journal of Curriculum Studies, 46*(2), 201–224. doi: 10.1080/00220272.2013.790480.

Scriven, M. (1967). The methodology of evaluation. In R. E. Stake (Ed.), *AERA monograph series on curriculum evaluation.* Chicago: Rand McNally.

Smallwood, M. L. (1935). An historical study of examinations and grading systems in early American universities. *Harvard Studies in Evaluation, Vol. 24.* Cambridge, MA: Harvard University Press.

Smith, A. G. (1911). A rational college marking system. *Journal of Educational Psychology, 2,* 383–393.

Smith, J. K., & Lipnevich, A. A. (2009). Formative assessment in higher education: Frequency and consequence. In D. M. McInerney, G. T. L. Brown, & G. A. D. Liem (Eds.), *Student perspectives on assessment: What students can tell us about assessment for learning* (pp. 279–296). Charlotte, NC: Information Age.

Smith, J. K., & Smith, L. F. (2009). The impact of framing effect on student preferences for university grading systems. *Studies in Educational Evaluation, 35*(4), 160–167.

Smith, J. K., Smith, L. F., & De Lisi, R. (2001). *Natural classroom assessment.* Thousand Oaks, CA: Corwin.

Spooren, P., Brockx, B., & Mortelmans, D. (2013). On the validity of student evaluation of teaching: The state of the art. *Review of Educational Research, 83,* 598–642.

Starch, D., & Elliott, E. (1912). Reliability of the grading of high school work in English. *School Review, 21,* 254–295.

Starch, D., & Elliott, E. C. (1913). Reliability of grading work in mathematics. *School Review, 21,* 254–259.

Winter, R. (1993). Education or grading? Arguments for a non-subdivided honours degree. *Studies in Higher Education, 18,* 363–377.

Conclusion: Where Do We Go from Here?

Thomas R. Guskey and Susan M. Brookhart

In this book, we reviewed and summarized the extensive knowledge base on grading and reporting student learning that has been accumulated over the past century. We now come to some crucial questions: What should we do with it? How can we use this vast body of research evidence? Specifically, where do we go from here?

It is easy to be overwhelmed by this massive collection of evidence. In approaching the task of reviewing and summarizing all these investigations, we recognized it was too much for one or two people to take on. That is why we assembled a team of distinguished scholars to synthesize the areas of research described in each chapter. In reading their work, you undoubtedly realized the enormity of the undertaking, how thoughtfully they approached the challenge, and how brilliantly they accomplished the task. Now we turn to the implications of their summaries for better practice.

Several themes emerged as we examined these distinguished scholars' reviews and summaries. Some of these themes confirm ideas that have been generated in reviews of other aspects of teaching and learning, particularly those associated with curriculum development and assessment practice. Other emerging themes are unique to aspects of grading and reporting. In every instance, however, these themes offer insights that can guide efforts to implement more effective grading and reporting policies and practice.

In this Conclusion, we describe these emerging themes along with their implications for practice. Our descriptions, however, are not meant to be conclusions. Rather, they represent starting points. We hope our discussion of these themes serves to deepen your understanding of each author's ideas. More important, we hope your reading and examination will lead you to see other themes that are just as significant and just as meaningful. We hope you will add your themes to this list and use them in your work to implement better grading policies and practice.

Start with Clear Learning Goals

Recall that in the Introduction we defined "grades" as "the symbols assigned to individual pieces of student work or to composite measures of student performance created for report cards and other summary documents." We added, "Grades can be letters, numbers, figures, or any set of descriptors that designate different levels of performance." For grades to be accurate descriptors of student performance, however, we must first be clear about what performance is being described. The reviews in Chapters 1, 2, and 8 show that the meaning of grades historically has not been clear, and that has led to difficulties. Grades cannot be interpretable until those who use them understand what they are intended to mean. Specifically, we must begin with clearly articulated student learning goals. Chapter 6 emphasizes this point, reminding us that we always must begin by describing clear learning goals for all students.

The premise of accurate and meaningful grading, similar to the basis of effective teaching and learning in any context, is congruence among the major elements of the teaching and learning process: *curriculum, instruction, assessment,* and *grading.* In other words, these four basic elements must be aligned and consistent, each building on the others. The first step in that process is the articulation of clear learning goals that identify what students should learn (content) and be able to do (cognitive behaviors or processes).

Effective learning goals *must* include both of these components. To separate "content goals" from "process goals" is not only a fool's errand—it's inaccurate and erroneous. Students *must* be able to do something with the content. At the simplest level, they may be expected only to know or recall what they learned. At a more complex level, we might expect students to apply what they learned in new or different contexts, transfer skills to new problems or situations, or synthesize ideas and concepts to develop new insights and understandings. Similarly, process skills *must* be performed in relation to content. As Gardner (2006) makes clear, "You can't think out of the box until you have a box" (p. 86). Student learning goals that specify components of both content and process must be developed and then shared with everyone involved: students, families, teachers, school leaders, and community members.

Clear learning goals bring meaning to discussions about curriculum rigor, college and career readiness, and global citizenship. They clarify the difference between memorizing factual information and developing enduring understandings. An emphasis on "essential questions" or "power standards" similarly shifts the focus to deeper, more complex, and higher-level cognitive skills (Guskey, 2016). The key issue with regard to grading and reporting is that clearly articulated learning goals must come first. They provide the foundation from which descriptions of student performance build and derive meaning.

The Importance of Appropriate Feedback

We know that grades are not essential to the instructional process. Teachers can teach many things very well without grades. In addition, students can and do learn many things very well without grades (Brookhart, 1993; Guskey, 1994, 1996). Nevertheless, grades can serve to enhance both teaching and learning if we focus on their use as feedback (formative) rather than as evaluative judgments (summative), especially early in a grading period or academic term. The review in Chapter 4 shows that most teachers intend grades to provide feedback to students on their learning.

Students do need regular and specific feedback on their learning progress in order to improve. This feedback lets students know how well they are doing in mastering identified learning goals and what should be their next steps on the path to mastery (Hattie & Timperley, 2007). Teachers typically gather information to offer this feedback through formative classroom assessments. These assessments can take any form, from short quizzes and compositions to demonstrations or performance. Scores derived from these formative classroom assessments are meaningless, however, unless related to some estimate or judgment of the quality of students' performance. Specifically, students need to know how their performance compares to what was expected, and what next steps need to be taken to reach mastery.

In essence, grades are really nothing more than labels attached to different levels of student performance. They identify how well students performed and answer the question students always ask: "How am I doing?" These labels can be letters, numbers, words, or symbols. They serve important formative purposes by helping students know where they are in meeting particular learning goals. When paired with individualized guidance and direction for improvement, they also help direct learning progress.

To serve this formative purpose, however, two essential consequences of grades must be changed. First, we must help students and their parents understand that grades do not reflect *who* you are as a learner, but *where* you are in your learning journey—and *where* is always temporary (Guskey, 2017). Knowing where you are is essential to improvement. Informed judgments from teachers about the quality of students' performance can help students become more thoughtful judges of their own work. Granted, a grade, number, or symbol offers only a shorthand description of where students are, and additional information is essential to direct progress. But when accompanied by guidance on how to do better, it provides the basis for improvement.

Second, we must never use grades to sort, select, or rank students. Too often, grades represent a student's relative standing among classmates. In most schools, grades provide the basis for determining class rank and selecting the class valedictorian. When used for these sorting and ranking purposes, students see grades as scarce rewards offered to a select few rather than as recognition of learning success attainable by all. Doing well does not mean learning excellently; it means outdoing your classmates. Helping others is discouraged, because for one student to move up in rank, another student must move down (Guskey, 2014).

Students need honest information from their teachers about the quality and adequacy of their performance in school. Parents need to know how well their children are doing and whether or not grade-level or course expectations are being met. Although grades should never be the only information about learning that students and parents receive, they can be a meaningful part of that information. When combined with guidance to students and parents on how improvements can be made, grades can become a valuable tool in facilitating students' learning success.

Accuracy and the Number of Grade Categories

The accuracy of any measure depends on the precision of the measurement instrument. A sophisticated stopwatch, for example, can very accurately measure the time an individual takes to run a 100-meter race. The instruments we use to measure student learning, however, are far less accurate and precise, as the review in Chapter 1 showed.

Measurement experts identify precision by calculating the *standard error of measurement*. This statistic describes the amount by which a measure might vary from one occasion to the next, using the same device to measure the same trait. For example, suppose the standard error on a 20-item assessment of student learning is plus or minus two items. This indicates that over multiple administrations of the assessment, the same student might get one or two more items right or wrong, simply due to imprecision in the measurement instrument (i.e., the assessment). That may not seem like much, but using a percentage grading scale with 100 distinct categories of student performance, that would be a range of 20 percentage points—a difference in most cases of at least two letter grades.

Many educators assume that because the percentage grading scale has 100 classification levels—or categories—it is more precise than a scale with just a few levels (such as *excellent, satisfactory*, and *poor*). But in the absence of a truly accurate measuring device, adding more gradations to the measurement scale offers only the illusion of precision.

When students are assigned to grade categories, classification accuracy is the most important aspect of reliability. Setting more cutoff boundaries (levels or categories) in a distribution of scores means that more cases will be vulnerable to fluctuations across those boundaries and, hence, to more error (Dwyer, 1996). A student is statistically much more likely to be misclassified as performing at the 85 percent level when his true achievement is at the 90 percent level (a difference of five percentage categories) than he is of being misclassified as scoring at a *satisfactory* level when his true achievement is at an *excellent* level. In other words, with more levels, more students are likely to be misclassified in terms of their performance on a particular assessment.

Overall, the large number of grade categories in the percentage grading scale and the fine discrimination required in determining the differences among categories allow for the greater influence of subjectivity, more error, and diminished reliability. The increased precision of percentage grades is truly far more imaginary than real. When well constructed, grading scales with fewer categories that describe clearly distinct levels of student mastery or proficiency are not only more reliable, but also offer students better information to guide improvements.

Multiple Grades Clarify Meaning and Accuracy

Combining disparate measures into a single, overall score or grade rarely yields anything useful or meaningful. We have frequently offered the example of combining measures of height, weight, diet, and exercise into a single number or grade to represent a person's physical condition. Most would consider this absurd. They would wonder how anyone would think the combination of such diverse measures (that is, scales of inches, pounds, calorie intake per day, and number of minutes of exercise per day) yielded anything meaningful. Yet every day, teachers combine equally diverse measures of students' performance in school into a "hodgepodge grade" (Brookhart, 1991, p. 36) that is just as confounded and impossible to interpret as a physical condition grade that combines height, weight, diet, and exercise—and no one questions it (Guskey, 2013). The reviews in Chapters 3 and 4 show how different teachers use different combinations, based on their own ideas of what particular measures a grade should reflect.

Every marking period, teachers gather evidence on students' performance from scores attained on major examinations, compositions, and classroom quizzes. They record data on students' homework completion, class participation, and punctuality in turning in assignments. Some teachers gather additional information on students' behavior in class, collaboration with classmates, respect, and effort. They then enter these data into a computer grading program that calculates a single number or grade that is recorded on a report card.

A more useful and meaningful description of students' performance includes multiple grades. At a minimum, it provides grades that distinguish *product, process,* and *progress* learning criteria (Guskey, 1996). The reviews in Chapters 5 and 7 show that much work needs to be done in order for teachers and administrators to embrace this concept and learn to do it well. However, when such reforms are made, the outcome is usually more clarity about both the grading process and the meaning of grades.

Product criteria reflect how well students have achieved specific learning goals, standards, or competencies. These might be determined by students' performance on major examinations, compositions, projects, reports, or other culminating demonstrations of learning. Product criteria describe students' academic achievements—that is, what they have learned and are able to do because of their experiences in school.

Process criteria describe student behaviors that facilitate or broaden learning. These may be things that *enable* learning, such as formative assessments, homework, and class participation. They also may reflect *extended learning* goals related to collaboration, responsibility, communication, perseverance, habits of mind, or citizenship. In some cases, process criteria relate to students' *compliance* with class procedures, like turning in assignments on time or not interrupting during class discussions.

Progress criteria show how much students have gained or improved. Sometimes these are referred to as "value-added" criteria. Although related to product criteria, progress criteria are distinct. It would be possible, for example, for students to make outstanding progress but still not be meeting course academic goals or achieving at grade level. It also would be possible for highly skilled and talented students to show they have achieved the product criteria without making notable progress or improvement.

Although these types of learning criteria vary in their importance depending on the subject area and grade level, all three are essential to school success. Meaningful communication about that success, however, requires that they be reported separately. In other words, students must receive different grades for whatever product, process, and progress criteria are considered most important in their learning.

Ironically, reporting multiple grades for these different criteria does not require extra work for teachers. In fact, it's less work. Teachers already gather evidence on different product, process, and progress criteria. They keep detailed records of students' scores on various measures of achievement, as well as formative assessment results, homework completion, class participation, collaboration in teamwork, and so on. By simply reporting separate grades for these different aspects of learning, teachers avoid the dilemmas involved in determining how much each should be weighted in calculating a single grade.

Reporting multiple grades on the report card and on the transcript further emphasizes to students that these different aspects of their performance are all important. Parents gain advantages because the report card now provides a more detailed and comprehensive picture of their child's performance in school. In addition, because product grades are no longer tainted by evidence based on students' behavior or compliance, those grades more closely align with external measures of achievement and content mastery, such as AP exam results and ACT or SAT scores—a quality that college and university admissions officers have been shown to favor.

The biggest challenge for teachers and school leaders rests in determining what particular product, process, and progress criteria to report. This requires deep thinking about the learning criteria that are most important to students' success in school and beyond.

From a practical perspective, it also involves finding an acceptable balance between providing enough detail to be meaningful but not so exhaustive that it creates a bookkeeping burden for teachers.

Summary

Grading and reporting are much more a challenge in effective communication than simply a task of tallying data on students' performance. Starting with clear learning goals, focusing on the important feedback function of grades, limiting the number of grade categories, and providing multiple grades that reflect product, process, and progress criteria will greatly enhance the meaning and accuracy of that communication. These strategies arise from a century of research on grading. All focus on helping grades reflect more meaningful information about students' learning and, therefore, are more useful to students, parents, and educators interested in ensuring learning success. Without adding to the workload of teachers, these simple strategies can do much to improve the effectiveness of grading and reporting. They guide teachers in providing more meaningful information, facilitate communication between school and home, and offer specific direction in efforts to improve students' learning.

References

Brookhart, S. M. (1991). Grading practices and validity. *Educational Measurement: Issues and Practice, 10*(1), 35–36.

Brookhart, S. M. (1993). Teachers' grading practices: Meaning and values. *Journal of Educational Measurement, 30*(2), 123–142.

Dwyer, C. A. (1996). Cut scores and testing: Statistics, judgment, truth, and error. *Psychological Assessment, 8*(4), 360–362.

Gardner, H. (2006). *Five minds for the future.* Cambridge, MA: Harvard University Press.

Guskey, T. R. (1994). Making the grade: What benefits students. *Educational Leadership, 52*(2), 14–20.

Guskey, T. R. (1996). Reporting on student learning: Lessons from the past—Prescriptions for the future. In T. R. Guskey (Ed.), *Communicating student learning: 1996 yearbook of the Association for Supervision and Curriculum Development* (pp. 13–24). Alexandria, VA: ASCD.

Guskey, T. R. (2013). The case against percentage grades. *Educational Leadership, 71*(1), 68–72.

Guskey, T. R. (2014). Class rank weighs down true learning. *Phi Delta Kappan, 95*(6), 15–19.

Guskey, T. R. (2016, October 14). Standards-based learning: Why do educators make it so complex? [Blog post]. *Education Week Blog.* Retrieved from http://blogs.edweek.org/edweek/finding_common_ground/2016/10/standards-based_learning_why_do_educators_make_it_so_complex.html

Guskey, T. R. (2017, September 10). Don't get rid of grades. Change their meaning & consequences! [Blog post]. *Education Week Blog.* Retrieved from http://blogs.edweek.org/edweek/leadership_360/2017/09/dont_get_rid_of_grades_change_their_meaning_and_consequences.html

Guskey, T. R. (2018, February 4). Multiple grades: The first step to improving grading and reporting. [Blog post]. *Education Week Blog.* Retrieved from http://blogs.edweek.org/edweek/leadership_360/2018/02/multiple_grades_the_first_step_to_improving_grading_and_reporting.html

Hattie, J., & Timperley, H. (2007). The power of feedback. *Review of Educational Research, 77*(1), 81–112.

Index

Note: Page references followed by an italicized *f* indicate information contained in figures.

About the Authors

 **Dr. Thomas R. Guskey** is senior research scholar at the University of Louisville and professor emeritus in the College of Education at the University of Kentucky. A graduate of the University of Chicago, he began his career in education as a middle school teacher and school administrator in Chicago Public Schools. He later became the first director of the Center for the Improvement of Teaching and Learning, a national educational research center. Dr. Guskey served on the National Commission on Teaching & America's Future and the task force to develop National Standards for Staff Development, has been named a fellow in the American Educational Research Association (AERA)—the association's highest honor—and was awarded AERA's prestigious Relating Research to Practice Award. He was also named the 2010 Jason Millman Scholar by the Consortium for Research on Educational Assessment and Teaching Effectiveness (CREATE). He is author or editor of 24 award-winning books and more than 250 book chapters and articles. His most recent books include *On Your Mark: Challenging the Conventions of Grading and Reporting* (2015); *Reaching the Highest Standard in Professional Learning: Data* (with Roy & Von Frank, 2014); *Answers to Essential Questions About Standards, Assessments, Grading, and Reporting* (with Jung, 2013); and *Benjamin S.*

Bloom: Portraits of an Educator (2012). He can be reached at guskey @uky.edu or www.tguskey.com.

Dr. Susan M. Brookhart is professor emerita in the School of Education at Duquesne University and an independent educational consultant and author based in Helena, Montana. She was the 2007–2009 editor of *Educational Measurement: Issues and Practice* and is currently an associate editor of *Applied Measurement in Education*. She is author or coauthor of 18 books and more than 70 articles and book chapters on classroom assessment, teacher professional development, and evaluation. She serves on the editorial boards of several journals and on several national advisory panels. She has been named the 2014 Jason Millman Scholar by the Consortium for Research on Educational Assessment and Teaching Effectiveness (CREATE) and is the recipient of the 2015 Samuel J. Messick Memorial Lecture Award from ETS/TOEFL. Dr. Brookhart's research interests include the role of both formative and summative classroom assessment in student motivation and achievement, the connection between classroom assessment and large-scale assessment, and grading. She also works with schools, districts, regional educational service units, universities, and states doing professional development. Dr. Brookhart received her PhD in educational research and evaluation from The Ohio State University, after teaching in both elementary and middle schools. She can be reached at suebrookhart@gmail.com.

Dr. Sarah M. Bonner is associate professor in the School of Education at Hunter College, City University of New York, where she teaches in programs in teacher preparation, educational psychology, and instructional leadership. Her scholarly work includes research on teacher beliefs about grading and assessment. She has also been involved in a multiyear project to study the effects of peer-facilitated instruction on secondary school students' achievement. In a recent project, she led a design team of researchers and teachers to develop and study formative assessment tasks for computer science classrooms. She can be reached at smbonner@gmail.com.

Dr. Alex J. Bowers is associate professor of education leadership at Teachers College, Columbia University, where he works to help school leaders use the data they already collect in schools in more effective ways to help direct schools' and districts' limited resources to specific student needs. His research focuses on the intersection of effective school and district leadership, organization and HR, data-driven decision making, student grades and test scores, student persistence, and dropouts. His work also considers the influence of school finance, facilities, and technology on student achievement. He can be reached at bowers@exchange.tc.columbia.edu.

Dr. Peggy P. Chen is associate professor in educational psychology programs at Hunter College and the Graduate Center, the City University of New York. She has published and coauthored articles in scholarly journals as well as chapters in books. Her research centers on academic self-regulation, with a focus on middle and high school students' learning of mathematics, and classroom assessment, with a focus on inservice and preservice teachers' grading beliefs and practices and how teachers provide feedback to their students. Dr. Chen is currently developing a class assessment model that incorporates learning theories and is researching students' self-regulated learning behaviors and thinking processes in computer science classes. She can be reached at ppchen@hunter.cuny.edu.

Dr. Lee Ann Jung is clinical professor at San Diego State University and founder of Lead Inclusion. She is a consultant to schools worldwide in the areas of inclusion, assessment and grading, intervention, and measuring progress. Before her career in higher education, Dr. Jung worked for eight years as a teacher and then an administrator. She is a former full professor and director of International Partnerships at the University of Kentucky. Dr. Jung is author of six books and more than 45 journal articles and chapters. Most recently, she authored *From Goals to Growth: Intervention and Support in Every Classroom* (2018). Dr. Jung is also past chair for the Classroom Assessment special interest group for the American Educational Research Association. She can be reached at www. leadinclusion.org or ljung@sdsu.edu.

Dr. Laura J. Link is assistant professor of educational leadership in the College of Professional Studies at Purdue University Fort Wayne. She is coauthor of *Cornerstones of Strong Schools: Practices for Purposeful Leadership* and author of several articles and professional papers on school leaders, grading, and assessments. Dr. Link leads K–16 research-practice partnerships and has twice won her college's Community Engagement Award. Dr. Link served in many K–12 central office and school-based leadership roles and has taught elementary school, middle school, high school, and college students. While assistant superintendent of teaching and learning in Memphis, Tennessee, she was one of seven district administrators charged with leading the largest school district merger in U.S. history. She can be reached at linkl@pfw.edu.

Dr. James H. McMillan is professor in the department of foundations of education at Virginia Commonwealth University, where he teaches courses in research methods and assessment. He received his doctorate from Northwestern University in educational psychology. Dr. McMillan is editor of the *Sage Handbook of Research on Classroom Assessment*, coeditor of the upcoming volume *Classroom Assessment and Measurement*, and author of *Using Students' Assessment Mistakes and Learning Deficits to Enhance Motivation and Learning* and *Classroom Assessment: Principles and Practice That Enhance Student Learning and Motivation*. He received the 2017 Jason Millman Scholar Award from the Consortium for Research on Educational Assessment and Teaching Effectiveness (CREATE). His recent research has focused on student perceptions of assessment as related to self-regulation and motivation. He can be reached at jmcmillan@vcu.edu.

Dr. Jeffrey K. Smith is professor in the College of Education at the University of Otago in New Zealand. Prior to this role, he was professor and chair of the educational psychology department at Rutgers University, where he had been a faculty member for 29 years. From 1988 through 2005, he also served as head of the Office of Research and Evaluation at The Metropolitan Museum of Art. He studies educational assessment and the psychology of aesthetics. He was awarded the Rudolf Arnheim Award for Outstanding Achievement in Psychology and the Arts from the American Psychological Association and the Gustav Theodor Fechner Award for Outstanding Contributions to Empirical Aesthetics from the International Association of Empirical Aesthetics. He received his AB from Princeton University and his PhD from the University of Chicago. He can be reached at jeffreyksmith@gmail.com.

Dr. Lisa F. Smith is professor and head of the School of Social Sciences at the University of Otago in New Zealand. Her research focuses on assessment issues related to both standardized and classroom testing, preservice teacher efficacy, and the psychology of aesthetics. Dr. Smith is on the editorial board of several peer-reviewed journals and is author or coauthor of more than 125 publications. She has received two lifetime achievement awards: the Rudolf Arnheim Award for Outstanding Achievement in Psychology and the Arts from the American Psychological Association, and the Gustav Theodor Fechner Award for Outstanding Contributions to Empirical Aesthetics from the International Association of Empirical Aesthetics. She also has been recognized with teaching awards in both hemispheres. She can be reached at professor.lisa.smith@gmail.com.

Dr. Megan Welsh is associate professor in the School of Education at the University of California–Davis, where she teaches courses in assessment, measurement theory, and research methods. Dr. Welsh conducts research in the areas of standards-based grading, test validity, behavioral assessment, and standards-based assessment. Her research has been supported by numerous grants from the U.S. Department of Education, the National Science Foundation, and the McDonnell Foundation. Before working in academia, Dr. Welsh was a 3rd and 4th grade teacher in Oakland, California; a district assessment specialist; and an education policy researcher. She received her PhD in educational psychology from the University of Arizona and has a master's degree in public policy analysis from the University of California–Berkeley. She can be reached at megwelsh@ucdavis.edu.

Related ASCD Resources

At the time of publication, the following resources were available (ASCD stock numbers appear in parentheses).

Print Products

Changing the Grade: A Step-by-Step Guide to Grading for Student Growth by Jonathan Cornue (#118029)

Charting a Course to Standards-Based Grading: What to Stop, What to Start, and Why It Matters by Tim R. Westerberg (#117010)

Classroom Assessment and Grading That Work by Robert J. Marzano (#106006)

Grading Smarter, Not Harder: Assessment Strategies That Motivate Kids and Help Them Learn by Myron Dueck (#114003)

How to Use Grading to Improve Learning by Susan M. Brookhart (#117074)

Rethinking Grading: Meaningful Assessment for Standards-Based Learning by Cathy Vatterott (#115001)

For up-to-date information about ASCD resources, go to **www.ascd.org.** You can search the complete archives of *Educational Leadership* at **www.ascd.org/el.**

PD Online

Grading Smarter, Not Harder—PD Online Course (#PD16OC005M)

Using Data to Determine Student Mastery (Reimagined) (#PD14OC001S)

ASCD myTeachSource®

Download resources from a professional learning platform with hundreds of research-based best practices and tools for your classroom at http://myteachsource.ascd.org/.

For more information, send an e-mail to member@ascd.org; call 1-800-933-2723 or 703-578-9600; send a fax to 703-575-5400; or write to Information Services, ASCD, 1703 N. Beauregard St., Alexandria, VA 22311-1714 USA.

WHOLE CHILD
TENETS

The ASCD Whole Child approach is an effort to transition from a focus on narrowly defined academic achievement to one that promotes the long-term development and success of all children. Through this approach, ASCD supports educators, families, community members, and policymakers as they move from a vision about educating the whole child to sustainable, collaborative actions.

What We Know About Grading relates to the **supported** and **challenged** tenets. *For more about the ASCD Whole Child approach, visit* **www.ascd.org/wholechild.**

1 **HEALTHY**
Each student enters school healthy and learns about and practices a healthy lifestyle.

2 **SAFE**
Each student learns in an environment that is physically and emotionally safe for students and adults.

3 **ENGAGED**
Each student is actively engaged in learning and is connected to the school and broader community.

4 **SUPPORTED**
Each student has access to personalized learning and is supported by qualified, caring adults.

5 **CHALLENGED**
Each student is challenged academically and prepared for success in college or further study and for employment and participation in a global environment.

LEARN. TEACH. LEAD.